Global Financial Crisis and Indian Economy

Global Financial Crisis and Indian Economy

Dr. Anil Kumar Thakur
Honorary Secretary and Treasurer,
Indian Economic Association (IEA)
Department of Applied Economics & Commerce,
College of Commerce, Patna (Bihar)

Dr. Ram Naresh Thakur
Head of the Department,
Post Graduate Centre of Economics
And Director, Gandhian Studies Centre
Samastipur College, Samastipur
(L.N. Mithila University, Darbhanga
Bihar - 848134

GRP

GLOBAL RESEARCH PUBLICATIONS
NEW DELHI (INDIA)

First Published – 2011

ISBN: 978-81-89630-20-1

Published by

GLOBAL RESEARCH PUBLICATIONS
4830/24, 1st Floor, Ansari Road
Darya Ganj, New Delhi-110002 (India)
Phone : 23245225. Fax : 91-11-23272135
E-mail: globalresearchpublications@gmail.com, grpindia@vsnl.net

CONTENTS

PREFACE

This book "Global Financial Crisis and Indian Economy" is based on the deliberations made under the 92nd Annual conference of Indian Economic Association. The theme was there 'The Impact of Global Recession'. The themes of this book includes global meltdown and its impact on various sectors on the economies of the various countries of the world – specially on the Indian Economy. Fundamentally, the crisis could be ascribed to the persistence of large global imbalances, which in turn, were the outcome of long periods of excessively loose monetary policy in the major advanced economies during the early part of this decade. Global imbalances have been manifested through a substantial increase in the current account deficit of the U.S.A mirrored by the substantial surplus in Asia, particularly in China, and in oil exporting countries in the Middle East and Russia. The ongoing global financial crisis can be largely attributed to extended periods of excessively loose monetary policy in the U.S. over the period 2002-04. The global financial crisis has affected the international money, credit, equity and foreign exchange markets. The impact of the financial crisis is likely to have negative effects on the agricultural sector and food security. The world is in the midst of a severe financial crisis, meaning a crisis that will exact a huge cost in terms of lost economic growth. It is not true, however, that all financial crises are severe. There is a high probability of a financial crisis having an impact on the real economy when there is disruption of the banking sector. India will not escape unscathed in the present crisis because its economy has become more integrated with the rest of the world over the past decade and a half.

Overseas finance has become increasingly important for Indian corporates and the drying up of such finance is bound to tell on their destinies. Though emerging market economies, including India, do not have direct or significant exposure to stressed financial instruments and troubled financial institutions, they are facing significant indirect impact of the financial crisis. There are number of lessons that can be drawn from crisis. The impact of the global showdown on India's economy is impacting the employment scenario. In fact, the rising joblessness in India has assumed worrisome proportions. With overall economic growth sharply slowing down, the ranks of those without work are growing by the day. Many people were rendered jobless in 2008-09, according to a survey made by the 'Ministry of Labour and Employment'. India could lose up to 1.5 million jobs during the period. Recession is equally big opportunity as robust economic growth. The global economic crisis has definitely taken a toll of India's economic performance. In fact, India, unlike other over exposed countries, has potential of its resilience to cope up with the global recession. The macro-economic fundamentals of Indian economy are sound. The growth rate is still reasonably high. The inflation is under control.

We are grateful to Dr. C. Hanumantha Rao, in whose guidance the conference and all the sessions took place and remained success. We are also thankful to Dr. Sukhdeo Thorat whose presence made the sessions bright and glorious. We are indebted to Dr. Manmohan Singh, Honorable Prime Minister of India, his inauguration and humble presence, who spared his time after heavy engagements amidst service of nation. We are thankful to Shri Naveen Patnaik, Honourable Chief Minister of Orissa for his humble presence and delivering lecture. We are also thankful to great economists of India, Dr. B.B. Bhattacharya, Vice-Chancellor of Jawaharlal Nehru University, New Delhi, Dr. S. Mahendra Dev, Dr. U.R. Pachmukhi, Dr. R. K. Sen, Prof. Yosoda Samug Sundram and many others. We are thankful to all paper writers and the all delegates who participated in the conference and that session.

Anil Kumar Thakur
Ram Naresh Thakur

INTRODUCTION

This book 'Global Financial Crisis and Indian Economy' is an out come of the 92nd annual conference of Indian Economic Association held at KIIT University, Bhubaneshwar, from 27 to 29 December, 2009. There was a session of 'Impact of Global Recession' (Theme -II out of IV themes). This book contains twenty two articles consisting of 37 paper-writers.

Rishi Vivek Dhar and *Sweta Upadhya* have explained India's reintegration into the world economy with higher trade/GDP ratio and increased dependence on external capital flows, has made her more vulnerable to global crises, but the pursuit of gradual reform and prudent regulations have minimised the negative impact of both the Asian and more recently the 'Trans Atlantic' financial crisis. *Harjinder Singh* and *Aman Deep Verma* have stressed that there has been a slow down in the services sector growth which has been our prime growth engine for the previous years mainly in construction, transport, communication, trade and hotels etc. They conclude once the global economy begins to recover India's turn around will be sharper and swifter, backed by strong fundamentals and untapped growth potential. *Suman Pamecha* and *Jasleen Sethi* have analysed that there silence of the Indian Financial Sector in the face of the worst global financial crisis since the 1930's can also be attributed to our approach to financial globalization. *Preeti Mishra* has discussed universal banking in India and global meltdown. She explains how universal banks give to economics of scale and scope to banks and at the same time it provides convenience to consumers through its one stop-shop. *Halima Sadia Rizvi* has shown how the two prominent economies of BRIC conclave India and China are reeling under the impact of the global recession. India and China are predicted to be the future super powers of the world. *Alka Agrawal, Anurag Srivastava* and *Satyendra Kumar* have analysed in detail the causes of global financial crisis and its impact on Indian economy. There is gloomy forecast that the U.S. sub prime mortgage crisis might convert into recession that could be as great as the Great Depression of 1930s that last over a decade. The sub prime crisis that started in 2004 and 2005 and extended to the current economic cycle world over. *K.G. Suresh Kumar* and *N. Chandra Gowda* have explained the case study of Karnatka economy about medium term fiscal plan for recession control. *Amiya Kumar Mohapatra* has made an analytical study of socio-economic impact of recession on employee in detail. *A. Sangamithra* and *N. Savitha* have analysed the global financial crisis and its impact on Indian economy how the turmoil in the international financial markets and advanced economies, which started around mid-2007, has exacerbated substantially since August 2008. *Jitendra Ahirrao* and *Shankar Ambhore* have expressed their views on the impact of global slowdown on Indian economy with special reference to agriculture sector. *M.S. Gupta* and *Asha Singh* have elaborated that the economic slowdown of the advance countries which started around mid – 2007, as a result the sub prime crisis in U.S.A., led to the spread of economic crisis across the globe resulting into significant changes in the global financial landscape. *S.K. Sharma* has discussed how the U.S. economy which is the largest consumer in the world is under severe economic recession. Some of the prominent American firms like the Lehman Brothers and others which had their business all over the world collapsed in the share market during the first half of 2009. *Manjushri Gupta, Parul Saxena* and *Anjila Gupta* have assimilated that the worst global financial crisis since the great depression has witnessed failures and collapses of major financial institutions in the U.S. and Several European Countries. *Baij Nath Singh* has expressed his opinion on the impact of the crisis on Indian banking sector. He has also studied the conditions and situations to take lessons for future. *B.N. Singh* and *Anuradha Verma* have emphasized the global economic crisis along with its wide effects on Indian economy and human resources. *O.P. Shukla* and *Vinayak Kant Mishra* have shown the impact of global economic crisis on Indian economy. They have analysed how the economy which had witnessed high growth till 2007, has slowed down. The GDP growth rate of the year 2008 has decelerated significantly. According to *Sobha Jain* the present financial crisis has been called the most serious financial crisis since the Great Depression with its global effects characterized by the failure of Key businesses, declines the consumer wealth estimated in the trillions of U.S. dollars, substantial financial commitments incurred by government and a significant decline in economic activity. *R.C. Mishra* and *K.C. Mishra* have overviewed the current financial crisis. According to them since current financial crisis had affected the Indian economy, it is imperative to take necessary steps to bring recovery to the economy. *Chandeshwari Tiwary* observes that inflation whether imported or non-imported has become mostly a regular feature of Indian economy since independence specially under the plans having different impacts on the economy good for the rich and bad for the poor, increasing the gap between the two; causing social, economic and political problems. *Hemlata* has stated that the crisis is not merely financial; it is a crisis of the real economy. It is not meekly banking, insurance and stock-markets which are in crisis. There is a crisis in the real economy. The *Ranjit Kumar Singh* and *Rameshwar Prajapati* have suggested much more creative and imaginative policy response are required. *Brajesh Srivastava* has stated that the financial market crisis has led to the collapse of major financial institutions and is now beginning to impact the real economy in advance economy.

We sincerely apologise to the learned writers whose papers could not be included in the present volume. This book will be fruitful for the academicians, research scholars, policy makes and financial administrators.

Anil Kumar Thakur
Ram Naresh Thakur

1

India and the Global Slowdown–New Vulnerabilities

Rishi Vivek Dhar, Shweta Upadhyay

Introduction

"We in India have been fortunate in having weathered the global downturn better than many others. Our growth rate, which was close to 9 percent in the previous 5 years, will fall below 7 percent in 2008-09. Like other countries, we have made aggressive use of both monetary and fiscal policy, with a total fiscal stimulus or expansion of the fiscal deficit above the planned level of almost 4 percentage points of GDP in 2008-09. We hope to be able to achieve a similar growth rate in 2009-10, with continuing reliance on monetary and fiscal policy. We recognize the importance of fiscal sustainability and it is our firm intention to return to a fiscally sustainable path after 2010. The additional fiscal stimulus we have undertaken will raise our debt to GDP ratio by a few percentage points above what it would otherwise have been, but this is relatively modest compared to what would have happened had our banks suffered a financial crisis. Effective regulation of the banking system has gained us much more than any additional strain imposed by temporary fiscal expansion. Besides, since most of the fiscal stimulus will be directed to increased investment in infrastructure, it will in the medium term contribute

to growth and thus help reduce the debt ratio automatically. Expansionary policy at home in an environment where exports are weak and private capital flows have dried up would normally lead to pressure on the balance of payments. In our case this has been partly offset by the fall in oil prices, but even so, India's current account deficit in 2009-10, is likely to be about 1.4 percent of GDP. We expect to be able to finance this without difficulty and in any case our strong foreign exchange reserves position enables us to cope with any shortfall in capital flows we may experience" Prime Minister Man Mohan Singh summed up the official thinking in India on the impact of the Trans-Atlantic financial crisis and the global economic slowdown in above words, Speaking at the London Summit of the G-20.

In underscoring the new 'post-reform' resilience of the economy, we do take account of new vulnerabilities that could hurt the growth process. The first is the higher trade/GDP ratio and the consequent increased dependence on the global market in both goods and services. The second is the increased importance of foreign capital inflows–portfolio, direct investment, external commercial borrowing (ECB) of Indian private corporate sector and private remittances by overseas Indians. While India's recent growth acceleration benefited from this external connectivity, the global crisis would hurt economic growth in the near term on account of the importance of these linkages.[3]

In a candid rejection of the so-called "decoupling thesis", namely that higher growth based on domestic savings and investment, and the greater reliance on domestic demand has 'decoupled' the Indian economy from the global economy, RBI Governor told the Confederation of Indian Industry, "The reason India has been hit by the crisis, despite mitigating factors, is clearly India's rapid and growing integration into the global economy. The contagion of the crisis has spread to India through all the channels – the financial channel, the real channel, and importantly, as happens in all financial crises, the confidence channel"[4].

Both public and private sector companies in India have become more dependent on the capital market for securing equity and debt finance, and India's equity market is fully integrated with global markets although the debt market is not. Indian companies are estimated to have raised US$41 billion (net of repayment) as overseas debt through external commercial borrowing and fully convertible commercial debentures.18 Even in the period October to December 2008 Indian companies were able to raise a total of US$4.5 billion from global debt markets. But these flows are expected to weaken, given the increased risk aversion in global markets. The decline in global merchandise trade has also slowed down the growth of India's exports, and for the first time in seven years export growth has been negative in the first quarter of 2009.

Table 1
Geographical Direction of India's Exports

Region	*1980-81*	*1990-91*	*2001-02*	*2007-08*
E.U.	21.6	27.5	22.7	21.2
USA	11.1	14.7	20.9	12.7
Africa	5.2	2.1	3.2	7.1
L. America	0.5	0.4	2.1	3.5
Asia (non oil)	13.4	14.3	21.4	25.8
OPEC	11.1	5.6	10.9	16.4

Source: Economic Survey, Ministry of Finance, Government of India, various issues

Apart from these macro linkages and the overall increase in the trade/GDP ratio, the changes in the geographical pattern of trade also points to an increased vulnerability to a slowdown. The depreciation of the Rupee is a reflection of these external vulnerabilities. India has had to draw down its foreign exchange reserves through the last quarter of 2008 and the first quarter of 2009 largely in defiance of the Rupee. While India's reserves are denominated in a basket of currencies, the United States dollar is the principle foreign currency in which India's external transactions are denominated. The United States and the European Union still account for over a third of India's exports, but Asia's share has increased in recent years. The shares of Japan and Russia have gone down, but those of China, South Korea and the Association of Southeast Asian Nations

(ASEAN) economies have increased. Each of these economies has experienced a slowdown in growth and a consequent decline in trade.

The growth of inward remittances from expatriate Indian workers, especially in the Persian Gulf region, and earnings from information technology and software services exports have increased the importance of services exports to India's balance of payments management. While low-skilled manpower exports are mainly to the OPEC member countries of the Persian Gulf and Middle East, high skilled services exports are mainly to the United States and other OECD economies. In 2008-09, inward remittances amounted to US$55 billion, while export earnings from information technology and business process outsourcing business were estimated to be US$47 billion.

The information technology, information technology services and business process outsourcing industry is now estimated to account for almost six percent of India's GDP. Two-thirds of the US$72 billion business is accounted for by exports, mainly to Trans-Atlantic economies. While spokespersons of the National Association of Software and Service Companies (NASSCOM) have expressed optimism that their exports would not be hurt if developed economies do not resort to protectionist measures, since firms in OECD economies would increase their demand for lower cost Indian software services in a downturn, NASSCOM has forecast a reduction in export earnings in 2009-10.[5] Growth in information technology-enabled services exports is expected to be around 15 percent in 2009 10, compared to annual growth rates of around 25 percent in recent years.

While this optimism about future growth prospects has been dented by recent events, there is as yet no anti-globalisation or protectionist sentiment in India. However, such protectionism in the OECD economies and the pursuit of 'beggar-my-neighbour' policies by its economic partners may make India less sanguine about globalisation, given the new external vulnerabilities.

India and the Least Developed Countries

India's growth acceleration since 2003 has also enabled it to adopt a more liberal stance towards other Least Developed Countries (LDCs) in Asia and Africa. The policy of non-reciprocal trade liberalisation involving duty-free access was extended to all African LDCs at the India-Africa Summit in New Delhi in April 2008, and to the so-called 'CMLV' countries in Southeast Asia (Cambodia, Myanmar, Laos and Vietnam). There are clearly two distinct strands of Indian strategic policy defining these initiatives. On the one hand, India's traditional policy of building bridges with other developing countries and promoting South-South cooperation; on the other hand, the need to keep pace with China in providing aid and assistance to other developing countries, especially the LDCs.

Liberal unilateral trade concessions, even if to the LDCs, would come under attack from producers' lobbies and politicians in a slow-growing India. For example, India's trade concessions to Vietnam, a friendly country, in commodities such as coffee have already come in for sharp attack from even the Communist Party-led state government of Kerala, where coffee growers have political clout. Apart from unilateral trade concessions, India has also stepped up aid and technical assistance to other developing countries. The Indian external aid budget has increased substantially in recent years, with a significant share of it going to Afghanistan and Bhutan[6]. While strategic interests in South Asia and traditional commitment to South-South cooperation drive India's aid budget, competition for influence with China, both within South Asia and in the developing world as a whole, is also a major driver. India's growth acceleration in the past decade has enabled it to find the resources for such aid. Any deceleration in growth and consequent fiscal pressures would impose constraints. This would most certainly be an adverse strategic consequence of the extant economic slowdown.

India's Relationship with USA and China

At a bilateral level, India's economic rise has shaped its relationship with the United States and China. It is an appreciation of the strategic importance of sustained growth of a free market democracy in the developing world, and the assurance of energy security for it that helped define an improvement in India-United States relations in recent years, especially during the Bush Administration. The United States came to appreciate that India's economic success within the framework of a secular and plural democracy is of strategic importance to all open societies and open economies.

President Obama's first important statement on United States-India relations, conveyed through a letter written when he was still a candidate in the presidential elections, to Prime Minister Man Mohan Singh, adopted a forward-looking and supportive position on United States-India relations, underscoring the importance of India's democratic development. Obama said, "I would like to see United States-India relations grow across the board to reflect our shared interests, shared values, shared sense of threats and ever-burgeoning ties between our two economies and societies...Imagine our two democracies in action: Indian laboratories and industry collaborating with American laboratories and industry to discover innovative solutions to today's energy problems. That is the kind of new partnership I would like to build with India as President."[7]

In dealing with the economic crisis the United States has moved closer to China, while in dealing with terrorism it has become more dependent on Pakistan.[8] It is, therefore, possible that these remarks do not any longer fully reflect the world view of President Obama. The United States continues to share common interests with India. The United States and India have a shared stake in reducing their dependence on imported petroleum and natural gas, and in the development of nuclear and non-conventional energy. Given India's low per capita domestic availability of energy and other natural resources, ensuring access to these resources is vital to India's development process and national security.

The global economic downturn offers an opportunity for the world's largest democracies and market economies to work together to strength the foundations of open societies and open economies, by creating a global order that is supportive of India's developmental aspirations. If the Obama Administration builds on the foundations laid by the Clinton and Bush Administrations to build a strategic partnership with India, the United States could play the same role in India's rise as it did in the post-war reconstruction of Japan and Western Europe, on the one hand, and the rise of the 'East Asian Tigers' and China, on the other.

The United States offered such a 'benign' economic environment for the reconstruction of post-war Western Europe and East Asia. Post-war Germany, Japan and South Korea owe their economic rise to supportive United States policies. Even the so-called 'Asian Tigers' - Hong Kong, Taiwan and Singapore - benefited from helpful United States economic and security policies. The United States economic support also helped many of the 'economies in transition' in Eastern Europe. Indeed, in the past two decades United States policies have facilitated the rise of China. The United States investments in China, access to United States markets for China's exports, United States support for China's membership of the World Trade Organisation have all played an important role, apart from China's own domestic policies, in boosting China's economic performance.

How open the United States remains towards India, keeping her markets open, being liberal with H1-B visas, being supportive in multilateral economic institutions, will have a bearing on India's growth process. The United States-India Chief Executive Officers (CEO) Forum was launched in July 2005 precisely with the intention of strengthening economic relations between the two countries. Just as many in Europe and Asia saw the United States as a partner in their progress, India too must have the opportunities that enable her to view the United States as such.

The United States strategy in Asia will also shape the strategic environment within which India is trying to improve its economic prospects. Stabilising the economy is also vital for India to deal with the instability of its neighbourhood. Apart from Pakistan, Sri Lanka too is in turmoil and both Nepal and Bangladesh remain potentially unstable polities. In each of these countries we see China's growing influence and interest. China has also arrived in the Indian Ocean with its naval fleet and is once again flexing its muscles on the status of Arunachal Pradesh. Its influence is growing in Pakistan, Nepal, Sri Lanka, Myanmar and Bangladesh. Chinese leaders have visited the Indian Ocean islands of Seychelles and Mauritius, and China is probing the newly democratic Bhutan.

Against the background of a rising China that is increasingly influential in her troubled neighbourhood India cannot afford to see a weakening of its own growth process that underpins her strategic capabilities.

The bigger challenge for India, however, is to ensure that the current global economic slowdown does not constrain it from catching up with China. Without doubt the rise of China is India's main long term strategic challenge. Already China's influence in Asia is rising. China had long overtaken India as the main business partner of many South Asian economies, not to mention East and Southeast Asia.[9] China has also emerged as a major source of external financial support through its contribution to the Chiang Mai Initiative and direct financial assistance to various countries. The two Asian giants are already engaged in a race for resources and markets in Asia and Africa, with China far ahead of India. A deceleration in China's growth could blunt the edge of this competition. But it will not go away. Rather, it is likely to accentuate as India catches up in the growth race. As a consequence of the current global slowdown, we can conjecture three alternative scenarios of regional growth.

First, India is able to recover more easily than China, due to its lower dependence on global markets and lower exposure to the United States economy; second, India is unable to regain its growth momentum, while China is; and third, no relative change in the status of India and China in the world economy. How the global slowdown impacts this bilateral relationship will shape the overall strategy of both the Asian powers. It will also impact on their relations with other Asian economies as well as Western powers. It will shape the process of institution-building in Asia, and the structure of regional economic and security architecture. The resolution of the problem of the savings-consumption imbalance between China and the United States will have a profound impact on the emerging global strategic balance. A United States-China 'condominium' could alter India's strategic environment and options.

A United States-China condominium could go beyond the management of global imbalances and crises. If it encapsulates multilateral trade negotiations and discussions on global warming and climate change, it would have an even greater impact on India's strategic environment. India seeks a benign global environment for trade and investment that will enable it to sustain higher rates of economic growth.

India's strategic perspective on trade and climate change negotiations has been defined in the framework of economic development, employment generation and poverty eradication. So far India and China have been able to work together on these issues. If China breaks ranks and arrives at an understanding with the United States that does not meet India's needs, India would have no option but to join ranks with other developing countries and other powers to secure its own interests. Here too the United States could adopt a supportive stance towards India or adopt postures that would revive old North-South divisions on global economic issues. The global economic slowdown has increased the salience of trade and climate change negotiations since the outcomes of these negotiations will shape the overall environment for India's economic development. India has often been portrayed as a 'spoiler' both in the Doha Round and in the climate change negotiations. This is not true. India has a 'strategic stake' in multilateralism on both counts. However, its priority lies in defending the environment for economic growth and poverty eradication. Without a 'development' dimension to the trade and climate change negotiations, India would be hard put to join a multilateral agreement.

Finally, India would want to see how the changing relationship between the United States and China would shape global negotiations on trade, finance and climate change, and impact on dealing with the challenges of food and energy security. The United States and India have a shared stake in reducing their dependence on imported petroleum and natural gas, and in the development of nuclear and non-conventional energy. Given India's low per capita domestic availability of energy and other natural resources, ensuring access to these resources is vital to India's development process and national security.

India's as a Re-emerging Economy

The Indian economy is on a long-term path of accelerating economic growth. Madison's Organisation for Economic Co-operation and Development (OECD)-funded study of historical trends in the national income of major world economies shows that at the beginning of the 18th century Europe, China and India had more or less equal shares of the world's GDP and the two Asian economies have been recovering their lost space, albeit at a different pace, over the past half century.[10] The Indian economy has grown at an annual average of 3.5 percent between 1950 and 1980, close to six percent between 1980 and 2004, and close to nine percent since 2004 India's more recent growth acceleration, since the early 1990s, has followed a shift in the macroeconomic policy framework, with greater external and internal economic liberalisation. India's economic rise as a 'free market democracy' and her reintegration into the global economy, creating new relationships of inter-dependence both globally and regionally, have shaped her strategic and foreign policies.

India's management of the 'triple crises' – fiscal, balance of payments and financial crises–experienced sequentially between the late-1980s and the mid-1990s, set the stage for India's response to the Asian and, more recently, the 'Trans-Atlantic' financial crises..

(1) The 'fiscal crises' of the 1990s. Responding to an unsustainable rise in budgetary and fiscal deficits, India adopted a fiscal stabilisation Programme, subsequently enacting a Fiscal Responsibility and

Budget Management Act, thus ensuring a reduction in revenue and fiscal deficits. However, the recent fiscal stimulus packages put in place in response to the current slowdown have forced the government to breach the provisions of the Fiscal Responsibility and Budget Management Act.

(2) An external payments crisis in 1991. India has since undertaken transformative changes in her trade, tariff and foreign investment policies. These have helped improve India's external economic profile, including a reduction in external debt to GDP ratios, an increase in trade/GDP and foreign investment/GDP ratios, and, most importantly, enabled India to accumulate foreign currency reserves. India's increased openness to global trade and capital flows has, however, increased her vulnerability to global crises and recession.

(3) The financial sector crisis of the early 1990s, which included a stock market crash and problems in the banking sector. India has since undertaken comprehensive financial sector reforms, put in place a world class regulatory and supervisory system for the equities market and the financial and banking sectors recapitalized banks and improved their asset position.

While undertaking these internal reforms, India opted for gradualism in external sector liberalisation, adopting full currency convertibility only on the current account and eschewing it on the capital account. This defined the context for India's exposure and response to the Asian and Trans-Atlantic financial crises. The cumulative impact of the reforms undertaken since 1991 has been to make the Indian economy more resilient to external shocks, even as it has become more open to external flows, enabling India to sustain an acceleration of its economic growth within a more open economy framework.

India's low inflation tolerance (the average rate of inflation for 50 years, 1950-2000, has been around eight percent) has meant that fiscal and monetary policies have been largely conservative, with brief episodes of high inflation and fiscal laxity. It was the easing up of this fiscal conservatism that contributed to the 1990 crisis. Although India returned to a more conservative approach in fiscal policy, the current crisis has forced the government to adopt a liberal fiscal stance.[11]

In his authoritative review of India's new economic policies Panagariya concludes, "India has had a history of maintaining a relatively stable macroeconomic environment...",[12] and says of India's external sector management in recent years, "The judicious handling of the monetary and exchange rate policies must be largely credited with price stability in the domestic market and a broadly competitive exchange rate that facilitated a healthy growth of international trade". In short, India's experience with handling the triple economic crises it confronted in the early 1990s has helped put in place a regime of policies that have contributed to an acceleration of economic growth and a strengthening of the Indian economy. This has helped India deal with the current slowdown with a greater degree of confidence.

Closing the Two Gaps: A Change

In the past India's growth process has been constrained by what economists referred to as the 'two gaps'–a domestic savings gap and an external financing gap. Rising domestic savings and increased inflow of foreign capital have helped bridge both gaps, contributing to higher growth. For a long time India's savings rate was below 20 percent, even as East and Southeast Asian economies saw their savings rates exceed 30 percent. In the 1990s, India caught up and its more recent growth acceleration has been facilitated by a sharp rise in savings and investment rates.

Traditionally India has bridged the 'external gap' through foreign aid and concessional debt. However, after 1991 India reduced its dependence on aid and debt flows, and has allowed private capital flows to bridge the gap. The share of foreign investment in India's GDP has gone up and foreign capital inflows have increased on account of higher remittances from overseas Indians.

Table 2
Growth Rate of GDP & Investment & Savings Rates

Financial Year	*GDP Growth Percent*	*Investment/ GDP (%)*	*Savings/ GDP (%)*
2000-01	4.4	24.3	23.7
2001-02	5.8	22.8	23.5
2002-03	3.8	25.2	26.3
2003-04	8.5	28.2	29.8
2004-05	7.5	32.2	31.7
2005-06	9.5	35.5	34.3
2006-07	9.7	35.9	35.6
2007-08	9	37.4	37.8
2008-09	7.1	35.5	35.9

Source: Prime Minister's Economic Advisory Council, Government of India, 2009.

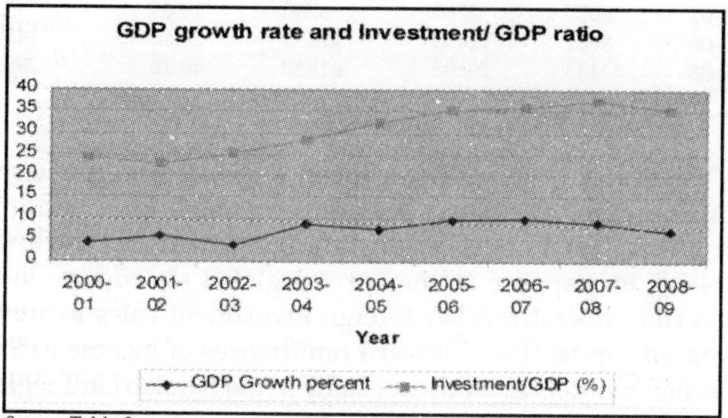

Source: Table-2

Figure 1

Following the Asian Financial Crisis and, more importantly, after facing economic sanctions in the wake of the 1998 nuclear tests, imposed among others by the United States and Japan, India chose to accumulate foreign exchange reserves as a hedge against risk of currency shortage. This explains the sustained rise in foreign currency assets since 2000.

The share of external trade in India's national income has doubled since 1991. (Table 5) India's trade/GDP ratio, at over 33 percent, is higher than that of the United States (around 25 percent). While increased trade dependence has made India more vulnerable to external shocks, her relatively low export dependence compared to other newly industrialising economies in Asia (China's trade/GDP ratio is close to 80 percent) has helped to limit the negative impact of a global slowdown.

Table 3
Foreign Investment & Income Flows into India

Year	*Foreign Direct Investment (US$ Million)*	*Portfolio Investment (US$ Million)*	*Total Foreign Investment (US$ Million)*	*Net Private Income Transfers (US$ Billion)*	*Foreign Currency Assets (US$ Billion)*
1990-91	97	6	103	2.07	2.24
1995-96	2144	2748	4892	8.51	20.81
2000-01	4029	2760	6789	12.85	39.55
2005-06	8961	12492	21453	24.46	145.11
2007-08	32435	29395	61830	40.78	299.23

Source: R.B.I. data base

The policy of ensuring reduced dependence on external debt flows has, therefore, been accompanied by a policy of increased openness to investment and income inflows. (Table 4) In response to the current global slowdown, India has further liberalized her foreign investment rules to attract increased capital flows. Inward remittances of income earned by Indian workers abroad, especially in the Persian Gulf region,

Table 4
Trends in Trade/GDP Ratio

Year	*Exports/ GDP (%)*	*Imports/ GDP (%)*	*Trade/ GDP (%)*
1980-81	6.2	9.8	16
1985-86	5.6	8.5	14.1
1990-91	7.3	9.9	17.2
1995-96	11.2	14.5	25.7
2000-01	13	14.7	27.7
2007-08	13.5	21.2	34.7

Source: Economic Survey, Ministry of Finance, Government of India, (various Issues).

have increased in importance as a source of foreign currency earnings for India. Nearly 3.5 million Indians work in the member-countries of the Gulf Cooperation Council. They send home monthly remittances which constitute a bulk of the US$40 billion that India received in 2007-08, and the US$55 billion it is estimated to receive in 2008-09.

Increased openness and external integration have made the Indian economy more efficient, increasing India's share in world trade from 0.5 percent in 1991 to over 1.0 percent by 2008. India has also been able to draw on foreign savings. However, for these very reasons, the current global slowdown could be expected to have a higher negative impact on India's economic growth compared to the Asian crisis of 1997-98 or earlier episodes of global recession. Already India's trade deficit and current account deficit have gone up, and India has had to draw down its foreign exchange reserves defending the rupee, which has depreciated against the dollar by close to 30 percent in the past year, with a sharp fall in February 2009. From a national security perspective, it is relevant to note that India's policy of external economic liberalisation after 1991 has focused on increasing non-debt inflows, including foreign equity and inward private remittances. India has never pursued a mercantilist trade policy. Rather, it has always run a trade deficit that has been financed by inflows on the capital account. These inflows have contributed to an accumulation of foreign currency reserves.

Fiscal Policy Changes

Higher economic growth has enabled India to reduce its budgetary and fiscal deficits over the past decade. This has also created the fiscal space for increased public investment in infrastructure development, defense modernisation and the development of strategic capabilities, including maritime. The current slowdown will undoubtedly exert a fiscal pressure on such strategic investments. However, a large part of such spending would naturally go into counter-cyclical safety nets and employment generation programmes. This would reduce the funds available for defence and strategic modernisation.

The Indian government can view some of the defence spending as part of the fiscal stimulus. However, given the high import intensity of defence spending in India, and the capital intensive nature of defence modernisation, there are limits to how much defence spending can be a counter-cyclical activity.

To sum up, while India's reintegration into the world economy in the 1990s has made her more vulnerable to global crises, her pursuit of gradual reform and prudent regulation seem to have helped her minimise the negative impact of the Trans-Atlantic financial crisis and the global economic slowdown. From a strategic policy perspective, therefore, India can claim that her model of "gradual" and "graduated" economic liberalisation, and of risk averse prudential regulation in the banking and financial sector have helped limit her exposure to the Asian and Trans-Atlantic financial crises and the subsequent global economic slowdown.

Banking and Finance

A third wave of financial sector reform was initiated by the bursting of the dotcom bubble and its impact on the Indian stock market. India's decision to attract foreign currency inflows through the capital market by opening up the stock market to foreign institutional investors also forced the authorities to undertake institutional reform. Consequently, India put in place a more efficient and transparent regulatory system for the equities market and the banking and financial sectors.[13] The relatively high standards of governance and institutional credibility of the Reserve Bank of India (RBI) and the Securities and Exchange Board of India have also been effective.

RBI Governor, D. Subba Rao has claimed that, "The Indian banking system has had no direct exposure to the sub-prime mortgage assets or to the failed institutions. It has very limited off-balance sheet activities or securitized assets." The RBI has been credited with taking pre-emptive action that has minimised the vulnerability of Indian banks to the ripple effects of the United States sub-prime crisis and the crisis in the equities market. In fact, in an early public statement on this, former RBI Governor, Y. V. Reddy claimed: Financial stability in India has been achieved through perseverance of prudential policies which prevent institutions from excessive risk taking, and financial markets from becoming extremely volatile and turbulent. As a result, while there are orderly conditions in financial markets, the financial institutions, especially banks, reflect strength and resilience. While supervision is exercised by a quasi-independent Board carved out of the RBI Board, the interface between regulation and supervision is close in respect of banks and financial institutions, and on market regulation, a close coordination with other regulators exists "

On the basis of the findings, in order to equip the banking system to be better positioned to meet the adverse impact of interest rate risk, banks were advised in January 2002 to build up an Investment Fluctuation Reserve (IFR) within a period of five years. The prudential target for the IFR was five percent of their investments in 'Held for Trading' (HFT) and 'Available for Sale' (AFS) categories. Banks were encouraged to build up a higher percentage of IFR up to 10 percent of their AFS and HFT investments. This counter-cyclical prudential requirement enabled banks to absorb some of the adverse impact when interest rates began moving in the opposite direction in late 2004. Banks have been maintaining capital charge for market risk as envisaged under the Basel norms since end-March 2006

Conclusion

If India can return to the more recent high growth trajectory of eight to nine percent annual economic growth and sustain it over a decade, it will be on course to emerge as a great Asian power. The challenge before India in the next half a decade is to regain this momentum at a time when the global economy is likely to be less hospitable than it has been over the past half decade. In this sense, the global economic slowdown has imposed new constraints on India's economic rise. However, these are not insurmountable obstacles given the high domestic savings and investment ratios and the potential of the home market for sustaining high growth.

India's reintegration into the world economy, with a higher trade/GDP ratio and increased dependence on external capital flows, has made it more vulnerable to global crises, but the pursuit of gradual reform and prudent regulation have minimised the negative impact of both the Asian and, more recently, the 'Trans-Atlantic' financial crises. From a strategic policy perspective, India can claim that her model of "gradual" and "graduated" economic liberalisation, and of risk averse prudential regulation in the banking and financial sector have helped limit her exposure to the 'Great Recession'. India's major economic vulnerabilities remain internal, with weak public finances and inadequate investment in social and economic infrastructure.

An economically stronger India has felt encouraged to pursue a policy of 'asymmetric' or non-reciprocal economic liberalisation towards less developed countries, including those in its neighbourhood. Any deceleration in growth and consequent fiscal pressures would impose constraints on such non-reciprocal trade liberalisation and foreign aid

It is clear that the second Congress government will keep its focus on sustaining high rates of investment and economic growth. This is in keeping with Prime Minister Man Mohan Singh's vision of defining India's rise in terms of its economic performance. The global economic slowdown has only underlined the importance of India's economic performance for its global standing. The '10-point' Charter of the new government balances considerations of equity with those of efficiency. As a 'free market democracy', Indian public policy will have to pay equal attention to both considerations

Footnotes

1. Department of Economics, University of Allahabad, Allahabad- 211001
2. Department of Economics, University of Allahabad, Allahabad- 211001
3. Rajiv Kumar, Mathew Joseph, Dony Alex, Pankaj Vashisht, Debosree Banerjee, Indian Economic Outlook, 2008-09 and 2009-10, ICRIER Working Paper No. 234. March 2009. Available at: www.icrier.res.in
4. D. Subba Rao, Governor, Reserve Bank of India, "India–Managing the Impact of the Global Financial Crisis", 29 March 2009. Available at: http://www.rbi.org.in/scripts/BS_SpeechesView.aspx?Id=413

5. Report on Information Technology Software and Services–Performance and Prospects, 2009. National Association of Software Services Companies.
6. Dweep Chanana, "India as an Emerging Donor", Economic and Political Weekly, 21 March 2009.
7. Barack Obama, "Letter to Prime Minister Man Mohan Singh," 23 September 2008, available at http://en.wikisource.org/wiki/Barack_Obama's_Letter_to_Prime_Minister_Manmohan_Singh.
8. Paul Richter, "U.S. appeals to China to help stabilize Pakistan", Los Angeles Times, 24 May 2009. Available at: http://www.latimes.com/news/nationworld/nation/la-fg-us-china-pakistan25-2009may 25, 0, 6047766.story.
9. Baru- (2006)
10. Angus Madison, The World Economy: A Millennial Perspective, OECD, Paris, 2001
11. Vijay Joshi and IMD Little, India: Macroeconomics and Political Economy, 1964-1991, Oxford University Press, New Delhi, 1994
12. Arvind Panagariya, India: The Emerging Giant, Oxford University Press, New Delhi, 2008.
13. Y.V. Reddy, 'Monetary and Financial Sector Reforms in India: A Practitioner's Perspective', in Kaushik Basu (Ed.) India's Emerging Economy, Oxford University Press, 2004.

2

Global Financial Crisis and India's External Sector

Harjinder Singh, Amandeep Verma

Introduction

The Present Global Financial Crisis can be traced to the transformation of the US and global finance in the 1970's. The "originate and sell model" of banking is responsible to a larger extent for this chaos in the financial world. The complexity of the financial sector, resulting from financial integration at many levels-markets, institutions and instruments - has meant that there are multiple elements to the crisis as it unfolds. American financial sector was example of a highly regulated and stable financial system. The Glass - Steagall Act (GSA) which was introduced in 1933 has established the Federal Reserve System. The Wall Street crash of 1929 and the depression that followed had concentrated minds in the US Govt. as to how banks should behave in the future. As a result proposals of Carter Glass and Henry Steagall were generally well received. Broadly, the principal feature of the act was to create two classes of banks i.e. commercial and investment. The Glass Steagall Act 1933 aimed to prevent commercial banks from selling securities in failing Companies to cover debt. A new study shows that securities offered by investment banks before 1933 failed more often than those offered by commercial banks. Under Clinton administration it was repealed by Gram Leach-Billey Act 1999. This demolished the regulatory walls of Glass Steagall, allowing all banks to engage in investment and underwriting.

It was generally perceived in India that there would be negligible impact of financial crisis on Indian economy because of strong fundamentals of the economy and the well regulated banking system. This argument was emphasized by the Finance Minister and others even when other developing countries in Asia clearly experienced significant negative impact, through transmission of stock market turbulence and domestic credit squeeze. That country in which foreign ownership of banks is already well advanced and have merged banking and investment functions, the effect have been more marked. However in India financial liberalization has not been carried out to the full extent. It is slightly better protected from financial meltdown because of the larger role of the nationalized banks and other controls on domestic finance.

According to decoupling theory it was generally perceived that emerging economics will remain unscathed because of their substantial forex, improved policy framework, and relatively healthy banking sector. However it stands totally invalided today reinforcing the notion that in a globalised world no country can be an island. India too has been impacted by the crisis by much more than it was suspected earlier. India's integration into the world economy over the last decade has been rapid. Going by the common measure of globalization India's external trade as a proportion of GDP, grew from 21.2 percent in 1997-98 to 34.7 percent in 2007-08 so far as financial integration is concerned the ratio of external transactions (gross capital in-flows plus gross capital outflows) to GDP, this ratio has more than doubled from 46.8% in 1997-98 to 117.4% in 2007-08. Indian corporate sector's access to external funding has markedly increased in the last five years. In the five year period 2003-08, the share of investment in India's GDP rose by 11 percent points. Corporate savings financed roughly half of this but a significant portion of the balance financing came from external sources. Although funds were available in the domestic market yet investors preferred foreign markets because funds were cheaper as compared to domestic market. In the year 2007-08 India received capital inflows amounting to over 9% of GDP as against a current account deficit in the balance of payments of just 1.5% of GDP. These capital flows, in excess of current account deficit, evidence the importance of external financing and depth of India's financial integration.

This slowdown in global demand and credit market shocks adversely impacted India's BOP in 2008-09 (April December) It was marked by widened trade deficit, a record level of current account deficit (CAD) and lower net capital inflows. During the third quarter of 2008-09, export growth turned negative for the first time since 2001-02, while import growth touched a single digit. Except FDI and NRI deposits, all other components of capital flows declined in net terms. There was lower capital account surplus during April-December 2008 due to large net outflows under portfolio investment and large repayments under short term trade credit. Reflecting these developments, India's foreign exchange reserves on BOP basis declined by US $ 20.4 billion, the foreign exchange reserves stood at US $ 253 billion.

International Developments

Global economic activity contracted with advanced economies experiencing their sharpest declines in the post world war II period, notwithstanding the policy efforts. The impact is visible not only in financial markets but also the real economy across the globe. Global outlook remains uncertain mainly because of financial market turmoil affecting real economy more adversely than previously anticipated, according to forecast released by the International Monetary Fund (IMF) on March 19, 2009. World output is projected to contract by 0.5-1.00 percent in 2009 as compared with growth of 3.2 percent in 2008, before recovering gradually in 2010. According to the IMF, the US economy is projected to contract by 2.6 percent in 2009 as against an increase of 1.1 percent in 2008, as households respond to depreciating real and financial assets and tightening financial conditions. The Japanese GDP has already shown contraction by 4.6 percent in the fourth quarter of 2008 reflecting sluggish domestic demand and sharp decline in exports and business investment Real GDP in Japan is projected to record a decline of 5.8 percent in 2009 as the support to growth from net export is expected to decline further.

The growth rates in the emerging and developing economics, which were earlier considered to be resilient to the global financial disruptions are also projected to slow appreciably to 1.5 - 2.5 percent in 2009 (7-8 percent in 2008). Growth rate of China will come down to 6.7 percent in 2008 from 9 percent in 2008. Growth rate for India is placed at 5.3 percent for 2009-2010 (6.3 percent in 2008-09) by the IMF. The impact on the financial crisis is already in evidence in the currency and equity markets and capital outflows from emerging economics. However the macroeconomic impact on the EME's including India has so far been contained somewhat by the strength of domestic demand. According to IMF projections, world trade volume is expected to decline by 9 percent in 2009; however trade volume of emerging and developing economics is projected to decline marginally by 0.8 percent. The world trade organization has also projected that the collapse in global demand will drive exports volume down by 9 percent in 2009, the biggest contraction since the world war - II.

Impact on India's External Sector

There was adverse impact on India's external sector particularly during the second half of the year reflecting the impact of global financial crisis on India. World merchandise exports in dollar terms grew by 22.6.1 during January - September 2008 but subsequently declined during October December 2008 by 10.1 percent according to IMF's International Financial Statistics. The decline in exports could be due to declining demand, falling production and sharp shrinkage in credit to finance trade according to WTO. Exports from advanced countries sharply declined reflecting the impact of well entrenched recession. Exports from emerging and developing economies grew during 2008 upto September, however a sharp decline occurred during October 2008 which subsequently got worsened with rapid fall in export growth due to deteriorating external demand, sharp fall in commodity prices and severe constraints in accessing trade credit in the international markets.

Merchandise Trade

The impact of global slowdown was felt more severely on India's external demand, evident in the negative growth of merchandise exports that set in the third quarter of 2008-09. Imports growth also declined as domestic activity showed down rapidly. During April–February (2008-09) exports recorded a lower growth of 6.4 percent than 28.4 percent a year ago. Imports during 2008-09 (April–February) also recorded a lower growth due to deceleration in growth of petroleum, oil and lubricants (POL) and Non-POL imports. So far as commodity wise export data, is concerned during April November 2008, engineering goods and Chemical related products showed higher growth in exports while agriculture and allied products ores and minerals, textile and textile products, gems and jewellery and petroleum products showed deceleration.

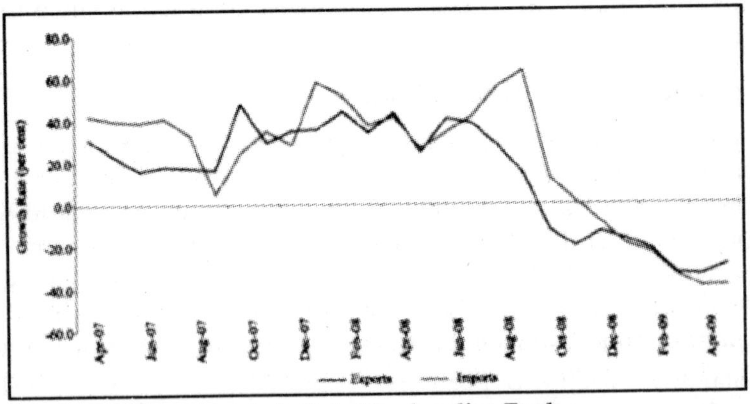

Chart 1: India's Merchandise Trade

Table 1
India's Merchandise Trade

(US $ Billion)

Item	*2008-09R*	*2008-09 R*	*2009-10 P*
		April-May	
1	2	3	4
Exports	168.7	31.6	21.8
Oil	24.9 *	5.5	..
Non-oil	128.1 *	26.1	..
Imports	287.8	51.5	32.0
Oil	93.2	19.2	7.8
Non-oil	194.6	32.3	24.2
Trade Balance	-119.1	-19.9	-10.2
Balance	..	-6.1	..
Exports	3.4	33.0	-31.2
Oil	2.4 *	27.2	..
Non-oil	7.4 *	38.8	..
Imports	14.3	30.3	-38.0
Oil	16.9	73.3	-59.6
Non-oil	13.2	24.1	-25.0

R: Revised. P: Provisional.
*: April-February... : Not Available
Source: DGCI&S.

Exports of Principal Commodities

Exports of principal commodities were affected by slowdown in the US as is evident from Table 2. It got worsened in the year 2008-09 (April-February) due to global recession. Gems and Jewellery (G&J) sector which has been identified as one of the thrust sector under special focus initiation under the Foreign Trade Policy 2004-09 was affected by the global financial crisis resulting in decline of 3.7 percent during 2008-09 (April-Feb.).

Imports of Principal Commodities

OPEC had the highest share in India's imports, followed by developing countries and the OECD countries. China was the single largest source of imports, with a share of 10 percent in total imports followed by Saudi Arabia, the UAE, the US, Iran and Switzerland. There was relatively less change in the imports of principal commodities as is evident from Table 3.

Table 2
Exports of Principal Commodities

	US $ billion			Variation (Per cent)		
	2007-08	2007-08 R	2008-09 P	2007-08	2007-08	2008-09
Commodity Group		*April-February*			*April-February*	
1	2	3	4	5	6	7
Primary Products	27.5	24.1	23.2	39.8	38.6	-3.6
of which:						
a) Agriculture and Allied Products	18.4	16.1	16.0	45.1	44.2	-0.9
b) Ores and Minerals	9.1	7.9	7.2	30.2	28.4	-8.9
Manufactured Goods	102.9	91.6	100.9	21.2	20.2	10.1
of which:						
a) Chemicals and Related Products	21.2	18.5	20.5	22.2	18.9	10.9
b) Engineering Goods	37.4	32.9	40.7	26.3	24.4	23.5
c) Textiles and Textile Products	19.4	17.4	17.7	11.8	10.7	1.4
d) Gems and Jewellery	19.7	17.9	17.2	23.2	25.3	-3.7
Petroleum Products	28.4	24.3	24.9	51.8	42.6	2.4
Total Exports	163.1	143.6	153.0	29.0	26.6	6.6
Memo:						
Non-oil Exports	134.8	119.3	128.1	25.1	23.8	7.4

R: Revised. P: Provisional.
Source: DGCI&S.

Table 3
Imports of Principal Commodities

	US $ billion			Variation (Per cent)		
	2007-08	2007-08 R	2008-09 P	2007-08	2007-08	2008-09
Group/Country		*April-February*			*April-February*	
1	2	3	4	5	6	7
Petroleum, Petroleum Products & Related Material	79.7	70.6	86.4	39.5	35.3	22.4
Edible Oil	2.6	2.4	3.2	21.4	24.2	32.8
Iron and Steel	8.7	8.0	8.8	35.3	40.3	9.7
Capital Goods	70.8	52.7	58.0	50.5	39.3	10.2
Pearls, Precious and Semi-Precious Stones	8.0	7.2	12.8	6.5	9.4	76.5
Chemicals	9.9	9.1	11.4	26.5	27.5	25.4
Gold and Silver	17.9	16.4	18.0	22.0	24.9	10.1
Total Imports	251.7	216.2	263.3	35.5	33.1	21.8
Memo:						
Non-oil Imports	171.9	145.7	176.9	33.7	32.0	21.4
Non-oil Imports excluding Gold and Silver	153.9	129.3	158.9	35.1	33.0	22.9
Mainly Industrial Inputs*	141.7	117.1	139.1	35.4	30.8	18.7

R : Revised. P : Provisional.
* : Non-oil imports net of gold and silver, bulk consumption goods, manufactured fertilizers and professional instruments.
Source : DGCI&S.

Balance of Payment's (Current Account)

Global financial crisis set in around August 2007. In the initial stages India was not significantly affected by the global financial crisis as it received huge FII's inflows of US$ 22.5 billion during September 2007 to January 2008. This led to belief in the decoupling theory that the emerging economies might remain insulated from the crisis and provide an alternative engine of growth to the world economy. However it was proved unfounded as the global financial crisis intensified and spread to emerging economies through capital and current account routes of balance of payments (BOP). It began to impact India through slowing down and reversal of capital flows. The portfolio flows to India (net) turned negative due to sale of equity stakes by FII's to replenish overseas cash balances. It had a negative impact on stock market and exchange rates through creating a supply demand imbalances in the foreign exchange market. Due to shrinkage in global demand and trade India's current account deficit increased to US$ 36.6 billion in April -December 2008 from US $ 15.5 billion in April December 2007 mainly led by larger trade deficit on account of higher growth in imports coupled with a slowdown in export growth. Merchandise exports increased by 17.5 % during April December 2008 from 21.9% in April December 2007). The lower growth of exports mainly reflected negative growth of 10.4% during the third quarter due to global economic slowdown. Overall the trade deficit was higher at US$ 105.3 billion during April - December 2008 as compared with US$ 69.3 billion in April - December 2007.

Invisibles

Gross invisibles receipts witnessed a lower growth of 18.8 percent during April–December 2008 which was 30.1% in the corresponding period of the previous years mainly due to slow growth in travel, business services and investment income receipts. Similarly invisible payments also showed a lower growth of 8.7 % in April December 2008 against 13.2% in April December 2007. Largely on account of slowdown in payments relating to travel, software services and a number of business and professional services. Net invisible increased by 28.1 percent during April-December 2008, primarily led by receipts under transfers and software services.

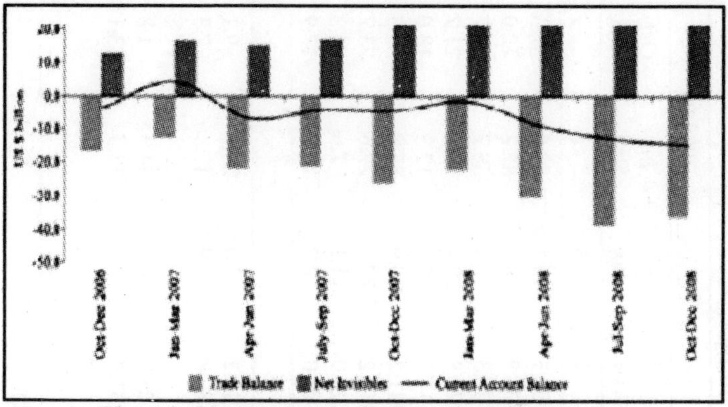

Chart 2: Movements in India's Current Account

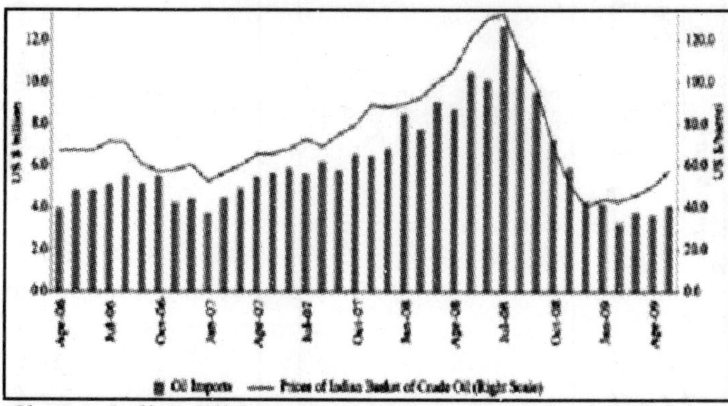

Chart 3: India's Oil Imports and International Crude Oil Prices

Capital Account

The adverse impact of global financial crisis was felt in terms of reversal of FII inflows and decline in long term and short term debt flows. Capital inflows can be classified by instrument (debt or equity) and maturity (short term or long term). The main components of capital account include foreign investment loans and banking capital, foreign investment comprising FDI and portfolio investment represents non-debt liabilities, while loans and banking capital including NRI deposits are debt liabilities. The net capital inflow during 2008-09 (April-

Table 4
India's Balance of Payments (US $ billion)

Item	*April-March*			*2008-09 P*			
	2007-08 PR	*2008-09 P*	*2007-08 PR Jan-Mar*	*Apr-Jun*	*Jul-Sept*	*Oct-Dec*	*Jan-Mar*
1	2	3	4	5	6	7	8
Exports	166.2	175.2	52.5	49.1	49.0	37.3	39.8
Imports	257.8	294.6	74.9	80.5	87.7	72.0	54.4
Trade Balance (1-2)	-91.6	-119.4	-22.3	-31.4	-38.7	-34.7	-14.6
Net Invisibles	74.6	89.6	20.8	22.4	26.2	21.7	19.3
Current Account Balance (3+4)	-17.0	-29.8	-1.5	-9.0	-12.5	-13.0	4.7
Gross Capital Inflows	433.0	302.5	141.2	90.9	85.0	69.5	57.1
Gross Capital Outflows	325.0	293.3	115.2	79.7	77.5	73.7	62.4
Net Capital Account (6-7)	108.0	9.1	26.0	11.1	7.6	-4.3	-5.3
Overall Balance (5+8)#	92.2	-20.1	25.0	2.2	-4.7	-17.9	0.3
Memo							
Export growth (%)	28.9	5.4	47.2	43.0	28.0	-9.1	-24.2
Import growth (%)	35.2	14.3	55.8	42.9	47.3	7.3	-27.3
Trade balance (as a % of GDP)	-7.8	-10.3					
Invisible receipts growth (%)	29.7	9.4	28.8	30.3	34.3	1.8	-16.6
Invisibles payments growth (%)	18.7	-1.4	31.9	13.5	14.4	3.1	-24.7
CAD as a % of GDP	1.5	2.6					
Foreign exchange reserves (as at end-March)	309.7	251.7					

#: Overall balance also includes errors and omissions apart from items 5 and 8.
PR: Partially Revised. P: Preliminary. CAD: Current account deficit. Source : DGCI&S.

Table 5
Invisibles Gross Receipts and Payments

(US $ billion)

	Invisibles Receipts				*Invisibles Payments*			
	April-March		*Jan-Mar*		*April-March*		*Jan-Mar*	
Item	*2007-08 (PR)*	*2008-09 (P)*	*2007-08 (PR)*	*2008-09 (P)*	*2007-08 (PR)*	*2008-09 (P)*	*2007-08 (PR)*	*2008-09 (P)*
1	*2*	*3*	*4*	*5*	*6*	*7*	*8*	*9*
Travel	11.3	10.9	3.6	2.7	9.3	9.4	2.8	2.6
Transportation	10.0	11.1	3.2	2.9	11.5	12.8	3.4	2.5
Insurance	1.6	1.4	0.5	0.3	1.0	1.1	0.3	0.3
Govt. not included Elsewhere	0.3	0.4	0.08	0.08	0.4	0.8	0.06	0.4
Miscellaneous	66.7	77.5	18.6	18.2	30.3	27.3	11.9	7.5
Of which								
Software	40.3	47.0	12.8	11.2	3.1	2.8	0.7	0.5
Non-Software	26.4	30.5	5.8	7.0	27.3	24.5	11.1	7.0
Transfers	44.3	47.0	14.5	10.0	2.3	2.7	1.0	0.4
Of which								
Private Transfers	43.5	46.4	14.2	9.8	1.8	2.3	0.9	0.3
Income	14.3	14.3	4.7	3.4	19.2	18.8	4.9	4.6
Investment Income	13.8	13.5	4.5	3.2	18.1	17.5	4.6	4.3
Compensation of Employees	0.5	0.8	0.2	0.2	1.1	1.3	0.3	0.3
Total (1 to 7)	148.6	162.6	45.2	37.7	74.0	73.0	24.3	18.3

P : Preliminary. PR : Partially Revised.
Source: DGCI&S.

December) was only US$ 15.3 billion. Capital account balance of US$ 16.1 billion (1.8% of GDP) during 2008-09 (upto Q_3) represented a decline of 80.5 percent from US$ 82.7 billion during corresponding period in 2007-08.

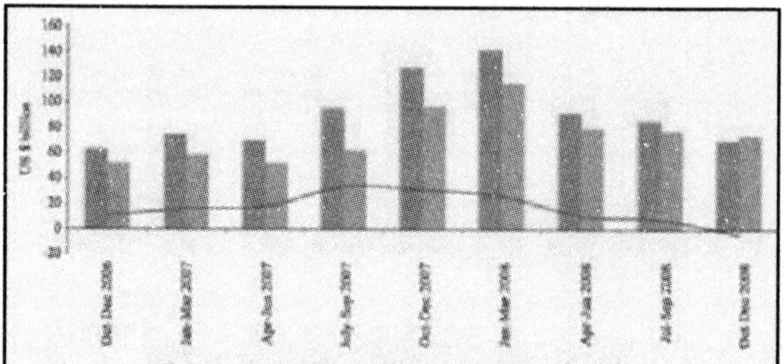

Source: DGCI&S

Chart 4: Movements in Capital Inflows and Outflows

Foreign Exchange Reserves

Foreign exchange reserves are an important component of the balance of payments and an essential element in the analysis of an economy's external position. Major fallout of the global financial crisis has been the reversal of portfolio flows. Together with the widening trade deficit, such outflows have upset the supply-demand balance in the foreign exchange market, leading to decline in the rupee exchange rate vis-à-vis US dollar. A sharp expansion in CAD in Q3 of 2008-2009 along

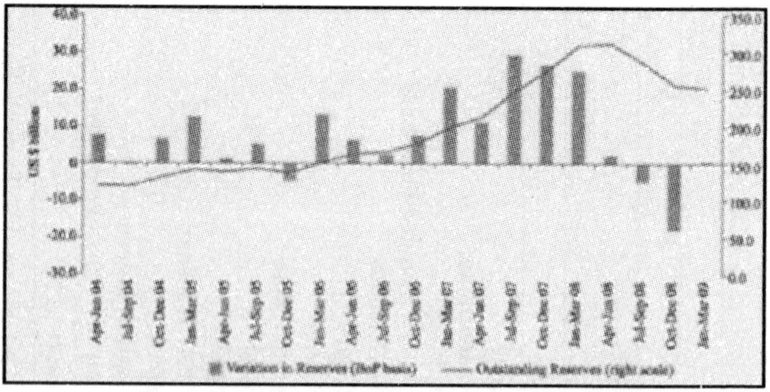

Chart 5: India's Foreign Exchange Reserves

Table 6
Foreign Exchange Reserves(US $ million)

End of Month	*Gold*	*SDR*	*Foreign Currency Assets**	*Reserve Position in the IMF*	*Total (2+3+4+5)*	*Memo: Outstanding Net Forward Sales (-)/Purchases (+) of US dollar by the Reserve Bank at the end of the month*
1	2	3	4	5	6	7
March2000	2,974	4	35,058	658	38,694	(-) 675
March 2005	4,500	5	135,571	1,438	141,514	-
March 2006	5,755	3	145,108	756	151,622	-
March 2007	6,784	2	191,924	469	199,179	-
March 2008	10,039	18	299,230	436	309,723	(+) 14,735
March 2009	9,577	1	241,176	981	251,735	(-) 2,042
April2009	9,231	1	241,487	983	251,702	(-) 1,071
May 2009	9,604	1	251,456	1,245	262,306	(+) 131
June 2009	9,800	1	254,093	1,248	265,142	-
July 2009#	9,800	1	255,138	1,248	266,187	-

* : Exclude US $250 million invested in foreign currency denominated bonds issued by IIFC (UK) since March 20, 2009.
# : As on July 17, 2009. – : Not Available.
Source: DGCI&S.

with net capital outflows resulted in the outgo of foreign exchange reserves to the extent of US$ 17.9 billion (exchange valuation). This level of decline in reserves was the highest during any one quarter in earlier years. As a result of this, foreign exchange reserves on BOP basis (i.e. excluding valuation) declined by US$ 20.4 billion in April December 2008 as against accretion of US$ 76.1 billion in April – December 2007.

India's foreign exchange reserves were US$ 252.0 billion as at the end of March 2009, showing a decrease of US$ 57.7 billion over end March 2008. The foreign exchange reserves, however increased to US$ 253 billion as on April 10, 2009.

Govt. Measures

India has been hit by the crisis through all the channels i.e. financial, real and the confidence channel. India's financial market–equity markets, money markets, forex markets and credit markets–had come under pressure from a number of directions. There was liquidity crunch and reversal of capital flows. So far as real channel is concerned it was marked by slump in demand for exports. Finally banks became cautious about lending. The failure of Lehman Brothers in mid-September and many big financial institutions led to uncertainty in the financial world. This contagion spread to emerging economics and to India too Both Govt. of India and Reserve Bank of India announced a series of measures. The main aim of the monetary policy was to maintain normalcy in the functioning of money and credit markets. It aimed at maintaining liquidity in rupee, to augment foreign exchange liquidity and to maintain credit delivery on track so as to keep the momentum of growth. It was reversal of RBIs policy of monetary tightening due to inflationary pressures in the economy. It included conventional as well as unconventional measures. Interest rates were aggressively reduced and there was upward adjustment of the interest rate ceiling on the foreign currency deposits by non-resident Indians substantially relaxing the external commercial borrowings regime for corporate, and allowing non-banking financial companies and housing financing companies access to foreign borrowings.

Among the unconventional measured taken by the RBI were a rupee dollar swap facility for Indian banks to give them comfort in managing short term funding requirement, expanding the lendable resources available to apex finance institutions for refinancing credit extended to small industries, housing and exports.

In the year 2003, Fiscal Responsibility and Budget Management Act were passed to bring fiscal sustainability. However recognizing the depth of and impact of the financial crisis, the central govt. invoked the emergency provisions of the FRBM Act to seek relaxation from the fiscal targets and launched two fiscal packages in December 2008 and January 2009. These fiscal packages amounting to 3% of GDP, included additional public spending particularly capital expenditure, govt. guaranteed funds for infrastructure spending, cuts in indirect taxes, expanded guarantee cover for credit to micro and small enterprises and additional support to exporters. These stimulus packages were in addition to already announced expanded safety net for rural poor, a farm loan waiver package and salary increases for government staff.

Conclusion & Suggestions

Real GDP growth of India has moderated in the first half of 2008-2009. There has been a slow down in the services sector growth which has been our prime growth engine for the last five years mainly in construction, transport, communication, trade and hotels etc. For the first time in seven years exports have declined during October-December 2008. All these factors suggest that growth moderation may be steeper and more extended than earlier projected.

However India has several advantages in facing this crisis. Most notably there has been fall in the inflation as measured by wholesale price index. It will induce consumption demand and reduce input costs for corporate. Fall in prices of crude oil and fertilizers will reduce size of subsidies thus opening up fiscal space for infrastructure spending. From the external sector perspective, it is projected that imports will shrink more than exports keeping the current account deficit modest. India's comfortable reserves position provides confidence to overseas investors.

During the last five years India achieved a nine percent growth driven by domestic consumption and investment even as share of net exports has been rising. It was due to a growing entrepreneur spirit, rise in productivity and increasing savings. However the global crisis will slowdown India's growth trajectory. There is a period of painful adjustment ahead of us. Once the global economy begins to recover India's turn around will be sharper and swifter, backed by strong fundamentals and untapped growth potential.

Reference

Acharya, Shankar (2009), 'Global Financial Crisis: Asian View' Business Standard, 12 Feb.

Chandraskhar, CP, Ghosh Jayati (2008), "India and the Global Financial Crisis" Business Line, Oct.

Economy Survey 2008-09, Ministry of Finance Department of Economic Affairs, Economic Division, Govt. of India, Oxford University Press.

Mohan, Rakesh 'Global Financial Crisis and Key Risks-Impact on India'. www.rbi.org.in

Ram Mohan, T.T. (2009), 'The Impact of the Crisis on the Indian Economy' Economic and Political Weekly, March.

Randall Wray, "Financial Markets Meltdown: What Can be Learn from Mynski? Public Policy Brief No. 94, 2008, the Economics Institute of Bard College, www.boylevy.org.

RBI Website: www.rbi.org.in

Reddy Y.V. (2009), "India and the Global Financial Crisis- Managing Money and Finance, Orient Black Swan, New Delhi.

Sunanda Sen (2008), "De-regulated Finance and the India Economy" in Alternate Economic Survey of India.

Sunanda Sen, "Global Financial Crisis- A Class 'Ponzi' Affairs?" Working Paper No. 2008/12 ISID, New Delhi.

3

Global Financial Crisis & its Impact on India

Suman Pamecha, Jasleen Sethi

Global Financial Crisis

The global financial crisis of year 2007-2008 was the most severe happened in last 80years. It has affected the whole world. The economic activity of the developing nations has declined by 15% and those of the developed nations declined by almost 23%. The worst hit economies have been in Eastern Europe and Central Asia and producers of capital goods. The economists have found in the studies that the global GDP has declined by 5% below the usual growth potential and this has happened for the first time after the World War II. There was a steep decline in trade in the countries of East Asia and these countries have suffered huge losses as production reduced, prices declined and there country's currency depreciated. In India, Over 500,000 jobs were lost in just the last three months of 2008 in export oriented sector alone.

The global financial crisis of 2008-2009 is an ongoing major financial crisis. It became prominently visible in September 2008 with the failure; merger or conservator ship of several large United States based financial firms.

Beginning with failures of large financial institutions in the United States, it rapidly evolved into a global crisis resulting in a number of European bank failures and declines in various stock indexes, and large reduction in market value of equities and commodities worldwide. The crisis has led to a liquidity problem and the deleveraging of financial institutions especially in the United States and Europe, which further accelerated the liquidity crisis. World Political leaders and national ministers of finance and central bank directors have coordinated their efforts to reduce fears but the crisis is ongoing and continues to change, evolving at the close of October into a currency crisis with investors transferring vast capital resources into stronger currencies such as the yen, the dollar, and the Swiss France, leading many emergent economies to seek aid from the International Monetary Fund. The crisis was triggered by the sub-prime mortgage crisis and is an acute phase of the financial crisis of the 2007-2008.

Types of Financial Crisis

Banking Crisis

When a bank suffers a sudden rush of withdrawals by depositors, this is called a bank run. Since banks lend out most of the cash they receive in deposits, it is difficult for firm to quickly pay back all deposits if these are suddenly demanded, so a run may leave the bank in bankruptcy, causing many depositors to lose their savings unless they are covered by deposit insurance. A situation in which bank runs are widespread is called a systematic banking crisis or just a banking panic. A situation without a widespread bank runs, but in which banks are reluctant to lend, because they worry that they have insufficient funds available, is often called credit crunch.

Speculative Bubbles and Crashes

Economists say that a financia! asset exhibits a bubble when its price exceeds the present value of the future income be received by owning it to maturity. If most market participants buy the asset primarily in hopes of selling it later at a higher price, instead of buying it for the income it will generate, this could be evidence that a bubble is present. If there is a bubble, there is also a risk of crash in asset prices: market participants will go on buying only as long as they expect others to buy, and when many decide to sell the price will fall. However, it is difficult to tell in practice whether an asset's price actually equals its fundamental value, so it is hard to detect bubbles reliably. Some economists insist that bubbles never or almost never occur.

International Financial Crisis

When a country that maintains a fixed exchange rate is suddenly forced to devalue its currency because of a speculative attack, this is called a currency crisis or balance of payment crisis. When a country fails to pay back its sovereign debt, this is called a sovereign default. While devaluation and default could both be voluntary decisions of the government, they are often perceived to be the involuntary results of a change in investor sentiment that leads to a sudden stop in capital inflows or a sudden increase in capital flight.

Wider Economic Crisis

A downturn in economic growth lasting several quarters or more is usually called a recession. An especially prolonged recession may be called a depression, while a long period of slow but not necessarily negative growth is sometimes called 'economic stagnation'. Since these phenomena affect much more than the financial system, they are not usually considered financial crisis. But some economists have argued that many recessions have been caused in large part by financial crisis. One important example is the great Depression, which was preceded in many countries by bank runs and stock market crashes. The sub prime mortgage crisis and the bursting of other real estate bubbles around the world are widely expected to lead to recession in the United States and a number of other countries in 2008.Nonetheless, some economists' argue that financial crises are caused by recessions instead of the other way around. Also, even if a financial crisis is the initial shock that sets off a recessions, other factors may be more important in prolonging the recession.

Bank Run (Banking Panics)

A bank run (also known as a run on the bank) occurs when a large number of bank customers withdraw their deposit because they believe the bank is, or might become, insolvent. As a bank run progresses, it generates its own momentum, is kind of self-fulfilling prophecy as more people withdraw their deposits, the likelihood of default increases, and this encourages further withdrawals. This can destabilize the bank to the point where it faces bankruptcy.A banking panic or bank panic is a financial crisis that occurs when many banks suffer runs at the same time.

Stock Market Crash

A stock market crash is a sudden dramatic decline of stock prices across a significant cross-section of a stock market. Crashes are driven by panic as much as by underlying economic factors. They often follow speculative stock market bubbles.

Stock market crashes are in fact social phenomena where external economic events combine with crowd behavior and psychology in a positive feedback loop where selling by some market participants drives more market participants to sell. Generally speaking, crashes usually occur under the following conditions: a prolonged period of rising stock prices and excessive economic optimism, a market where Price to Earnings ratios exceed long-term averages, and extensive use of margin debt and leverage by market participants.

There is no numerically specific definition of a crash but the term commonly applies to steep double digit percentage losses in a stock market index over a period of several days. Crashes are often distinguished from bear markets by panic selling and abrupt, dramatic price declines. Bear markets are periods of declining stock market prices that are measured in months or years. While crashes are often associated with bear markets, they do not necessarily go hand in hand.

Economic Bubble

An Economic Bubble (sometimes referred to as a speculative bubble, a market bubble, a price bubble, a financial bubble, or a speculative mania) is "trade in high volumes at prices that are considerably at variance with intrinsic values".

While some economists deny that bubbles occur, the cause of bubbles remains a challenge to those who are convinced that asset prices often deviate strongly from intrinsic values. While many explanations have been suggested, it has been recently shown that bubbles appear even without uncertainty, speculation, or bounded rationality. Most recently, it has been suggested that bubbles might ultimately be caused by processes of price coordination or emerging social norms. Because it is often difficult to observe intrinsic values in real-life markets, bubbles are often identified only in retrospect, when a sudden drop in prices appears. Such a drop is known as a crash or a bubble burst. Both the boom and the bust phases of the bubble are examples of a positive feedback mechanism, in contrast to the negative feedback mechanism that determines the equilibrium price under normal market circumstances. Prices in an economic bubble can fluctuate erratically, and become impossible to predict from supply and demand alone.

Currency Crisis

A currency crisis is also called a balance-of-payments crisis, occurs when the value of a currency changes quickly, undermining its ability to serve as a medium of exchange or a store of value. It is a type of financial crisis and is often associated with a real economic crisis. Currency crisis can be especially destructive to small open economies or bigger, but not sufficiently stable ones. Government often takes on the role of fending off such attacks by satisfying the excess demand for a given currency using the country's own currency reserves or its foreign reserves.

Sovereign Default

A sovereign bond is a bond issued by a national government. Bonds issued by national governments in the country's own currency are also referred to as government bonds.

Nations with very high or unpredictable inflation or unstable exchange rates often find it uneconomic to issue bonds in their own currencies and so far forced to issue bonds denominated in more stable foreign currencies. This raises the issue of sovereign default if the nation cannot afford to repurchase the necessary foreign currency at bond repayment time. Due to the risk of default, investors require the bonds to be issued with a higher yield. This makes the debt more expensive to service, increasing risk of default. In the event of default, unlike a corporation or even a municipal subdivision, a nation cannot file for bankruptcy. But on the rare occasions a default occurs, just as in defaults on corporate bands, recent practice has been that the defaulting borrower presents an exchange offer to its bond holders in an effort to restructure the sovereign debt.

A Systemic Banking Crisis

It is the one where all or almost all of the banking capital in a country is wiped out. The resulting chain of bankruptcies can cause a long economic recession. Much of the Great Depression's economic damage was caused directly by bank runs. Several techniques can help to prevent bank runs. They include temporary suspension of withdrawals, the organization of central banks that act as a lender of last resort, the protection of deposit insurance systems such as United States Federal Deposit Insurance Corporation and governmental bank regulation. These techniques do not always work: for example, even with deposit insurance, depositors may still be motivated by beliefs they may lack immediate access to deposits during bank reorganization.

Causes of Financial Crises

It is often observed that successful investment requires each investor in a financial market to guess what other investors will do. J.M. Keynes compared financial markets to a beauty contest game in which each participant tries to predict which model other participants will consider most beautiful.

Furthermore, in many cases investors have incentives to coordinate their choices. For example a depositor in ICICI Bank who expects other depositors to withdraw their funds may expect the bank to fail, and therefore has an incentive to withdraw too. Economists call an incentive to mimic the strategies of others strategic complementarities. It has been argued that if people or firms have a sufficiently strong incentive to do the same thing they expect others to do, then self-fulfilling prophecies may occur. For example, if investors expect the value of the yen to rise, this may cause its value to rise; if depositors expect a bank to fail this may cause it to fail. Therefore, financial crises are sometimes viewed as a vicious circle in which investors shun some institution or asset because they expect others to do so.

Sub Prime Lending

In addition to the easy credit conditions, there is evidence that both government and competitive pressures contributed to an increase in the amount of sub prime lending during the years preceding the crisis. Major U.S banks and government sponsored enterprises (Like Fannnie Mac) played an important role in the expansion of higher-risk lending,

The term sub prime refers to the credit quality of particular borrowers, who have weakened credit histories and a greater risk of loan default than prime borrowers, The value of U,S sub prime mortgages was estimated at $ 1.3 trillion as of March 2007with over 7.5 million first-lien sub prime mortgagees outstanding.

Sub Prime mortgages remained below 10% of all mortgage originations until 2004, when they spiked to nearly 20% and remained there through the 2005-2006 peak of the United States Housing Bubble. A proximate event to this increase was the April 2004 decision by the U.S Securities and Exchange Commission (SEC) to relax the net capital rule, which encouraged the largest five investment banks, encouraged the largest five investment banks to dramatically increase their financial leverage and aggressively expand their issuance of mortgage-backed securities.

Leveraged Investment

It means borrowing to finance investments, is frequently cited crisis. When a financial institution invests its own money, it can, in the very worst case, lose its own money. But when it borrows in order to invest more, it can potentially earn more from its investments, but it can also lose more than all it has. Therefore leverage magnifies the potential returns from investment, but also creates a risk of bankruptcy. Since bankruptcy means that a firm fails to honor all its promised payments to other firms, it may spread financial troubles from one firm to another.

The average degree of leverage in the economy often rises prior to a financial crisis.

Asset-Liability Mismatch

Another factor believed to contribute to financial crisis is asset-liability mismatch, a situation in which the risks associated with an institution's debts and assets are not appropriately aligned. For example, commercial banks offer deposit accounts which can be withdrawn at any time and they use the proceeds to make long-term loans to business and homeowners. The mismatch between the bank's short-term liabilities (its deposits) and its long-term assets (its loans) is seen as one o the reason bank runs occur (when depositors panic and decide to withdraw their funds more quickly than the bank can get back the proceeds of its loans).

In an international context, many emerging market governments are unable to sell bonds denominated in their own currencies, and therefore sell bonds denominated in US dollars instead. This generates a mismatch between the currency denomination of their liabilities (their bonds) and their assets (their local tax revenues), so that they run a risk of sovereign default due to fluctuations in exchange rates.

Regulatory Failures

Governments have attempted to eliminate or mitigate financial crises by regulating the financial sector. One major goal of regulation is transparency: making institutions' financial situation publicly known by requiring regular reporting under standardized accounting procedures. Another goal of regulation is making sure institutions have sufficient assets to meet their contractual obligations, through reserve requirements, capital requirements, and other limits on leverage.

Fraud

Fraud has played a role in the collapse of some financial institutions, which companies have attracted depositors with misleading claims about their investment strategies, or have embezzled the resulting income.

Many rogue traders that have caused large losses at financial institutions have been accused of acting fraudulently in order to hide their traders. Fraud in mortgage financing has also been cited as one possible cause of the 2008 sub-prime mortgage crisis; governmental officials stated on September 23, 2008 that the FBI was looking into possible fraud by mortgage financing companies Fannie Mae & Freddie Mac, Lehman Brothers, & insurer American International Group.

Ecopathy

Swedish psychologist Torbjorn K A Eliazon has proposed a new psychological concept of Ecopathy, when economic smartness or greed crosses the borders to an extreme speed and computational proposal unit. Ecopathy_is an economic understanding without moral values, here the word 'more' has become a central existential position and have no ulterior border in the same manner as that of drug abusers or people denying humanity and mortality. Ecopathy can be both existing in an individual subject (as a personality disorder) and been developed as a structurally built-in-operative within organizations.

Contagion

Contagion refers to the idea that financial crises may spread from one institution to another, as when a bank run spreads from a few banks to many others, or from one country to another, as when currency crises, sovereign defaults, or stock market crashes spread across countries. When the failure of one particular financial institution threatens the stability of many other institutions, this is called systemic risk.

Recession Effects

Some financial crisis have little effect outside of the financial sector, like the Wall Street Crash of 1987, but other crises are believed to have played a role in decreasing growth in the rest of the economy. There are many theories why a financial crisis could have a recessionary effect on the rest of the economy. These theoretical ideas include the 'financial accelerator', 'flight to quality' and 'flight to liquidity' model. Some third generation models of currency crises explore how currency crises and banking crises together can cause recessions.

Self- Fulfilling Prophecy

A self-fulfilling prophecy is a prediction that directly or indirectly causes itself to become true by very terms of the prophecy itself.

"The self-fulfilling prophecy is, in the beginning, a false definition of the situation evoking a new behavior which makes the original false conception come 'true'. This specious validity of the self fulfilling prophecy perpetuates a reign of error. For the prophet will cite the actual course of events as proof that he was right from the very beginning."

In other words, a prophecy declared as truth when it is actually false may sufficiently influence people either through fear or logical confusion, so that their reactions ultimately fulfill the once-false prophecy.

Impact of the Crisis on India

There was no direct impact of the Lehman failure on the domestic financial sector in view of the limited exposure of the Indian banks; however, following The Lehman failure, there was a sudden change in the external environment. As in the case of other major EME's there was a sell-off in domestic equity markets by portfolio investors reflecting developing.

Consequently there were large capital outflows by portfolio investors during September-October 2008, with concomitant pressure in the foreign exchange market. While foreign direct investment flows exhibited resilience, access to external commercial borrowings and trade credits was rendered somewhat difficult. On the whole, net capital inflows during 2008-09 were substantially lower than in 2007-08 and there was a depletion of reserves. However a large part of the reserve loss (US $33 billion out of US $54 billion) during April-December 2008 reflected valuation losses

While the overall policy approach has been able to mitigate the potential impact of the turmoil on domestic financial markets and the economy, with the increasing integration of the Indian economy and its financial markets with rest of the world, there is recognition that the country does face some downside risks from these international developments. In India, the adverse effects have so far been mainly in the equity markets because of reversal of portfolio equity flows, and the concomitant effects on the domestic forex market and liquidity conditions. The macro effects have so far been muted due to the overall strength of domestic demand, the healthy balance sheets of the Indian corporate sector, and the predominant domestic financing of investment.

Least Impacted: Pharmaceuticals, Oil & Gas, FMCG, and Media & Entertainment

Mildly Impacted: Power equipments & Services, Auto, Retail, Logistics, Hospitality and tourism

Most Impacted: Banks, Financial Services, Real Estate, Infrastructure, Information Technology

Here some of the heads have been discussed:

Impact on the Indian Financial Services

The US sub-prime market crisis, which so far caused losses worth $181 billion to the world's top 45 banks by the end of financial year 2008, has started hitting Indian banks also. India's largest private sector bank ICICI Bank was the first bank to announce a loss of about Rs. 1056 crores owing to the sub prime crisis of US in the financial year 2008 results. The public sector banks have had a limited position in the structured products and therefore impact is expected to be minimal. However negative sentiments will hit harder. Punjab national Bank, Bank of India, State Bank of India, Bank of Baroda were major banks having an exposure to the instruments issued by Lehman and Merrill Lynch. However the banking sector in general will have to face tight liquidity conditions from further mark-to-market losses. The net non performing assets of entire banking sector are less than 2% and it is well capitalized. The capital adequacy ratio is around 13% as against the statutory requirement of 8 to 9%.

Impact on the Indian Banking System

A detailed study undertaken by the RBI in September 2007 on the impact of the sub-prime episode on the Indian banks had revealed that none of the Indian banks or the foreign banks, with whom the discussions had been held, had any direct exposure to the sub-prime markets in the USA or other markets. However, a few Indian banks had invested in the collateralized debt obligations (CDOs) / bonds which had a few underlying entities with sub-prime exposures. Thus, no direct impact on account of direct exposure to the sub-prime market was in evidence. However, a few of these banks did suffer some losses on account of the mark-to-market losses caused by the widening of the credit spreads arising from the sub-prime episode on term liquidity in the market, even though the overnight markets remained stable. Consequent upon filling of bankruptcy by Lehman Brothers, all banks were advised to report the details of their exposures to Lehman Brothers and related entities both in India and abroad. Out of 77 reporting banks, 14 reported exposures to Lehman Brothers and its related entities either in India or abroad. Overall, these banks' exposure especially to Lehman Brothers Holding Inc. which has filed for bankruptcy is not significant and banks are reported to have made adequate provisions.

Impact on the Real Estate

With the sudden collapse of world leading financial houses, the Indian real estate players who were already facing the problem of lack of funds due to economic slowdown & correction in prices would find it difficult to raise further funds. Among the US Financial Houses – Lehman Brothers was very bullish on Indian Reality Sector and had an investment in excess of US$ 700 million (maximum amongst peers). Lehman's real estate investments at project levels (including the big ones like DLF, Unitech & Future Capital) have been disbursed & it will not affect the ongoing projects. RBI's directive not to remit investments made by US financial houses in India without permission is also a step in positive direction and would restrict flight of capital. However, stocks of companies in which sunken financial institutions have a direct exposure (as FII investments especially Lehman) would see selling pressure. Stocks to get affected: Anant Raj Industries, Orbit Corporation, Ganesh Housing, DSK Kulkarni Dev, Ajmera Reality, Ansal Housing, Ansal Properties, Purvankara Projects.

Impact on Infrastructure

Global financial crisis has an adverse impact on the infrastructure companies as it disturbs the financial atmosphere for the companies which are in the growth stage. Lately, after having raised money through IPO's many Indian infrastructure companies have gone in for QIP issues with the financial majors across the world. Thus, the current situation might not affect the companies at the project implementation level, however we might see heavy selling pressure in the stocks of these companies by the sinking US financial institutions which have an exposure to these companies. Going forward, if there is no change in the scenario, fund raising by infrastructure companies could become a problem. Stocks to get affected are Reliance Infrastructure, Prajay Engg, Triveni Engg, Pratibha Inds, Unity Infra, BSEL Infra, Nagarjuna Construction, Sujana Tower, Madhucon Projects, Jyoti Structures, Action Construction.

Impact on Information Technology

USA as a region and Banking Financial Services and Insurance as a vertical are most critical for top Indian IT companies. There would be lesser probability of immediate cancellation of orders or vendor consolidation. Sales cycle would become longer and hence top line impact should be visible after two-three quarters due to this crisis. Large investment banks had significant discretionary IT spend, which should reduce now resulting in reduction of outsourcing pie.

Manufacturing and Retail, two other significant verticals for Indian IT companies would surely take a hit due to this gloom and hence would negatively impact the IT spend of companies in this vertical. Europe and APAC market would also get significantly impacted and though they are relatively lesser tapped in terms of IT outsourcing, they were a significant growth areas for Indian IT companies. Relocation of employees from these clients's project would be a big task. Negative on utilization as well as productivity. Perhaps pink slips would be the norm.

It's an irony. Tier 1 IT companies have USA and BFSI as biggest revenue earners, yet even in these turbulent times these companies are the safest bet. Companies having significant non USA focus (like Educomp having ~13% outside India revenue) could also be a good bet. These companies are focused on profitability and growth and have considerable revenue visibility. However these buys are for significantly longer term, at least more than 1-2 year. Currency will keep on playing its part and rupee may not be allowed to depreciate from its current levels (but then RBI can do only that much). Therefore rupee going up (perhaps after reaching 48-50 range) would again impact IT sector in the short term.

Impact on the Automobiles

In the event of credit crunch spreading to India from US, we might see auto sales getting impacted due to tougher credit availability. Auto companies have been seeing sluggish sales for the past few months due to higher interest rates and higher fuel prices: two wheelers have shown decent sales growth in the last 2 months, more due to the low base effect. It would get tougher for passenger and commercial vehicles and it might start impacting two wheeler vehicle sales negatively. Exports of auto companies might take some hit, however, the impact on exports might not have significant impact on the top-line of auto companies, as the percentage sales contribution from exports is less for Indian auto companies; but this might cause the auto companies to cut their export targets for the next two or three years.

Impact on the Hospitality, Travel and Tourism

Slowdown in travel demand: Travel budgets of companies have fallen this year by approximately 40% and a further fall of 10-15% is expected in the next 2 quarters, in spite of being a peak season of inbound travel hotels will face a difficulty in maintaining occupancies during the coming holiday season of Oct–Jan, falling from the current 75% to 68-70%. With increasing competition and room tariff wars, hotels will face a pressure on their profit margins. Growth in Average Rooms Rates are expected to slowdown from 16-21% to 5-9% around the year end festive season. Lack of investments in properties will limit the hotels from expansion plans. AIG bailout is likely to impact Indian Aviation as its subsidiary is among the world's largest aircraft leasers, which include Indian companies like Jet Airways, Kingfisher Airlines, Deccan Aviation and Spicejet.

Impact on the Pharmaceuticals

There is no direct exposure to the sector in terms of clients from the financial sector Jubilant, Dishman, Divi's & Vimta that get contracts from Innovator Big pharma companies can see increased volume as big companies look to hive off more manufacturing units and transfer high end R&D work to Indian companies. Generic companies have revenue streams from different geographies and thus no significant affect on the overall revenues. We continue to remain bullish on the Contract Manufacturing business model of pharma companies in India.

Impact on Fertilizers

In the event of credit crunch spreading to India as well, fertilizer sector might face trouble in working capital financing front. With rising subsidy bill, fertilizer sector is already into a bit of tight spot regarding working capital financing. Recently government of India (GOI) has announced an increase in the allocation to fertilizer subsidy to Rs.54, 000 crores from the earlier allocation of Rs.32, 000 Crores for 2008-08. This announcement came as a breather to the fertilizer industry. However, due to rise in oil prices in 2008-09 and higher levels of imported fertilizer inputs, subsidy payments have skyrocketed in the last four years from about Rs15,800 crores in 2004-05 to an estimated Rs120,000 crores in 2008-09, or 2% of the GDP. In this context, the GOI has to further increase the allocation for the fertilizer subsidies.

Impact on Oil & Gas

The least impacted are the oil marketing companies and mildly impacted are the private oil exploration companies. As sub-prime crisis deepens with the extinction of Wall Street giants, it would extend the pressure in the credit markets/lending segment of the banking sector. This along with massive job losses is likely to constrain consumer spending and thereby put pressure on demand for petro products. This demand destruction in the developed economies would put pressure on the crude oil prices. Falling crude prices would be broadly good for the Indian economy and the Indian oil sector. In case of private exploration companies as prices fall, realization of these companies is expected to fall, which would reduce their revenues and earnings growth. However, as the long term trend is up, the fall in prices would be temporary and thus would benefit these companies over a long period. While in case of Oil Marketing companies (OMCs) there is an an environment of rising oil prices and the limited pass-through of these through subsidies, OMCs are unable to benefit from higher prices. Their margins suffer and the subsidy burden increases which is shared among OMCs and ONGC. As oil prices cool off, their margins increases and the subsidy burden decreases, giving them flexibility to focus on long term growth plans.

Impact on the Consumer Driven Sectors

World Financial crisis has in turn affected the risk appetite for lending institutions. This has resulted in an increase in cost of capital and tight credit appraisal in the system. Due to this, Indian retail companies are facing problem in execution of Capex program. This will put brakes on the aggressive expansion of the companies in the sector.

Retail: Sizeable young population in India generates income from ITES/BPO and spends on Movies, Hotels, and Malls etc. With possible job losses in ITES/BPO, falling consumer confidence, personal consumption expenditure is expected to fall. This will reduce the customer traffic in organized retail outlets.

FMCG: As rural India is on radar of FMCG companies, the effect on these companies will not have major impact on their top-line. However, bottom-line might be under pressure as the premium products will not be favored in the market.

Logistics Sector: It would be impacted from the offshoot of the current crisis. Organized logistics is still a very nascent industry and requires continuous funding. FDI inflows which have rather remained unaffected by the credit crisis are the main source for funding the capex plans. Rail & Road Infrastructure: Built mostly through PPP or 100% government funding.

Shipping: Projects might get delayed in the rising interest rate scenario, otherwise is insulated from sub prime. Air Freight Logistics: Very small share in logistics space. No direct impact.

Media & Entertainment: The demand for news and entertainment will not be notably impacted by slow down in world economies. Recently, there has been a significant increase in investments in M&E sector which is not expected to significantly slow down due to the sector low price elastic nature. The Indian E&M is estimated at Rs. 513 billion in 2007, is projected to grow at 18% CAGR for the next 5 years to reach Rs. 1.157 trillion in 2012.

Conclusion

There silence of the Indian Financial Sector in the face for the worst global financial crisis since the 1930's can also be attributed to our approach to financial globalization. The key features of our approach have been reflected in a full, but gradual opening up of the current account but a more calibrated approach towards the opening up of the capital account and the financial sector. As far as the capital account is concerned, whereas foreign investment flows, especially direct investment inflows are encouraged, debt inflows in the form of external commercial borrowings are generally subject to ceilings and some end-use restrictions. Macro ceilings have also been stipulated for portfolio investment in government securities and corporate bonds. Capital outflows have also been progressively liberalized. Along with the calibrated approach to opening of the capital account, we have also practiced prudential regulation, particularly of banks to manage financial instability.

India has by-and-large been spared of global financial contagion due to the sub-prime turmoil for a variety of reasons. India's growth process has been largely domestic demand driven and its reliance on foreign savings has remained around 1.5 per cent in recent period. It also has a very comfortable level of forex reserves. The credit derivatives market is in an embryonic stage; the originate-to-distribute model in India is not comparable to the ones prevailing in advanced markets; there are restrictions on investments by residents in such products issued abroad; and regulatory guidelines on securitization do not permit immediate profit recognition. Financial stability in India has been achieved through perseverance of prudential policies which prevent institutions from excessive risk taking, and financial markets from becoming extremely volatile and turbulent. The Indian approach has focused on gradual, phased and calibrated opening of the domestic financial and external sector, taking into account reforms in the other sector of the economy. Financial markets are contributing to the efficient channeling of domestic savings into productive uses and are supporting domestic growth. These characteristics of India's external and financial sector management coupled with ample forex reserves coverage reduce the susceptibility of the Indian economy to global turbulence.

References

Reserve Bank of India (2008), Annual Policy Statement for the year 2008–2009, April.

Mohan, Rakesh (Deputy Governor RBI), Remarks prepared for IMF–FSF at Washington D.C.

Times of India

Journals/Articles

Elliot, Larry (2008), "Credit Crisis- How It All Began", The Guardian, August 5.

Norris, Floyd (2007), "A New Kind of Bank Run Tests Old Safeguards", The New York Times, August 10.

Robertson, Justin (2008), *1972*- US-Asia Economic Relations: A Political Economy of Crisis and the Rise of New Business Actors. Rout ledge. ISBN 9780203890523 (ebook)

Carney, Richard, ed. (2009), Lessons from the Asian Financial Crisis. Routledge.

Subbarao, Duvvri, "India-Managing the Impact of the Global Financial Crisis"

www.crisistalk.worldbank.org

www.nytimes.com

www.moneymorning.com

www.knowledgestorm.com

www.globalguru.com

www.news.bbc.co.uk

4

UNIVERSAL BANKING IN INDIA AND GLOBAL MELTDOWN

Preeti Mishra

This paper consists of V sections the, section I consists with the literature review on the universal banking and its experience worldwide. Section II consists of the genesis of universal banking in India and the failure of DFIs model , section III consists of rational of the research , scope of the research ,objective of the research, hypothesis of the research and research methodology. Section IV consists of case study of ICICI Bank .Section V consists of analysis and findings and the emerging issues in universal banking.

SECTION-I

Introduction

Universal banking is one of the most commonly used words in the banking industry today. It becomes pertinent to understand what it means as people have different notions about the same. According to Molyneux et al (1996) there is no clear definition of universal banking, but they describe it as a large commercial bank undertaking corporate, wholesale and retail banking, investment banking, securities and insurance business. A more theoretical definition is provided by Canals (1997) who defines universal banks as "........... those banks that offer a full range of products to a vast number of customers". Saunders and Walter (1994) add a third dimension to the definition that considers the geographic arenas where business is done.

In more recent research a stricter was used: the key feature of universal banking is their ability to hold equity shares large enough to monitor corporations as equity owner (Steinherr and Huveneers, 1994; Santos, 1998; Vander Vennet, 1998). In this way, these banks not only deliver the traditional banking products (attracting deposits to make loans), but may also engage in securities business and thus, may perform tasks which are normally considered to be the domain of financial markets.

In world we find two models of financing that is bank-based financing and market -based financing. Among these two the bank based financing is more prevalent in most of developing and developed economies like Germany, Japan and East Asia etc. The America has market based financing system but bank based financing is also present there. The basic difference between the two systems is that in one case the corporate entities directly approach the public for finance while in the second case they interact with the intermediary. So, there is dilemma for banks i.e. diversification of activities versus specialization. Now the banks have to decide the scope of their activities and weigh the advantages of scale and scope against those of flexibility, simplicity and specialization Universal Banking organizations may take a number of more or less distinct forms these are stylized[2] as follows:

(i) *Full Integration*– These types of banks provide a broad range of financial services i.e. banking, securities and insurance under a single corporate structure supported by a single capital base .there is at present no best example of this model.

(ii) *Bank Parent Structure*– It is Universal bank whose core business is taking deposits and making commercial loans. The Commercial bank is parent of subsidiaries engaged in variety of other financial services ranging from investment banking to insurance. Barclays Plc is the best Example of this version. India is also following this structure

(iii) *Holding Company Structure*– It involves the creation of holding company which controls affiliates engaged in commercial banking, investment banking, insurance and possibly other type of financial and non financial businesses .JP Morgan and CS Holding.

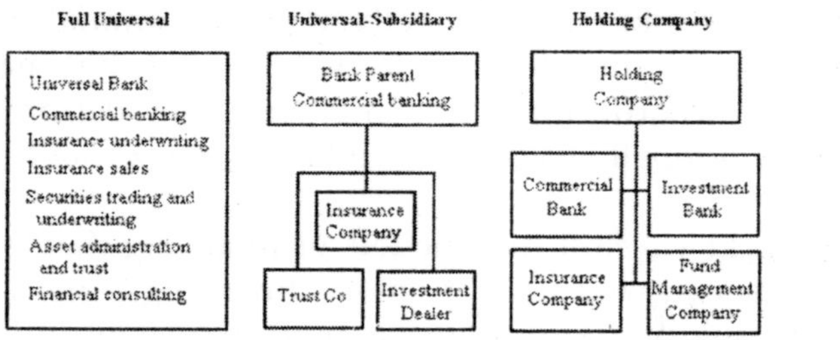

Source: Saunders and Thomas (2001)

Advantages of Universal Banking for Banks

Economies of Scale

the financial services is said to have high fixed cost so naturally there is ample potential for economies of scale. Empirical tests for the economies of scale and scope are beset with many conceptual difficulties and the present study do not give adequate support for the realization of economies of scale or scope in universal banks. However the comprehensive study done by the Saunders and Walters (1994) conclude that over some size ranges of banks, there appear to be the economies of scale gained from an institution's large scale. Other studies show that, profitability scope inherent in this model lie more on revenue generating side than on cost side.[3] These revenue synergies comes firstly from the enhanced ability of the managers to shift freely the resources among the activities which are highly demanded by the consumers. Secondly, by the joint marketing and selling of financial services.

Economies of Scope

On supply side scope economies leads to cost savings through sharing of overheads and joint production of generically similar group of financial products. On demand side the scope economies help the buyer by reducing the transaction cost i.e. providing all the services at same point like product, information, search, monitoring, contracting and pother services.

- *Increased Revenue Generation-* Since the universal banks are more leveraged and customers also prefer to have more information and types of product from the one-stop-shop this gives convenience to the consumer so increased selling of product will increase revenue
- *Increased Revenue Diversification-* As the universal banks are producing variety of financial products, so they have diversified portfolio.

Advantages of Universal Banking–Consumers Perspective

- One stop shopping (Super market)-providing savings in transaction and information cost. One conglomerate selling the financial services jointly would reduce the transaction cost, search cost and other problems faced by the consumers
- Greater opportunity for inter-generational risk sharing
- Suppression of "noisy" information

The cost and benefits of universal banking has been debated over several years. Mark Roe[4] has documented the populist sentiment that developed in US after the stock-market crash of 1929. It has ended the euphoria of investing, developed in post-world war scenario. It turned the public belief against the financial institutions. Most of the Banks were criticized for the role they have played which ultimately brought the demise of banking system. It is said that banks have taken the advantage of conflict of interest, as they issued the securities in companies with outstanding loan balances at times when the firms future prospects were not as positive as public believed . Issuing overpriced securities allowed the firms to liquidate the outstanding balances owed to banks. Ultimately the public outcry led to the legislation of Glass-Steagell Act[5] ,the landmark of 1933 which restricted underwriting by commercial banks and also required greater disclosure of information by firms.The Act has myriad effects over banking system as most of the banks were barred the activities like trading or underwriting securities. In the 1990s the debate over universal banking was revived as the model was working successfully in some of the countries like Germany and Switzerland ect. Advocates wanted the removal of restrictions; they gave the logic of efficiency of universal banking. Calomiris and Ramirez[6] argue that universal banking has four primary advantages over the current system in US; improved information gathering and monitoring, amelioration of conflicts among various claimants on the firm diversification benefits and more effective signaling. The recent wave of mergers in the financial sector all across the globe and particularly in India has intensified the scrutiny of this issue for its prospective pros and cons .Also the Sub -prime crisis in US (2007) , ripple effect of which are experienced along the globe in form of recession, urges the need of debate over the controversial issue of universal Banking. So characteristic and the success of universal banking depends mostly on following two factors

- specific countries diversification rules and regulatory norms
- the strengths of individual bank in enlarging the scope of the activities to various segments of financial industry

SECTION-II

Universal Banking in India

In India the financing was primarily bank based at the same time the government established the development financial institutes for industrial financing. Historically in Indian financial set-up it was the commercial banks which were meeting the short term working capital requirements of business at national and state level while DFIs took care of long term project finance requirements. DFIs were set up with the objective of providing term lending at concessional rate for the economic development. The DFIs were funded by the government so that they can provide the loanable funds to corporate at concessional rates.

This financing system was based on the fact that public investment would generate the demand in economy and bring about economic development. But the huge concessional lending has direct bearingt on fiscal deficit which began to increase. Since the DFIs were government funded so they lacked prudent lending and were also affected by the political interference. Most of their financing was for riskier projects having long gestation period. Also their was huge gap between their disbursement and sanction amount All these factors combined together lead to mounting NPAs on DFIs. In order to follow the policy of fiscal prudence the government decided to curtail the excessive government spending and the government funding to DFIs was ended. Now DFIs have to raise funds from market for lending purpose. As the market rates were high so they could not extend concessional lending. This has strained the DFIs model.

With the reforms in Indian banking system and thrusts on deregulation the low cost funds from official sources began drying up for the DFIs and the distinction between DFIs and banks become blurred. After the recommendation of Khan working Group and Narsimsham committee report in which the universal banking was advised as desirable goals for the DFIs ,two major DFIs ICICI (2002) and IDBI (2004) converted themselves into commercial banks primarily to tap low-cost funds and diversify their asset structure. It is said that converting to bank these DFIs could get access to the cheap and continuous source of funding i.e. current deposit and saving deposit. So the debate has turned to Universal banking vs Narrow banking. The universal banking model is seen as strategic solution for efficiency and competitiveness by most of the Indian policy makers.

In the Indian perspective the issue of universal banking is entirely different from the international context. The universal banking has been recently introduced not as policy initiative for development and growth but as solution, to the poor economic condition of DFIs, their mounting NPAs and increased cost of funding. So the important driver towards universal banking has been the access to low cost funds.

ICICI has become a first universal bank of India after its reverse merger with ICICI Bank in 2002, it is largest private sector bank. SBI has entered universal banking by entering into insurance and mutual fund services. HDFC is now into commercial banking and owns insurance joint venture wit Standard Assurance. Recently LIC has also increased its stake in Corporation bank and is planning to sell insurance to the customers. IDBI has also become a universal bank in 2004.So the universal banking is fast evolving in India. Many of the bnaks have entered the banc assurance like Bazaz- Allianz , Birla–Sunlife, Kotak-Mahindra etc

SECTION–IV

Case Study ICICI Bank

In the fiscal year 2002 ICICI Bank Ltd was the first universal bank in India. At that time bank has three key activities: corporate banking, retail banking and treasury operations. In corporate banking the ICICI bank' primary goal was to build a strong asset portfolio consisting mainly of working capital and term loans to large and well established Indian corporations as well as to the select middle market companies in growth industries . ICICI bank also required providing wide variety of fee-based corporate products and services like documentary credits, cash management services, cross- border trade services, stand by letter of credits and treasury based derivative products that helped ICICI bank to increase its non-interest based income. While to increase its corporate banking activities ICICI bank sought to capitalize on strong relationship that ICICI enjoyed with many of the India's leading corporations.

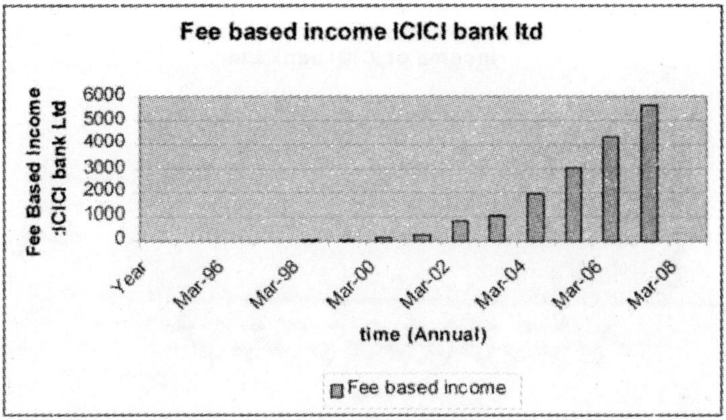

Diagram I: Trend in Fee–based Income of the ICICI Bank Ltd.

The above graph shows the high increase in the Fee based income of ICICI Bank after 2002 when it became universal bank.

The graph below of NIM shows that net interest margin remain flat 2007. Though the cost of fund has reduced but there is no significant increase in the interest margin it may be due to the increase in other kind of expenses.

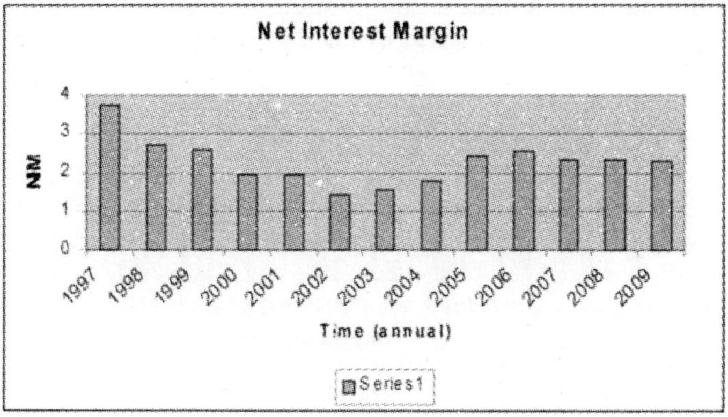

Diagram II: Trend in Net Interest Margin

In the Diagram–III we can see that income generation of ICICI bank is continuously increasing after 2002- So we can say that performance of ICICI as a universal bank has improved after becoming a universal bank.

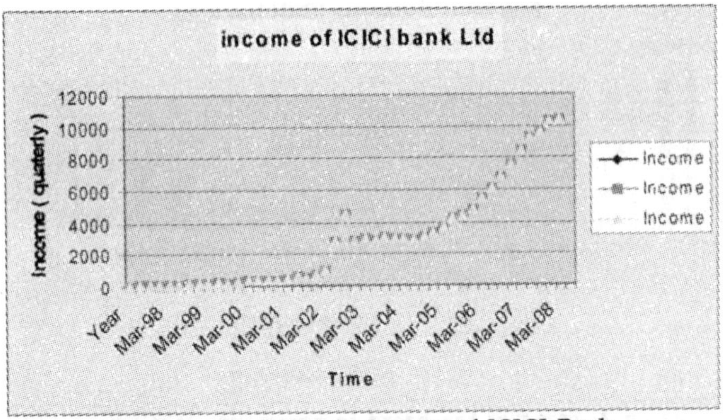

Diagram–III: Trend in Income of ICICI Bank

The strategy followed by the ICICI bank for aggressive expansion has been to target the retail sector with its efficient and speedy services. So technology has been the important factor in fulfilling the need of efficient management and dealing in multiple financial products and services at a time. Some of other Indicators of performance of bank are given below.

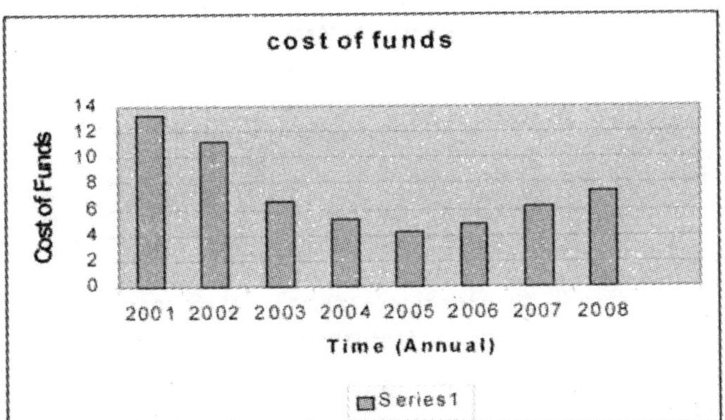

Diagram IV: Pattern of Cost of Funds for the ICICI Bank Ltd.

In the above graph we can see that the after entering the universal banking the cost of fund for ICICI bank has reduced steeply around 50%. So the objective of funds supply at cheaper rate is seemed to be fulfilled but the cost of fund started increasing after 2007, because, the market was in shortage of liquidity as the people were reluctant to invest after the global slowdown.

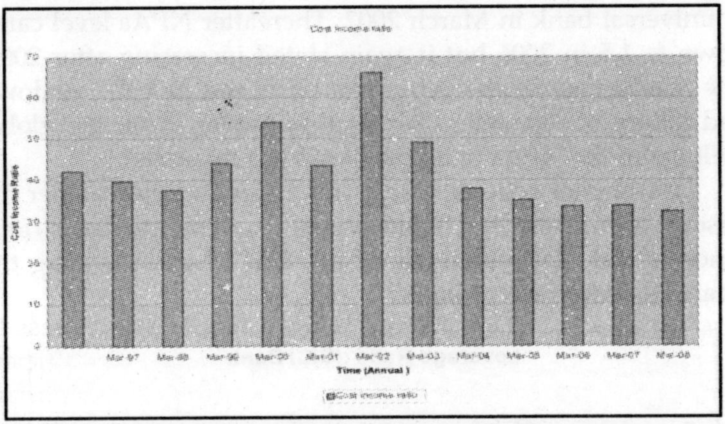

The graph shows the trend in cost income ratio, which was increased in Mar 2002 and there after started declining. Which shows the increasing efficiency of bank but it again started increasing after the sub prime crisis in 2007. This may be due to slowdown in the retail and the falling income of ICICI bank.

Table 1
Other Measures which Show the Soundness of Bank

Year	*Capital Adequacy Ratio*	*Tier I Capital*	*Tier II Capital*	*Leverage Ratio=Asset //capital*
Mar 97	13.04	0	0	4.026462
Mar 98	13.48	13.38	0.1	4.418916
Mar-99	11.06	7.32	3.74	9.145717
Mar-00	19.64	17.42	2.22	7.632084
Mar-01	11.57	10.42	1.15	11.00429
Mar-02	11.44	7.47	3.97	7.558621
Mar-03	11.1	7.05	4.05	9.374142
Mar-04	10.36	6.09	4.27	1.683991
Mar05	11.78	7.59	4.19	2.204212
Mar-06	13.35	9.2	4.15	2.719656
Mar-07	11.69	7.42	4.27	3.211449
Mar-08	11.32	3.6	-	3.751062
Mar-09	14.92	-	-	3.79434

If we look at the NPAs of ICICI then we find that there has been sharp rise in NPAs till 2001. Gross NPAs as the percentage of gross advance stood at 10.23% in 2001. ICICI converted itself to universal bank in March 2002. Thereafter NPAs level came down to 1.5 in 2006 but it again stated increasing after 2007. The reason may be the sub prime crisis and global slowdown and failure of repayment by retail borrower. After the global melt down the NPAs of all the banks has increased

Risk–capital adequacy and Tier I Tier II capital as per the Basel II norm show the banks ability to overcome the various kinds of risk Ratio analysis of the ICICI bank showing the financial soundness of banks

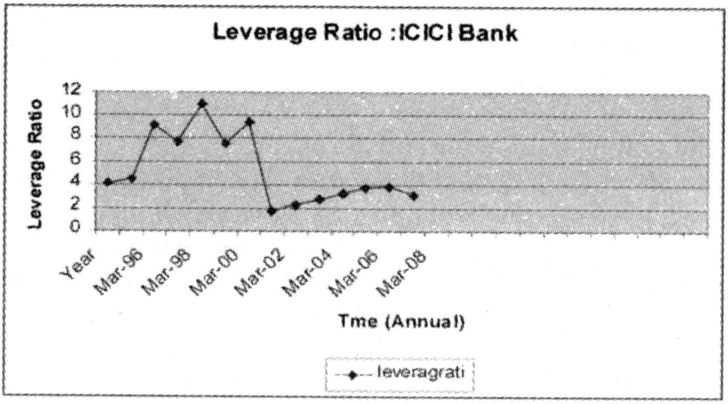

Leverage ratio is the ratio of asset to capital and it shows the asset growth over capital. Higher is the leverage ratio more leveraged is the bank which is one of advantage of universal banking means more growth of asset over given capital base. The graph shows the increasing trend in leverage ratio after March 2002. But it again started falling since March 2007. Its one of reason is the poor performance of retail sector after global recession.

SECTION–V

Emerging Issues

It is believed that full fledged universal banking in India will gain more market share from other players because of their potential to exploit economies of scale and scope, expert application of information technology and risk diversification. Influenced by actual performance of universal banks in India the policy makers are favouring more strategic alliances among the public sector banks and other financial sector players such as insurance companies and mutual funds which would help the public sector banks increase their product range and leverage more for economies of scale and reduce the cost. Most of them entered banc -assurance and have tie-ups in mutual fund distribution.

After the liberalization has refined market micro structure, modernized operations, and broadened investment choices unleashing competition among the intermediaries, who are restructuring themselves for their survival and growth. The financial landscape is increasingly witnessing (i) entry of some of the bigger banks into other financial segments like merchant banking, insurance, etc. which has made them financial 'conglomerates' like ICICI bank ltd, SBI, IDBI, HDFC etc (ii) emergence of several new players with diversified presence across major segments and (iii) possibility of some of the non-banking institutions in the financial sector acquiring large enough proportions to have a systemic impact.

The issue of conflict of interest is of more concern for international regulators in universal banking. It has always been a main impediment against the smooth functioning of the universal banking. Conflict of interest and corporate governance has been the prime cause of 1929 and the sub-prime crisis (2007). Since India allows only conglomerate route for universal banking so conflict of interest between deposit taking and underwriting is automatically removed and not of much concern. Also Section 20 of the Banking Regulation Act prohibits grants of loans and advances by a bank on security of its own shares. The problem of conflicts of interest can easily be checked out by creating reputation risks and; legal sanctions.

Similarly government can make some more sophisticated regulatory norms to avoid the concentration of economic power which is of more concern for the policy makers. The experience of ICICI and SBI with universal banking has proved that size does matter. There is tremendous scope for all the small scale banks in India to consolidate and increase their size to reap the benefits of economies of scale. But this may also lead to concentration of economic power; it needs to be taken care by supervisory and regulatory authority. The emergence of conglomerate groups and associated cross-linkages has brought following supervisory concerns:

1. The moral hazard associated with the 'Too-Big-To-Fail' position of many financial conglomerates is now leading to the conclusion that universal banks are 'Too- Big -To -Manage'
2. Possibility of Contagion effects on account of the 'holding out' phenomenon;
3. Sub prime crisis has heated up the debate that large banks are too big too be managed and saved and they incur heavy social cost beared by the nation and ultimately the world in this globalize era.
4. Universal banking Model is quite effective in promoting social welfare by reducing the corporate financing costs for ultimate borrowers[7].The world wide experience of universal banking shows that, the success of modern Universal Banks depends mostly on successful management as opposed to mere regulation. Strong leadership and well thought-out risk mitigation strategies will determine the success of the Universal Banking movement. Moreover with the increasing pace of globalization and financial innovation the complexities of financial product are ever increasing so the regulatory and supervisory norms should keep pace with the increasing complexities of financial products.

References

Ajit D. and Bangar R.D. (1997), "Banks in Financial Intermediation Performance and Issues-RBI-Occasional Papers, Sep.

Krishna Chitanya .V. (2005), "Universal Banking the Indian Perspective" Vol 5, AEEADE.

Walter Christian and Gerg Rich (Fall 1993), " The Future of Universal Banking" *Cato Journal* Vol.- 13 No-2 pp. 289-313.

Calomiris Charles.W. (1993), "Corporate Finance Benefits from Universal Banking : Germany and the United States 1870-1914", *WP -4408 NBER*, July, pp. 1-23.

Khatkhate Deena (1998) " Timing and sequencing of Financial Sector Reforms Evidence and Rationale" *Economic and Political Weekly*, July 11, pp. 1831-1840.

Radhakrishnan . R. (2003), "Banking Strategy: Universal Banking End of The Road?" *PNB Monthly Review*, Jan., pp. 23-33.

Ram Mohan T.T. "(2005), "Bank Consolidation Issues and Evidence" *Economic and Political Weekly*, March 19, 1151-1161.

Mathur K.B.L. (2005), "Market Orientation of Financial Sector-State as Facilitator" *Economic and Political Weekly*, March 19, *1136-1141*

Elsas Ralf, Hacktheral Andreas (2006), "The Anatomy of Bank Diversification", Electronic copy is available at :http//ssrn.com/abstract =968214, June, pp. 1-27.

Editor (2004 Feb 28) "Where are the DFIs?" , *Economic and Political Weekly* , pp 859-860

Kaul Reeta (2001), "Universal Banking" PNB Monthly Review, October, pp. 9-12.

Jhaveri Narendra (2004), "Resurrection of DFIs : Between Prudence and Push " *Economic and Political Weekly*, July 17, pp. 3309-3311

Ghosh D.N. (1998), "Narrow Banking The Fudging the Issue" *Economic and Political Weekly*, Oct 17, pp. 2694-2695.

Karunagaran A. (2005), "Should DFIs be Revived?" *Economic and Political Weekly*, March 19, pp. 1247-1253.

Chaitanya Krishna V. (2005), "Universal Banking the Indian Perspective", Regional and Sectoral Economic Studies Vol 5-I pp. 5-20.

Footnotes

1. Preeti Mishra, Academic Associate, Indian Institute of Management Ahmedabad, E-mail: preetimishra7sep@gmail.com
2. Walter Ingo Universal banking: A shareholder Perspective
3. Berger, Hancock and Humphrey-1993
4. Mark Roe, Political and Leagl restrainton ownership and control of public companies,27 J.FinEcon(1990)

5. Glass- Steagall act in US,separating the commercial banking and the universal banking
6. Calomiris and carlos, Financining the American corporation NBER WP-79 (1996)
7. A K Khandelwal EPW March 18, 2006

5

IMPACT OF GLOBAL RECESSION ON INDIA AND CHINA

Halima Sadia Rizvi

Introduction

Recessions, depressions and progressions are vital parts of the business cycle. The world of economics is not exceptions to this route in their pursuits of progress. At the moment they are reeling the conditions of recession/global meltdown or economic downturn.

Since coming to terms after the great depression of the 1930's, different world economies adopted different systems of economic governance prominent being free capitalist economies and regimented socialist economies. But in between were many countries that opted for the middle path of mixed economic policies in their pursuit of development.

The world witnessed major collapse of the regimentation during the decades of 1970's and 1980's, while capitalism with all its hollow grandeur surrendered during the 1990's and 2000's. Globalization in all its tentacles spread to all parts of the world to ensure equitable availability of resources and services and resulted in generating more inequalities both within and across nations. The worst hit was the human resource which neither retained its original talent and occupation, nor could emerge trained, professionally qualified or adequately equipped to face mammoth challenges faced by bitter competition.

The present study intends to peep into the function of the two supposedly emerging superpowers (China and India), their characteristic features, the advantages they possess and the shortcomings prevailing amongst them through the two major economic indicators of performance of exports and the role of Foreign Direct Investment.

The global recession is the most talked about news these days. Everyday the news headlines are about markets crashing, decreasing industrial growth and the overall negative economic situation of the world. The world according to some is going through an economic depression, some say the worst is over and yet others say that economic meltdown is just around the corner.

The crisis originated in the sub-prime housing loans in America. Many people with low income and bad credit history or as it is called NINJA-no income, no job, no assets were given loans. In the US, an estimated 8.8 million homeowners, nearly 10.8% of the total homeowners had zero or negative equity as of March 2008. This means that their homes were worth less than the mortgages paid on them. When eventually the bubble burst, many major investment banks found themselves in a terrible mess. Banks such as Bear Sterns, Lehman Brothers, Merrill Lynch Freddie Mac and Fannie Mae were all in deep trouble. The panic soon spread overseas. Banks became increasingly suspicious of the others ability to honor commitments. The liquidity crunch soon led to a situation where even the top companies were finding it difficult to find loans for their needs. No country can stay away from the effects of the economic slowdown. The crisis was brought about by the Sub prime housing loans in America but the entire world is feeling the pinch. Slated to be the next superpowers of the world, China and India are also feeling the ill-effects of the meltdown. Both the countries had high growth rates and were on the track to fulfill the predictions of superpowers, when the global recession played the spoilsport. The paper intends to compare the effects of the global phenomenon on both the emerging economies. However since the scope of the paper is limited, the study would focus on two aspects i.e., exports and foreign direct investment. Through an analysis of these figures, it would be interesting to see how the economies have fared in dealing with the crisis situation.

Global Recession

The global recession is affecting every country in the world and we are taking the example of India and china with simple comparing between both of them.

China

The Chinese economy began its liberalization process in 1978 and has not looked back ever since. The rapid growth rate of the economy made the nation one of the fastest growing markets to reckon with. The GDP has grown close to 10 % for half the decade. The country witnessed a growth rate of 9% in 2008. The country has a booming manufacturing sector that employs million and has enabled it to achieve its phenomenal success. According to Reuters, manufacturing constitutes 43% of the economy.

The figures are however changing rapidly. Economists at HSBC say that China would witness growth dipping as low as 6% - dangerously short of 8% which is widely regarded as the level required to generate enough jobs to absorb the new entrants. In January 2009, Reuters reported that China could face surging protests and riots as the rising unemployment levels are breeding discontent. The stable environment offered by the Chinese government was one of the main attractions for the foreign investments. If the stability crumbles, it could lead to widespread unemployment. A small article in China's Daily revealed that an estimated 600,000 migrant workers have left China's Guangdong Province due to unemployment in 2008. This Province has been the forefront of China's economic reform with more than 996,900 registered companies. The Chinese economy is an export led one. A look at the exports table shows that there has been a steady increase in the

Table 1
China's Trade with the World ($ billion)

	1999	*2000*	*2001*	*2002*	*2003*	*2004*	*2005*	*2006*	*2007*	*2008*
Exports	194.9	249.2	266.2	325.6	438.2	593.3	762.0	969.1	1,218.6	1,428.5
% change	6.1	27.8	6.8	22.4	34.6	35.4	28.4	27.2	25.7	17.2
Imports	165.7	225.1	243.6	295.2	412.8	561.2	660.0	791.6	955.8	1,133.1
% change	18.2	35.8	8.2	21.2	39.8	36.0	17.6	20.0	20.8	18.5
Total	360.6	474.3	509.8	620.8	851.0	1,154.6	1,421.9	1,760.7	2,173.8	2,561.6
% change	11.3	31.5	7.5	21.8	37.1	35.7	23.2	23.8	23.5	17.8
Balance	29.2	24.1	22.5	30.4	25.5	32.1	102.0	177.5	262.2	295.5

Note: PRC exports reported on an free-on-board basis; imports on a cost, insurance, and freight basis
Sources: PRC National Bureau of Statistics and PRC General Administration of Customs, China's Customs Statistics

percentage change in export from 1999 upto 2004. The country experienced phenomenal export growth during 2003 and 2004. Thereafter there has been a steady decline. The rate of change has therefore slowed down. The level of imports has also shown a similar trend- a steady increase till 2004 thereafter decline. The overall balance has not shown any drastic change over the decade.

Table 2
China's Top Import Suppliers 2008 ($ billion)

Rank	*Country/Region*	*Volume*	*% Change**
1	Japan	150.7	12.5
2	South Korea	112.2	8.1
3	Taiwan	103.3	2.3
4	United States	81.4	17.4
5	Germany	55.8	23.0
6	Australia	37.4	44.8
7	Malaysia	32.0	11.8
8	Saudi Arabia	31.0	76.6
9	Brazil	29.7	62.2
10	Thailand	25.6	13.2

*Percent change over 2007
Source: PRC General Administration of Customs, *China's Customs Statistics*

China imports many of its components from its neighboring countries as seen from the table above. Thus the recession reaches them too. About 70% of the imports are used as inputs for export oriented industries. As the table shows, Japan, South Korea and Taiwan are the chief importer to China. These economies get deeply affected when the imports decline.

As the largest recipient of FDI among all developing countries, China received a cumulative total of $692 billion from 1997 to 2007. In modern history of economic development no other country has ever benefitted as much as China did and continues to, from FDI. Foreign invested firms have played an important role in promoting China's exports. China's exports grew at phenonmenal rate and today, Made-in-China products can be found in every corner of the world. China's decision to promote FDI was based on the fact that in the early stages of economic reforms, the country was faced with severe shortage of capital. Moreover, the industry consisted of exclusively state owned enterprises with outdated technology and limited production capacities. Thus the Chinese government was determined to make use of FDI to overcome the capital deficiency, acquire advanced technology and promote exports.

The Asian Crisis dampened the economic growth of China's main FDI sources such as Korea and Japan leading to FDI growing by less than 1% in 1998 and declining in the following years. By 2001, annual FDI inflow shrank to $ 40.7 billion. The growth momentum however resumed in 2002 and FDI in China reached $46.8 billion- 15.24% higher than 2001 by 2007, it reached another record high of $74.8 billion. The rising FDI after 2001 was mainly due to China's official entry to the WTO in November 2001. With recession reducing the global income, a report in FDI Intelligence magazine predicts that there will be a decline of 13% in the number of FDI in 2009. According to the report; in China the growth has declined in 2008. A further decline is also predicted for 2009 as the sharp reduction in GDP growth reduces China's FDI market size by about $150 billion as compared to last year's prediction. The table below shows that the main sources of FDI in China are Hong Kong, Taiwan, Japan Korea and USA. Over the years, Hong Kong's share has decreased from 60.9% to 31.9%. Likewise, Taiwan and USA's share has declined. These economies have experienced the economic slowdown and are therefore cautious in their foreign investments.

Beijing announced a stimulus package of $586 billion in November in order to revive the economy. However the solution is not as simple as the package. China is an export driven economy and as such unless the situation of its export market improves, it can only grow on the basis of its domestic market and domestic investments. Export led growth models have been unsustainable and prone to volatile unwinding. There are numerous examples in the world such as the German attempt in 1960's, Japan in 1970's and East Asia in 1990's.

A possible outcome of the financial crisis for China is the return of the role of the state. The financial crisis seems to have heightened the state's role in the growth of the economy. This has been further emphasized by the fact that the western capitalist countries are funding bailouts and other financial assistance to the private companies facing the threat of closing down due to the crisis. The question remains whether this increased role would be a permanent feature or a temporary one until some economic stability is achieved. It is too soon to answer this as none of the models of state and market are close to a steady equilibrium.

Table 3
The Major Sources of Foreign Direct Investment in China: 1985-2006
(Value in billions US dollars, share in percentage)

	1985-1990		*1991-2000*		*2001-2006*	
	Value	*Share*	*Value*	*Share*	*Value*	*Share*
The World	15.9	100	327.7	100	343.5	100
Hong Kong	9.7	60.9	159.0	48.5	109.5	31.9
Taiwan	0.0	0.0	25.8	7.9	17.7	5.2
Japan	2.2	13.6	25.2	7.7	30.2	8.8
Korea	0.0	0.0	10.5	3.2	27.4	7.2
Singapore	0.2	1.3	16.8	5.1	13.0	3.8
USA	1.9	12.1	27.6	8.4	23.9	7.0
Germany	0.2	1.3	6.1	1.9	7.6	2.2
UK	0.2	1.2	8.4	2.6	5.2	1.5
France	0.1	0.9	4.0	1.2	3.4	1.0

Source: China Statistical Bureau

State Owned Enterprises SOE, were initially created as a means to provide jobs for the people. In times of the financial crisis, these SOE may gain more prominence and political importance. Job creation is once again a core concern and the state may find itself managing more industries. However, such state control also means greater accountability. A 1% decrease in a 9% GDP may not be of much concern among other nations but in China it could lead to riots and turmoil. As the crisis deepens, China may find that free market and democracy has certain benefits such as a buffer to public hostility in times of economic strain. The Chinese Communist Party will have to reinvent itself in these times of economic crisis and be more accountable to its people.

The study so far reveals that the stimulus packages announced by the Chinese government is not sufficient to bail out the manufacturing sector from the grips of the dual pressure of surplus production and growing unemployment. One of the main reasons have been the major imports from China are also in the grip of global slowdown. The direction of the stimulus package has to be multidimensional in order to pull Chinese economy out of this global disorder.

India

Although India attainted independence in 1947, it was only in the 1980's that the country was opened to the world markets. The growth rate was lower than that of China nevertheless, the country achieved 9% growth rate in 2008 and has maintained a steady path of development. Recession in the world market has however led to many plans unfulfilled. The country is facing heavy losses in the IT industry, car industry, investment banking and other sectors. The Federation of Indian Export Organization reports that the country has experienced the steepest decline in the export sector. Handicrafts declined by 54% in December 2008, gems and jewelry fell by 27% and textiles by 21%. These industries are the worst affected by the global meltdown. According to report by FICCI, the inventories industries like these have cut production by 10 to 50 % as compared to the previous year.

According to RBI governor Subba Rao, "The reason India has been hit by the crisis, despite mitigating factors is clearly India's rapid and growing integration into the world economy. The contagion of crisis has spread to India through all the channels-the financial channel, the real channel and importantly as happens in all financial crisis, the confidence channel."

The table below shows the growth rate of the economy. It can be clearly seen that the economy was growing rapidly from 2003 onward with the rate between 8 to 9%. It was in 2007-08 that the nation began to feel the effects of the recession.

The steady growth of the Indian economy has many reasons both interrelated and disconnected simultaneously. Political stability immediately after the 1990's reform package

Table 4
India's Growth Rate

Year	2000-01	2001-02	2002-03	2003-04	2004-05	2005-06	2006-07	2007-08	2008-09 A.E
GDP growth rate %	4.4	5.8	3.8	8.5	7.5	9.5	9.5	9.0	7.1

Source: Prime Minister's Economic Advisory Council, GOI, 2009

created a somewhat conducive business environment. The Indian inc made maximum use of liberalization measures. Information technology driven results were enormous though in absolute GDP terms, they were marginal. Manufacturing sector picked up after large scale disinvestment and the financial sector reformed played a pivotal role in the growth process.

The external sector too witnessed a major shift in terms of the basket of the composition o fits exports as well as the direction of foreign trade. India truly with in 15 years was on the road to be a strong emerging economy.

The following table shows the exports of India to the world. Although the volume has increased over the years, the average value as remained more or less the same over the period.

Table 5
India's Exports to the World

	India's Exports to World		*Average Value*	
Period	*(Rs. Million)*	*(US $ Million)*	*Rs. Per Euro*	*Rs. Per US $*
Apr-Oct 2005	2,494,969	56,928	54.09	43.81
Apr-Oct 2006	3,250,912	70,838	58.03	45.86
Apr-Oct 2007	3,477,939	85,583	55.73	40.68

Source: Calculated from India Trades, CMIE

Table 6
FDI to India

Year	*Total FDI Inflows*	*Percentage Change*
2000-01	4,029	-
2001-02	6,130	52 %
2002-03	5,035	-18 %
2003-04	4,322	-14%
2004-05	6,051	40%
2005-06	8,961	48%
2006-07	22,826	146%
2007-08	34,362	51%
2008-09	35,146	02%

Source: Department of Industrial Policy and Promotion, Ministry of Commerce and Industry.

The table reveals that FDI in India has been fluctuating throughout the years. 2002-04 witnessed a negative rate of change while 2006-07 was an extremely good year. Thereafter, the FDI slowed down and the year 2008-09 received only a 02% percentage increase. The uncertainties of the global markets finally caught up with the Indian economy. Both the private and public companies in India have become dependent on the capital market for finance. Indian companies are estimated to have raised $41 bn. as overseas debt. But these flows are expected to weaken given the increased risk aversion in the global markets.

Table 7
Country-wise FDI Inflow to India

Country	*FDI [in US$ millions]*	*Percentage share*
Mauritius	39,379	44.43
Singapore	8,070	8.99
USA	6,508	7.37
UK	5,289	5.94
Netherlands	3,700	4.19

Source: Department of Industrial Policy and Promotion, Ministry of Commerce and Industry

A country wise analysis shows that the top investor in India is from the small countries of Mauritius and Singapore. As the effect of the recession spreads to these economies, the FDI inflows get affected too hence the decreasing rate of change.

The Table 8 shows the various sectors that attract FDI in India. The services sector has received Rs.89,761 C as of May 2009, followed by computer software and hardware and telecommunication industry. However over the years, computer sector has received decreasing FDI along with the metallurgical industries. The rest of the sectors have only increased their share.

One of the main reasons India has been able to hold out so far from the really negative effects of recession is the fact that the Indian banks were more or less secured from the sub prime crisis. Major bank operations are still carried out by the Public Sector Banks who are extremely cautious in disbursing loans. The RBI has been credited with taking pre-emptive action that has minimized the vulnerability of Indian banks to the ripple

Table 8

Sectors Attracting FDI Inflows [Amount in Rs. Crores (US$ million)]

Ranks	*Sector*	*2006-07 (April-March)*	*2007-08 (April-March)*	*2008-09 (April-March)*	*2009-10 (April-May '09)*	*Cumulative Inflows (April '00 to May '09)*	*% age to total Inflows (In terms of rupees)*
1.	SERVICES SECTOR (financial & non-financial)	21,047(4,664)	26,589 (6,615)	28,411(6,116)	5,308(1,073)	89,761(20,322)	23 %
2.	COMPUTER SOFTWARE & HARDWARE	11,786(2,614)	5,623(1,410)	7,329(1,677)	733(149)	40,229(9,103)	10 %
3.	TELECOMMUNICATIONS (radio paging, cellular mobile, basic telephone services)	2,155(478)	5,103(1,261)	11,727(2,558)	3,055(612)	31,422(6,989)	8 %
4.	HOUSING & REAL ESTATE	2,121(467)	8,749(2,179)	12,621(2,801)	2,801(566)	26,583(6,078)	7 %
5.	CONSTRUCTION ACTIVITIES (including roads & highways)	4,424(985)	6,989(1,743)	8,792(2,028)	2,694(551)	24,871(5,742)	6 %
6.	AUTOMOBILE INDUSTRY	1,254(276)	2,697(675)	5,212(1,152)	497(101)	15,564(3,489)	4 %
7.	POWER	713(157)	3,875(967)	4,382(985)	777(159)	14,789(3,349)	4 %
8.	METALLURGICAL INDUSTRIES	7,866(173)	4,686(1,177)	4,157(961)	113(23)	11,618(2,746)	3 %
9.	PETROLEUM & NATURAL GAS	401(89)	5,729(1,427)	1,931(412)	869(174)	11,046(2,567)	3 %
10.	CEHMICALS(other than fertilizers)	930(205)	920(229)	3,427(749)	247(50)	9,814(2,184)	3 %

Source: Department of Industrial Policy and Promotion, Ministry of Commerce and Industry

effects to the sub-prime crisis. The RBI also took counter-cyclical and precautionary measures to limit the exposure of banks to high risk lending especially in real estate and housing. The banks were advised in January 2002 to build up and Investment Fluctuating Reserve within 5 years. The target for IFR was 5% of the investments. This requirement enabled the banks to absorb some of the adverse impacts when interest rates began moving in the opposite direction in 2004. Thus the country was able to forestall the ill-effects of recession though not for long enough.

Conclusion

A negative atmosphere, shortage of liquidity, decreased demand, reduced growth rates and uncertainties are the clear visible signs of economic depression. What started out as a small matter of sub prime loan defaulters has now become a global phenomenon and led to a global crisis.

India and China are poised to become superpowers of the world in just a few decades. The dream still remains. The countries have chosen different paths to deal with the current economic crisis and depending on how well the economy responds to the stimulus packages, the economy can recover soon enough. In fact the worst may be already over.

In order to insure faster recovery the country need to encourage more foreign investment incentives need to be offered to attracted capital inflow tax brakes could be extended to ten years or more this would ensure that foreign capital stays in the country for the time period and helps in the recovery process. Other benefits such as free or subsidized electricity supply less red tapes and bureaucratic delay could also be offered.

From an ideological point of view, the time to rethink and reanalyze the concepts of free markets and Capitalism is finally here. It is time for a new ideology to arise that would ensure that such crisis do not occur again. The free market regime in USA caused a ripple effect all over the world. The interconnectivity across markets ensured that no one was left behind in being dragged into the Crisis. It is therefore high time to rethink the philosophy of Capitalism. There need to be certain checks in place to ensure there is no repeat performance of the current situation.

References

Balfour Frederik (2009), "The Global Recession Slams China", in Business Week, 22 January 2009.

Baru Sanjaya (2009), "Strategic Implications of the Global Economic Crisis for India", ISAS Working paper No. 77, Singapore.

Report in FDI "The Shape of Things to Come: The FDI Outlook for 2009 and Performance Analysis for 2009" April/May.

Verma Sonia (2009), "Impact of Recession on India", wwww. merinews.com.

Xing, Yuqing (2008), "FDI China: Facts and Impact on China and the World Economy" IRI Working Paper 01-08, Japan.

http://seekingalpha.com/article/114131-is-china-s-recession-worse-than-we-thought, 11 January 2009.

McIntyre, Douglas. A. (2009), http://247wallst.com/2009/01/02/believe-it-or-not/

www.theindianblogger.com/problems/reasons-for-global-recession-in-plain-simple-english.

6

Causes of Global Financial Crisis and its Impact on Indian Economy

Alka Agarwal, Anurag Srivastava, Satyendra Kumar

The intensification of the global financial crisis, following the bankruptcy of Lehman Brothers in September 2008, has made the current economic and financial environment a very difficult time for the world economy, the global financial system and for central banks. The proximate cause of the current financial turbulence is attributed to the subprime mortgage sector in the USA. There is gloomy forecast that the US sub-prime mortgage crisis might convert into recession that could be as great as the Great Depression of 1930's that lasted over a decade. The sub-prime crisis that started in 2004 and 2005 is extended to the current economic cycle world over. In US, homeowners select a mortgage lender who gives the loan after inquiring the borrower's creditworthiness and the property that serves as collateral. The lenders resell these loans to investors or Wall Street firms, who in turn bundle thousands of mortgage loans from different lenders into mortgage backed securities. These securities are often sliced and diced into different structures like Collateralized Debt Obligations (CDO), rated by rating agencies like Moody's, S&P, Fitch etc. and are finally sold to institutional investors worldwide- mutual funds, banks, hedge funds, central banks and pension funds. The US mortgage-backed securities market is the largest fixed income market in the world, with over $8 trillion outstanding followed by US treasury market with around $5 trillion outstanding. These mortgages do not create any problem for lenders until the mortgagers fulfill their commitments in time. But with rising payment obligations, sub-prime mortgagers ran for foreclosures. Sub-prime mortgage refers to the lending by the banks and other financial institutions to borrowers with poor or no credit history or variable income flows. Borrowers with the higher-than-average risk profile because of low credit worthiness should have been charged a higher interest rate for loans but in the wake of optimistic enthusiasm. It did not happen and lending was done at rate lower than required. These loans are considered sub-prime.

Fundamentally, the crisis could be ascribed to the persistence of large global imbalances, which, in turn, were the outcome of long periods of excessively loose monetary policy in the major advanced economies during the early part of this decade (Mohan, 2007, Taylor, 2008).

Global imbalances have been manifested through a substantial increase in the current account deficit of the US mirrored by the substantial surplus in Asia, particularly in China, and in oil exporting countries in the Middle East and Russia (Lane, 2009).These imbalances in the current account are often seen as the consequence of the relative inflexibility of the currency regimes in China and some other EMEs. According to Portes (2009), global macroeconomic imbalances were the major underlying cause of the crisis. These saving-investment imbalances and consequent huge cross-border financial flows put great stress on the financial intermediation process. The global imbalances along with imperfections in financial markets because instruments to generate the specific crisis. Such a view, however, offers only a partial analysis of the recent global economic environment. The role of monetary policy in the major advanced economies, particularly that in the United States, over the same time period needs to be analysed for a more balanced analysis.

Monetary policy in the US and other advanced economies was eased aggressively. Policy rates in the US reached one per cent in June 2003 and were held around these levels for an extended period (up to June 2004). In the subsequent period, the withdrawal of monetary accommodation was quite gradual. An empirical assessment of the US monetary policy also indicates that the actual policy during the period 2002-06, especially during 2002-04, was substantially less active than what a simple Taylor rule would have required.

Excessively loose monetary policy in the post dot com period boosted consumption and investment in the US and, as Taylor argues, it was made with purposeful and careful consideration by monetary policy makers. As might be expected, with such low nominal and real interest rates, asset prices also recorded strong gains, particularly in housing and real estate, providing further impetus to consumption and investment through wealth effects. Thus, aggregate demand consistently exceeded domestic output in the US and, given the macroeconomic identity, this was mirrored in large and growing current account deficits in the US over the period. The large domestic demand of the US was met by the rest of the world, especially China and other East Asian economies, which provided goods and services at relatively low costs leading to growing surpluses in these countries. Sustained current account surpluses in some of these EMEs also reflected the lessons learnt from the Asian financial crisis. Furthermore, the availability of relatively cheaper goods and services from China and other EMEs also helped to maintain price stability in the US and elsewhere, which might have not been possible otherwise. Thus measured inflation in the advanced economies remained low, contributing to the persistence of accommodative monetary policy.

The emergence of dysfunctional global imbalances is essentially a post 2000 phenomenon and which got accentuated from 2004 onwards. The surpluses of East Asian exporters, particularly China, rose significantly from 2004 onwards, as did those of the oil exporters. In fact, Taylor (op. cit.) argues that the sharp hike in oil and other commodity prices in early

2008 was indeed related to the very sharp policy rate cut in late 2007 after the sub-prime crisis emerged.

Apart from creating large global imbalances, accommodative monetary policy and the existence of very low interest rates for an extended period encouraged the search for yield, and relaxation of lending standards. Even as financial imbalances were building up, macroeconomic stability was maintained. Relatively stable growth and low inflation have been witnessed in the major advanced economies since the early 1990s and the period has been dubbed as the Great Moderation. The stable macroeconomic environment encouraged underpricing of risks. Financial innovations, regulatory arbitrage, lending malpractices, excessive use of the originate and distribute model, securitisation of sub-prime loans and their bundling into AAA tranches on the back of ratings, all combined to result in the observed excessive leverage of financial market entities.

Components of the Crisis

As inflation started creeping up beginning 2004, the US Federal Reserve started to withdraw monetary accommodation. With interest rates beginning to edge up, mortgage payments also started rising. Tight monetary policy contained aggregate demand and output, depressing housing prices. With low/negligible margin financing, there were greater incentives to default by the sub-prime borrowers. Defaults by such borrowers led to losses by financial institutions and investors alike. Although the loans were supposedly securitized and sold to the off balance sheet special institutional vehicles (SIVs), the losses were ultimately borne by the banks and the financial institutions wiping off a significant fraction of their capital.

But, two events that were assumed to have a low probability in a booming market in fact happened: first, interest rates increased and second, home prices began falling. This led to sub-prime mortgages resetting at shockingly high rates, with homeowners missing payments and foreclosing accounts. As a result, financial institutions holding mortgage-backed securities incurred losses and had to sell their assets to meet margin calls.

The slides of sub-prime crisis dates back to 30 June 2004 when Federal Reserve began the cycle of interest rate hikes that increased the cost of borrowings from the lowest levels registered since 1950s. It has increased it 17 times in a row before it paused in July .

Prime facie it might appear that the prime cause of boom and bust was expansionary and contractionary monetary policy, but the fact of the matter is too much of decentralized decision making which is the inevitable feature of a market economy ; very little fiscal indulgence and lack of coordination between monetary, fiscal and BOP policies.

Prime Rates Charged by Banks in US

Date	*Interest Rate*	*Date*	*Interest Rate*
June 2004	4.00	July 2005	6.25
July 2004	4.25	Aug 2005	6.50
Aug 2004	4.50	Sep 2005	6.75
Sep 2004	4.75	Nov 2005	7.00
Nov 2004	5.00	Dec 2005	7.25
Dec 2004	5.25	Feb 2006	7.50
Feb 2005	5.50	Mar 2006	7.75
Mar 2005	5.75	May 2006	8.00
May 2005	6.00	July 2006	8.25

Source: Federal Reserve, Bureau of Economic Analysis

Finally, crisis broke out in March 2007, when the shares in New Century Financials, one of the largest sub-prime lenders in US were suspended amid fears that the firm is heading for bankruptcy. On April 2 2007, New Century Financials filed for bankruptcy after it was forced by its backers to purchase billions of dollars of bad loans. Another US-based sub-prime firm Accredited Home Lenders Holding said it would pass on $2.7 billion of its loans at a heavy discount. GE also decided to sell its sub-prime lending arm, WMC Mortgage, a subsidiary of GE Money, it brought in 2004. Bear Stearns, a Wall Street firm and the topnotch player in mortgage-backed securities market for over a decade, had to close down two hedge funds that lost over 95% of Net Asset Value (NAV).

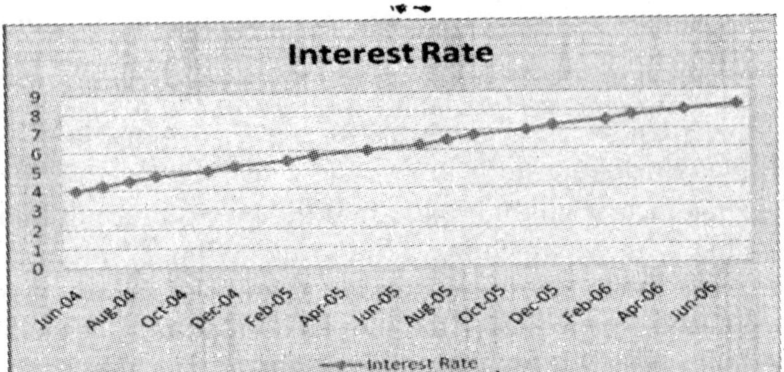

Source: Office of Federal Housing Enterprise Oversight

Graph 1: Prime Rates Charged by Banks in US

Impact on India

The initial impact of the sub-prime crisis on the Indian economy was rather muted. Indeed, following the cuts in the US Fed Funds rate in August 2007, there was a massive jump in net capital inflows into the country. The Reserve Bank had to sterilize the liquidity impact of large foreign exchange purchases through a series of increases in the cash reserve ratio and issuances under the Market Stabilisation Scheme (MSS). With persistent inflationary pressures emanating both from strong domestic demand and elevated global commodity prices, policy rates were also raised. Monetary policy continued with preemptive tightening measures up to August 2008. The direct effect of the sub-prime crisis on Indian banks/financial sector was almost negligible because of limited exposure to complex derivatives and other prudential policies put in place by the Reserve Bank. The relatively lower presence of foreign banks in the Indian banking sector also minimized the direct impact on the domestic economy. The larger presence of foreign banks can increase the vulnerability of the domestic economy to foreign shocks, as happened in Eastern European and Baltic countries.

There was also no direct impact of the Lehman failure on the domestic financial sector in view of the limited exposure of the Indian banks. However, following the Lehman failure, there was a sudden change in the external environment. As in the case of other major EMEs, there was a sell-off in domestic equity markets by portfolio investors reflecting deleveraging. Consequently, there were large capital outflows by portfolio investors during September-October 2008, with concomitant pressures in the foreign exchange market. While foreign direct investment flows exhibited resilience, access to external commercial borrowings and trade credits was rendered somewhat difficult. On the whole, net capital inflows during 2008-09 were substantially lower than in 2007-08 and there was a depletion of reserves. However, a large part of the reserve loss (US $ 33 billion out of US $ 54 billion) during April-December 2008 reflected valuation losses.

The contraction of capital flows and the sell-off in the domestic market adversely affected both external and domestic financing for the corporate sector. The sharp slowdown in demand in the major advanced economies is also having an adverse impact on our exports and industrial performance. On the positive side, the significant correction in international oil and other commodity prices has alleviated inflationary pressures as measured by wholesale price index. However, various measures of consumer prices remain at elevated levels on the back of continuing high inflation in food prices. Government finances, which had exhibited a noteworthy correction starting 2002-03, came under renewed pressure in 2008-09 on account of higher expenditure outgoes due to (i) higher international crude oil prices (up to September 2008) and the incomplete pass-through to domestic prices (ii) higher fertiliser prices and associated increase in fertiliser prices (iii) the Sixth Pay Commission award and (iv) debt waiver scheme. The fiscal stimulus packages involving additional expenditures and tax cuts have put further stress on the fisc. Reflecting these factors, the Central Government's fiscal deficit more than doubled from 2.7 per cent of GDP in 2007-08 to 6.0 per cent in 2008-09, reaching again the levels seen around the end of the 1990s. The revenue deficit at 4.4 per cent of GDP will be at its previous peak touched during 2001-02 and 2002-03. Primary balance again turned into deficit in 2008-09, after recording surpluses during the preceding two years. Net market borrowings during 2008-09 almost trebled from the budgeted

Table 1

Fiscal indicators of central government (Fiscal deficit, Primary Deficit, & Revenue Deficit, Actual and Estimated by Using Regression Analysis) % of GDP

Year	*Year*	*Gross FD*	*FD-esti*	*Gross PD*	*PD-esti*	*Gross RD*	*RD-esti*
1990-91	1	7.8	6.4	4.1	1.92	3.3	3.1147
1991-92	2	5.6	6.3	1.5	1.84	2.5	3.1194
1992-93	3	5.3	6.2	1.2	1.76	2.5	3.1241
1993-94	4	7	6.1	2.7	1.68	3.8	3.1288
1994-95	5	5.7	6	1.3	1.6	3.1	3.1335
1995-96	6	5.1	5.9	0.9	1.52	2.5	3.1382
1996-97	7	4.8	5.8	0.5	1.44	2.4	3.1429
1997-98	8	5.8	5.7	1.5	1.36	3	3.1476
1998-99	9	6.5	5.6	2	1.28	3.8	3.1523
1999-00	10	5.4	5.5	0.7	1.2	3.5	3.157
2000-01	11	5.7	5.4	0.9	1.12	4.1	3.1617
2001-02	12	6.2	5.3	1.5	1.04	4.4	3.1664
2002-03	13	5.9	5.2	1.1	0.96	4.4	3.1711
2003-04	14	4.5	5.1	0	0.88	3.6	3.1758
2004-05	15	4	5	0	0.8	2.5	3.1805
2005-06	16	4.1	4.9	0.4	0.72	2.6	3.1852
2006-07	17	3.5	4.8	-0.2	0.64	1.9	3.1899
2007-08	18	2.7	4.7	-0.9	0.56	1.1	3.1946
2008-09	19	6	4.6	2.5	0.48	4.4	3.1993
2009-10	20	5.5	4.5	1.8	0.4	4	3.204
	intercept	6.547895	intercept	2.127895	intercept	3.073684	
	slope	-0.11361	slope	-0.09075	slope	0.009173	
	R=	-0.56435	R=	-0.47341	R=	0.059431	
	R2=	0.318491	R2=	0.224118	R2=	0.003532	

Standard error of estimates of F.D.= 0.9486

Note : negative sign show surplus. 2009-10 Budget estimates

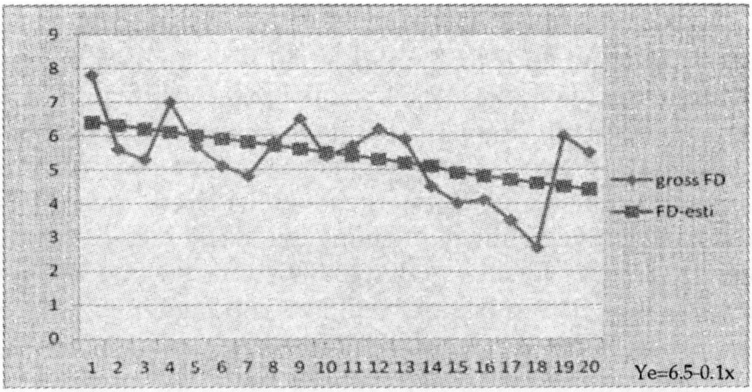

Graph 2: Gross Fiscal Deficit and Estimated Fiscal Deficit

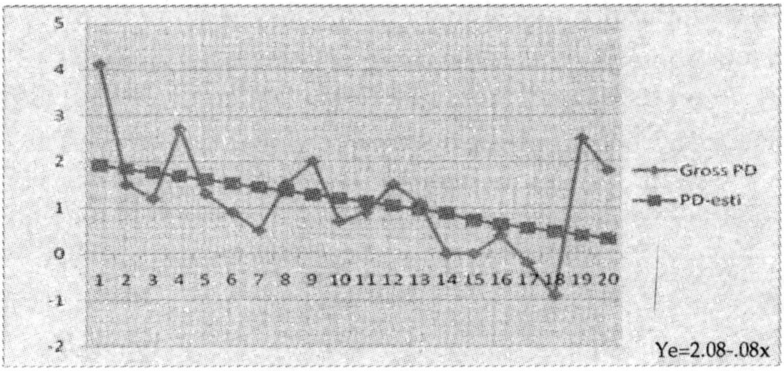

Graph 3: Gross Primary Deficit and Estimated Primary Deficit

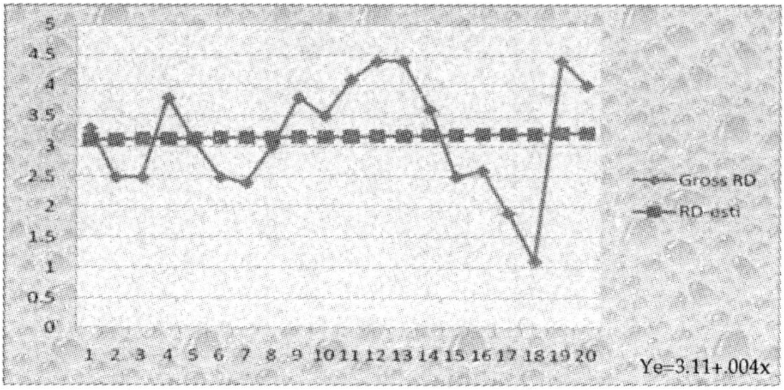

Graph 4: Gross Fiscal Deficit and Estimated Fiscal Deficit

Rs.1,13,000 crore to Rs.3,29,649 in the revised estimates (actual borrowings were Rs.2,98,536 crore as per Reserve Bank records) and are budgeted at Rs.3,08,647 crore (gross borrowings at Rs. 3,98,552 crore) in 2009-10. In view of the renewed fiscal deterioration, the credit rating agency Standard and Poor's has changed its outlook on long-term sovereign credit rating from stable to negative, while reaffirming the 'BBB-' rating. If bonds issued to oil and fertilizer companies are taken into account, the various deficit indicators will be even higher. Moreover, in order to boost domestic demand, the Government has announced additional tax sops subsequent to the interim vote-on-account budget putting further pressure on fiscal position. Thus, while the slowdown in the domestic economy may call for fiscal stimulus, fiscal maneuverability is limited.

H0 = There is no significant effect of global financial crisis on fiscal indicators like Fiscal Deficit of Central Govt.

H1 = There is significant effect of global financial crisis on fiscal indicators like Fiscal Deficit of Central Govt.

Year	*Gross FD*	*Year*	*Percentage*
1990-91	7.8	2000-01	5.7
1991-92	5.6	2001-02	6.2
1992-93	5.3	2002-03	5.9
1993-94	7	2003-04	4.5
1994-95	5.7	2004-05	4
1995-96	5.1	2005-06	4.1
1996-97	4.8	2006-07	3.5
1997-98	5.8	2007-08	2.7
1998-99	6.5	2008-09	6
1999-00	5.4	2009-10	5.5
x1	5.9	x2	4.81
s1	0.929755	s2	1.21239
	0.864444		1.469889
	8.644444		14.69889
	1.296852		
s=	1.140175		
tcal=	0.964912		
	2.236068		
tcal=	2.11		
ttab=	2.262		
	tcal<ttab		

5% level of significance and degree of freedom is 18.

F-test

Fcal=	1.627907	
Ftab=	3.18	d.f. =18

Fcal<Ftab so H0 is accepted.

it means the effect of global financial crisis had limited effect on Indian Economy in terms of very little average change in fiscal deficit of central government in the recession period.

Basically it was due to adherence to FRBM act on the on hand, *on the other hand limited exposure to* the world economy *as compared to others.*

However, the equity market felt that the jolt, but the monetary policy reacted quite promptly and the shocks could be lessened.

The Indian banks and financial system had only negligible direct exposure to the type of toxic assets that have Contaminated the Western countries' banking system. Bank's credit quality remains of high quality. Although bank credit growth was quite high at around 30 per cent per annum during 2004-07, it would appear that there was no significant relaxation of lending standards. Bank's loans to individuals for housing have been backed by prudent loan to value ratios. However, in view of the rapid credit growth to certain sectors, the Reserve Bank had pre-emptively tightened prudential norms (provisioning requirements and risk weights) for these sectors in order to safeguard financial stability.

Bank balance sheets remain healthy and adequately capitalised. Growth in bank credit remained strong up to October 2008 but has decelerated since. The financial system is working normally and accordingly there has been no need for any enhancement of government guarantee for bank deposits or banks' other liabilities. In view of the strong balance sheets and the transparency in the operations, there is no mistrust between banks and the inter-bank money market has been working throughout the period normally. Volumes in the money market have in fact grown over the past few months. There was some volatility in the call money rate, but this resulted from the sudden reversal in capital flows and resulting tightening of liquidity in September- October 2008. Thus, the Indian banking system is displaying none of the distresses that the Western banking system has exhibited since the start of the sub-prime crisis. While our banks do not have the problems of the type faced by the Western banking system, the global financial crisis has impacted us in other ways. The main impact over the past few months, especially following the collapse of Lehman Brothers in September 2008, has been the outcome of the reduction in net capital inflows and the significant correction in the domestic stock markets on the back of sell-off in the equity market by FIIs. The reduced foreign funding and the lackluster domestic capital market had put pressures on some segments of the financial system, such as NBFCs and mutual funds.

Conclusions

The ongoing global financial crisis can be largely attributed to extended periods of excessively loose monetary policy in the US over the period 2002-04. Very low interest rates during this period encouraged an aggressive search for yield and a substantial compression of risk-premia globally. Abundant liquidity in the advanced economies generated by the loose monetary policy found its way in the form of large capital flows to the emerging market economies. All these factors boosted asset and commodity prices, including oil, across the spectrum providing a boost to consumption and investment. Global imbalances were a manifestation of such an accommodative monetary policy and the concomitant boost in aggregate demand in the US outstripping domestic aggregate supply in the US. This period coincided with lax lending standards, inappropriate use of derivatives, credit ratings and financial engineering, and excessive leverage.

We have much less banking problems as our banks are still mostly in public sector and are well-capitalized. The Indian banking system has very limited exposure to the toxic assets that led to the downfall of the banks and financial institutions in the US and other advanced economies. The CRAR of all scheduled commercial banks (SCBs) taken together was 13.0 per cent at end-March 2008, well-above the regulatory requirement of 9 per cent. Asset quality of the domestic banks also remains satisfactory with net NPAs being only 1.0 per cent of net advances and 0.6 per cent of assets at end-March 2008. A more rigorous assessment of the health of commercial banks, recently undertaken by the Committee on Financial Sector Assessment (CFSA) (Chairman: Dr. Rakesh Mohan) (RBI, 2009), also shows that the commercial banks are robust and resilient. The single-factor stress tests undertaken by the CFSA reveal that the banking system can withstand significant shocks arising from large potential changes in credit quality, interest rate and liquidity conditions. These stress tests for credit, market and liquidity risk show that Indian banks are generally resilient. Given the ongoing financial crisis and its likely impact on the Indian economy, the CFSA conducted stress tests for the end of September 2008. Under the worst-case scenario (150 per cent increase in gross NPAs), the overall capital adequacy position of the banking sector would have declined to 10.6 percent in September 2008 - still well-above the regulatory requirement of 9 per cent. Thus, even under the worst case scenario, CRAR remains comfortably above the regulatory minimum. Our problems are mainly due to the sell-off by foreign institutional investors in the domestic equity markets leading to a sharp reduction in net capital inflows and the sharp slowdown in global economic activity and external demand. In view of the lower level of capital inflows, there were some pressures in the foreign exchange market. Consistent with its policy objective of maintaining orderly conditions in the foreign exchange market, the Reserve Bank sold foreign exchange in the market. While foreign exchange sales attenuated the mismatch in the foreign exchange market, these operations drained liquidity from the rupee market and accentuated pressures on the rupee liquidity. Accordingly, the Reserve Bank has been pro-actively managing liquidity since mid- September 2008 to assuage the liquidity pressures through a variety of measures noted above.

In view of these developments, the Reserve Bank, inter alia, reduced the cash reserve ratio (CRR) from 9 per cent

(September 2008) to 5 per cent by early January 2009 injecting nearly Rs.1,60,000 crore of primary liquidity in the system. Fresh issuances under MSS were stopped and buyback of existing MSS securities was also resorted to inject liquidity into the system. Simultaneously, in view of the adverse impact of the global slowdown on the domestic economy, policy rates were also cut - the reverse repo rate by 425 basis points from 9.00 per cent to 4.75 per cent and the reverse repo rate by 275 basis points from 6.00 per cent to 3.25 per cent.

However, a scrutiny of this crisis gives an opportunity to be cautions and vigilant in a phase when decoupling theory does not work, and we in India are also moving ahead towards more and more liberalization, privatization , Deregulation and marketization. The so called asymmetric information and moral hazard in back drop of market imperfection has compelled the pundits to focus on active macro intervention and regulation. Emerging economies have a lot to learn and practice.

References

Report on Trend and Progress, 2007-08, Reserve Bank of India

Committee on the Global Financial System (2009), Report of the Working Group on Capital Flows to Emerging Market Economies (Chairman: Rakesh Mohan), Bank for International Settlements, Basel.

Federal Reserve Bank of St. Louis (2009), Monetary Trends, April.
Group of Thirty (2009), "Financial Reform: A Framework for Financial Stability" (Chairman: Paul A. Volcker), Washington D.C.

Geneva Report (2009), "The Fundamental Principles of Financial Regulation", Geneva Reports on the World Economy 11 (by Markus Brunnermeier, Andrew Crocket, Charles Goodhart, Avinash D. Persaud and Hyun Shin).

G-20 (2009), "Working Group on Enhancing Sound Regulation and Strengthening Transparency (Co-Chairs: Tiff Macklem and Rakesh Mohan).

Haldane, Andrew (2009), "Why Banks Failed The Stress Test?", Bank of England.

Henry, Peter Blair (2007), "Capital Account Liberalization: Theory, Evidence, and Speculation", Journal of Economic Literature, Vol. XLV, December.

International Monetary Fund (2009a), "Group of Twenty: Note by the Staff of International Monetary Fund", January. — — — (2009b), "Initial Lessons of the Crisis", February. — — (2009c), World Economic Outlook, April.

Kohn, Donald (2008), "Monetary Policy and Asset Prices Revisited", Remarks at the Cato Institute's 26th Annual Monetary Policy Conference, November 19. Available at http://www.federal reserve.gov/newsevents/speech/kohn 2008 1119a.htm

Lane, Philip (2009), "Global Imbalances and Global Governance", Paper presented at the `Global Economic Governance: Systemic Challenges, Institutional Responses and the Role of the New Actors', Brussels, February.

de Larosiere Report (2009), "Report of the High-Level Group on Financial Supervision in the EU" (Chairman: Jacques de Larosiere), Brussels.

Mohan, Rakesh (2006a), "Coping With Liquidity Management in India: A Practitioner's View", Reserve Bank of India Bulletin, April. — — (2006b), "Evolution of Central Banking in India", Reserve Bank of India Bulletin, June — — (2007), "India's Financial Sector Reforms: Fostering Growth While Containing Risk", Reserve Bank of India Bulletin, December. Portes, Richard (2009), "Global Imbalances" in Mathias Dewatripont, Xavier Freixas and Richard Portes (Ed.), "Macroeconomic Stability and Financial Regulation: Key Issues for the G20", Centre for Economic Policy Research, London.

Obstfeld, Maurice (2009), "International Finance and Growth in Developing Countries: What Have We Learned?", Working Paper 14691, National Bureau of Economic Research, Cambridge, MA.

Reserve Bank of India (2009a), "India's Financial Sector: An Assessment" Committee on Financial Sector Assessment (Chairman: Rakesh Mohan), March. — — (2009b), "Macro economic and Monetary Developments during 2008-09", April.

Taylor, John (2009), "The Financial Crisis and the Policy Responses: An Empirical Analysis of What Went Wrong", Working Paper 14631, January, National Bureau of Economic Research.

Turner Review (2009), "The Turner Review: A Regulatory Response to the Global Banking Crisis" by Lord Turner, Chairman, Financial Services Authority, UK.

World Bank (2008), Global Development Finance 2008: The Role of International Banking, World Bank.

Bernanke, Ben (2009), "The Crisis and the Policy Response", Stamp Lecture at London School of Economics, January 13. Available at http://www.federalreserve.gov/newsevents/speech/bernanke20090113a.htm

7

Medium Term Fiscal Plan for Recession Control- A Study of Karnataka Economy

K.G. Suresh Kumar, N. Chandre Gowda

Economic Policy and the Business Cycle

The approach to the business cycle depends upon the type of economic system. Under a communist system, there is no business cycle since all economic activities are controlled by the central planners. Indeed, this lack of a business cycle is often cited as an advantage of a command economy. Both socialist and fascist economies have a mix of market and command sectors. Again, the command sector in these economies will not have a business cycle—while the market sector will display a cyclical activity. In a fullmarket economy—like the United States—the nation can suffer extreme swings in the level of economic activity.

The economic policies used by the government to smooth out the extreme swings of the business cycle are called stabilization policies, and are based on the theories of John Maynard Keynes. Writing in 1936 (the Great Depression), Keynes argued that the business cycle was due to extreme swings in the total demand for goods and services. The total demand in an economy from households, business, and government is called aggregate demand. Contracyclical policy is increasing aggregate demand in recessions and decreasing aggregate demand in overheated expansions.

In a market economy (or market sector) the government has two types of economic policies to control aggregate demand—fiscal policy and monetary policy. When these policies are used to stimulate the economy during a recession, it is said that the government is pursuing *expansionary* economic policies. And when they are used to contract the economy during an overheated expansion, it is said that the government is pursuing contractionary economic policies.

Fiscal Policy and Monetary Policy

1. Discretionary Fiscal Policy. Fiscal policy is changes in the taxing and spending of the federal government for purposes of expanding or contracting the level of aggregate demand. In recession, an expansionary fiscal policy involves lowering taxes and increasing government spending. In an overheated expansion, a contractionary fiscal policy requires higher taxes and reduced spending.

   The first way this can be done is through the federal budget process. However, this process takes so long—12 to 18 months—that discretionary fiscal policy cannot be matched with the business cycle. The Kennedy tax cut of 1964 and later the Ford tax increase of 1974 hit the economy just when the opposite contracyclical policy was needed. As a result, the federal government no longer uses discretionary fiscal policy.

2. Automatic Stabilizers. A second type of fiscal policy is built into the structure of federal taxes and spending. This is referred to as "nondiscretionary fiscal policy" or more commonly as "automatic stabilizers". The progressive income tax (the major source of federal revenue) and the welfare system both act to increase aggregate demand in recessions, and to decrease aggregate demand in overheated expansions.

3. Monetary Policy. Monetary policy is under the control of the Federal Reserve System (our central bank) and is completely discretionary. It is the changes in interest rates and money supply to expand or contract aggregate demand. In a recession, the Fed will lower interest rates and increase the money supply. In an overheated expansion, the Fed will raise interest rates and decrease the money supply.

These decisions are made by the Federal Open Market Committee (FOMC) which meets every six to seven weeks. The policy changes can be done immediately, although the impact on aggregate demand can take several months. Monetary policy has become the major form of discretionary contra cyclical policy used by the federal government. A source of conflict is that the Fed is independent and is not under the direct control of either the President or the Congress. This independence of monetary policy is considered to be an important advantage compared to fiscal policy.

Note that expansionary monetary policy is commonly called "easy money" while contractionary monetary policy is called "tight money". Other terms are also used.

The Medium Term Fiscal Plan Objectives

The Medium Term Fiscal Framework has provided the basis for devising fiscal strategies for the State on a multi year framework. This has yielded rich dividends as outlined in the previous paragraphs. The Medium Term Fiscal Plans of the State presented till now from 2001 have a common thread of fiscal objectives running through them. These fiscal objectives need to be emphasized in every medium term plan as they are the foundation for decision making. These guiding principles are as follows: -

- Widening the tax base while moderating the tax rates.
- Smart enforcement through use of Information technology and computerization.
- Reducing compliance cost and promoting tax payer friendly processes.

- Focused approach for recovery of arrears of revenue.
- Priority in allocation to Social Services and Infrastructure upgradation.
- Emphasis on decentralized and local solutions for implementation.
- Linking outlay to outcome to improve productivity of expenditure.
- Zero based budgeting to weed-out schemes which have outlived their utility. Consolidation of schemes to provide impetus to core programmes without spreading the resources thinly.
- Appropriate staffing and operational expenditure for service delivery sectors like health, education and regulatory functions.
- Prudent borrowing guided by affordability rather than availability as per the provisions of the Karnataka Fiscal Responsibility Act 2002.
- Bringing down the cost of debt by debt swapping, prepayment and adopting best debt management practices.
- Maintaining Government guarantee stock within the ceiling prescribed by the Ceiling on Government Guarantees Act, 1999 and extension of guarantees not on the basis of availability but through rigorous risk analysis.
- Upgradation and improvement of the existing system of Government transactions to facilitate real time monitoring, reconciliation, accountability and integrity of the financial system.
- Leveraging of Government assets, specially Government land, and assets of Public Sector Undertakings to generate surplus so as to finance physical infrastructure.
- Adoption of Public Private Partnership Route to attract more investment for infrastructure upgradation and to bring in managerial efficiency

Performance of Fiscal Indicators

After achieving a revenue surplus status in 2004-05, Karnataka Government has consistently striven to sustain and improve its fiscal parameters. Table 5 given belowshows the State's fiscal performance since 2004-05 in terms of various indicators comparing the actual achievement with targets set for each year. In respect of 2007-08 the likely performance as per the revised estimates is compared with the budget estimates.

As is evident from the figures in Table 5 the revenue balance position has improved substantially from 2004-05 onwards reaching a peak surplus of Rs.4152 crore in the financial year 2006-07. Thereafter there has been a downward shift in the revenue surplus even though it is still as high as Rs. 2981 Crore in 2007-08. This reduction in the revenue surplus is partially on account of implementation of the State's Fifth Pay Commission Award leading to higher expenditure under salaries and pensions head. This trend is likely to continue till the financial year 2008-09 during which arrears of the financial year 2006-07 are to be paid. It is expected to disburse almost Rs.2500 Crores in 2007-08 & 2008-09 over and above normal increases in revenue expenditure because of the revisionof salaries and pensions. To a certain extent, the revenue surplus has also come down in 2007-08 on account of substantial one time expenditure of Rs.1250 Crores on Farmers' Loan Waiver Scheme and the hike in the rate of Social Security Pensions from Rs.200/- per month to Rs.400/- per month which increased the revenue expenditure by almost another Rs.400 Crores. It is projected that from 2008-09 onwards, while financing operating expenditure, there will not be any abrupt increase in revenue expenditure and therefore it would be possible to achieve a secular increase in the revenue surplus. This revenue surplus achieved in the coming years will be available for funding higher expenditure on capital formation.

The Medium Term Fiscal Plan Targets Achieved

In the earlier Medium Terms Fiscal Plans the State had set for itself the target of phasing out off budget borrowings.

Fiscal Framework (Rs. Crores)

Item	*2004-05 BE*	*2004-05 A/c*	*2005-06 BE*	*2005-06 A/c*	*2006-07 BE*	*2006-07 A/c*	*2007-08 BE*	*2007-08 RE*
Revenue Receipts of which	25510	26570	29218	30352	35875	37587	40762	40840
State' Own Tax Revenues	14958	16072	18680	18632	22534	23301	26691	27218
Non Tax Revenues	4486	4472	4090	3875	4088	4098	1857	1802
Resources from the Centre -Devolution	3760	3878	3760	4213	4609	5374	6300	6300
- Grants	2306	2147	2688	3632	4644	4813	5914	5520
Revenue Expenditure of Which	25437	24896	28364	28041	34341	33435	39135	37859
Interest	3920	3794	4029	5750	4366	4236	4818	4718
Salaries	5751	5392	6169	5750	6724	6545	8547	8744
Pensions	2214	2157	2427	2237	2666	2496	3416	3296
Subsidies (Food, TransportHousing & Industry)	905	1145	1573	2099	1741	1991	2517	3027
Power Subsidy	1400	1724	1750	1821	1800	2370	2150	1950
Devolution to ULBs	799	798	1160	1159	1530	1639	1904	1904
Major O&M (Roads,Buildings &Irrigation)	401	333	513	262	1018	1011	810	1099
Other O & M (Edn,Health,RD,WS,Agr, Forest)	2444	2498	2778	2716	3438	3477	6161	6794
Administrative Expenditure	442	478	559	557	687	559	799	769
Other Revenue Expenditure	7163	6577	7406	7677	10372	9112	8014	5558
Capital Receipt (Non Debt)	30	47	30	124	45	60	749	263
Revenue Deficit	-73	-1673	-854	-2311	-1535	-4152	-1627	-2981
Expenditure on CapitalFormation	2502	3444	3774	3591	5088	6349	7523	8201
Fiscal Deficit	4247	3600	4714	3687	5211	4688	6305	6085
Total Debt Stock	48384	46117	52727	49794	56148	54676	61492	60588
Interest	3920	3794	4029	3765	4366	4236	4818	4718
Debt Services	5907	7823	4925	4576	5320	5986	6117	6018
Salary+Pension+Interest	11885	11343	12625	11751	13756	13278	16780	16758

Contd.

Item	*2004-05 BE*	*2004-05 A/c*	*2005-06 BE*	*2005-06 A/c*	*2006-07 BE*	*2006-07 A/c*	*2007-08 BE*	*2007-08 RE*
Gross Off Budget Borrowings	1035	838	899	1078	845	242	720	720
Net Off Budget Borrowings	-174	-347	-135	-816	-146	-1246	- -58	-74
Consolidated interest	4558	4485	4820	4508	5077	5299	5198	5053
Consolidated Revenue Deficit	565	-982	-63	-1568	-824	-3089	-1247	-2647
Consolidated Capital Formation	3537	4282	4673	4668	5933	6591	8243	8921
Consolidated Fiscal Deficit	4073	3553	4579	2871	5064	3442	6242	6011
Consolidated Debt Stock	55009	53412	59216	59274	61337	59717	66223	65302
Cnsldtd Rev Deficit/ GSDP	-0.38%	-0.66%	-0.04%	-0.92%	-0.44%	-1.64%	-0.57%	-1.23%
GSDP at Current Prices	147956	148521	166228	166228	186757	188274	220006	215282
INFLATION	5.00%	5.00%	5.00%	5.00%	4.00%	4.00%	5.00%	5.00%
GSDP Annual Real Growth	7.00%	7.00%	7.00%	7.00%	7.00%	7.00%	8.00%	8.00%
Revenue Receipts of which	17.24%	17.89%	17.58%	17.78%	19.21%	19.96%	18.53%	18.97%
State' Own Tax Revenues	10.11%	10.82%	11.24%	10.91%	12.07%	12.38%	12.13%	12.64%
Non Tax Revenues	3.03%	3.01%	2.46%	2.27%	2.19%	2.18%	0.84%	0.84%
Resources from the Centre- Devolution	2.54%	2.61%	2.26%	2.47%	2.47%	2.85%	2.86%	2.93%
- Grants	1.56%	1.45%	1.62%	2.13%	2.49%	2.56%	2.69%	2.56%
Revenue Expenditure of Which	17.19%	16.76%	17.06%	16.42%	18.39%	17.76%	17.79%	17.59%
Interest	2.65%	2.55%	2.42%	2.20%	2.34%	2.25%	2.19%	2.19%
Salaries	3.89%	3.63%	3.71%	3.37%	3.60%	3.48%	3.88%	4.06%
Pensions	1.50%	1.45%	1.46%	1.31%	1.43%	1.33%	1.55%	1.53%
Subsidies (Food,Transport,Housing & Industry)	0.61%	0.77%	0.95%	1.23%	0.93%	1.06%	1.14%	1.41%
Power Subsidy	0.95%	1.16%	1.05%	1.07%	0.96%	1.26%	0.98%	0.91%
Devolution to ULBs	0.54%	0.54%	0.70%	0.68%	0.82%	0.87%	0.87%	0.88%
Major O&M (Roads,Buildings &Irrigation)	0.27%	0.22%	0.31%	0.15%	0.54%	0.54%	0.37%	0.51%
Other O & M (Edn,Health,RD,WS,Agr, Forest)	1.65%	1.68%	1.67%	1.59%	1.84%	1.85%	2.80%	3.16%

Contd.

Item	*2004-05 BE*	*2004-05 A/c*	*2005-06 BE*	*2005-06 A/c*	*2006-07 BE*	*2006-07 A/c*	*2007-08 BE*	*2007-08 RE*
Administrative Expenditure	0.30%	0.32%	0.34%	0.33%	0.37%	0.30%	0.36%	0.36%
Other Revenue exp	4.84%	4.43%	4.46%	4.50%	5.55%	4.84%	3.64%	2.58%
Revenue Deficit	-0.05%	-0.05%	-0.51%	-0.51%	-1.35%	-0.82%	-2.21%	-0.74%
Capital Receipt (Non Debt)	0.02%	0.03%	0.02%	0.07%	0.02%	0.03%	0.34%	0.12%
Expenditure on CapitalFormation	1.69%	2.32%	2.27%	2.10%	2.72%	3.37%	3.42%	3.81%
Fiscal Deficit	2.87%	2.42%	2.84%	2.79%	2.79%	2.49%	2.87%	2.83%
Off Budget Borrowings/GSDP	0.70%	0.56%	0.54%	0.63%	0.45%	0.13%	0.33%	0.33%
Consolidated RevenueDeficit/GSDP	-0.38%	-0.66%	-0.04%	-0.92%	-0.44%	-1.64%	-0.57%	1.23%
Consolidated Capitalexpenditure/GSDP	2.39%	2.88%	2.81%	2.73%	3.18%	3.50%	3.75%	4.14%
Consolidated FiscalDeficit/GSDP	2.75%	2.19%	2.75%	1.68%	2.71%	1.83%	2.84%	2.79%
Consolidated Debt Stock/GSDP	37.18%	35.96%	35.62%	32.96%	32.84%	31.72%	30.10%	30.33%

In MTFP 2007-11 it was targeted to eliminate fresh off budget borrowings from 2008-09 by bringing them onbudget. It is heartening to note that this target will be achieved and borrowings of all special purpose vehicles which were earlier raised through the off-budget route will be brought on budget in 2008-09. This is also reflected in the revised estimates for 2007-08 which show that inspite of off-budget borrowings of Rs.835 Crores proposed in the budget estimates, Rs.733 Crores has been provided on budget during the year and only Rs. 102 Cr has been allowed for off-budget borrowing. With the complete elimination of fresh off-budget borrowings in 2008-09it is expected that the various special purpose vehicles would be able to focus more on project management and implementation. It would also facilitate transparent and effective debt management besides reducing the cost of debt servicing.

The Letter of Credit (LOC) System existing mainly in the Department of Public Works and Irrigation was a parallel system for drawal of funds from the Consolidated Fund bypassing the Treasury system. This was not only making monitoring of expenditure and consolidation of accounts difficult but was often leading to excess expenditure. After achieving the stabilization of the Treasury Computerization System, the State has been able to bring all LOC system transactions pertaining of public Works and Irrigation Departments on to the treasury network. There is further scope for improvement of the system by linking drawals to individual works instead of the budgetary head of account as is being done at present. This is a part of the medium term strategy to be implemented in the coming years.

The Zilla Panchayat Transactions are effected through the Zilla Panchayat Fund Accounts to which funds are transferred from the Consolidated Fund as per the link document. Even though all the drawals from Zilla Panchayat Fund Accounts are accounted for under the schemes mentioned in the link document, a system check to ensure that the drawals take place only against the schemes for which funds were transferred from Consolidated Fund was not in place so far. The consequence of this was temporary diversion of funds between schemes and delays in disbursement of salary in some cases. It was therefore targeted to bring scheme-wise budget control under the Zilla Panchayat Fund Accounts as was already being done for State sector schemes. Accordingly the Zilla Panchayat Budget Control has now been implemented throughout the State. The next step would be to bring this scheme-wise control for the Taluk Panchayat schemes also. It is targeted for implementation in a phased manner over the medium term fiscal plan period.

Focus Areas

The quality of expenditure and effectiveness in program implementation is an area which needs focussed attention. Though higher outlays are being provided in the area of public works, irrigation, energy, health and education, the productivity of expenditure needs to be substantially improved. Much more than increases in the outlay, this is expected to provide higher impetus to faster and inclusive economic growth. The spread of expenditure over the financial year at present indicates crowding of plan expenditure towards the last quarter and the last month. The Table given below shows that more than 30% of the plan expenditure is incurred in the month of March.

Year	*2004-05*	*2005-06*	*2007-08*
Plan Expenditure	9227.61	11290.10	14602.76
Plan Expenditure duringMarch	2432.61	3750.63	5405.20
% of March Expenditure to BE	26.36%	33.22%	37.01%

This back-loading of expenditure in the last month of a financial year compromises the quality of expenditure and also leads to spill over of expenditure to the next financial year. It makes fiscal marksmanship extremely difficult and also pushes expenditure into areas where absorptive capacity for expenditure is high even though they may not be the targeted sectors. It is therefore very important to institutionalize and build consensus on budgetary screening process which should mandate inclusion of new programmes in the budget only after thorough scrutiny and appraisal. Though this was suggested in the Medium Term Fiscal Plan 2006-10, decisive action needs to be taken on this issue.

The other issue which needs urgent attention is programme performance budgeting roll-out in all the departments. At present more than 2500 scheme heads are being utilized by the departments to implement a multitude of schemes. Several schemes have common objectives and often, the same target beneficiaries. Existence of a large number of schemes complicates monitoring and implementation and also compromises focused approach. Therefore, programme performance budgeting which would consolidate schemes into programmes and tie-up program implementation to inputs, outputs and outcomes is to be pursued vigorously. Though the same was part of 2007-11 MTFP and efforts were made to implement it in some departments, the progress is still in its early stages and departments need to be convinced to take this up on priority.

Management of Subsidies, especially Food and Power Subsidies is another critical area of importance. Being nonplan in nature, these expenditures do not get the attention they deserve. More than the substantial outlay it is the present delivery system of these subsidies which is a matter of concern. Food subsidy has acquired new dimensions on account of the recent signals of future decline in the availability of rice and wheat. Decentralization of procurement and diversification in procurement to include coarse food grains would throw-up new challenges in balancing food security concerns with appropriate procurement prices to be paid to the farmers. This may also provide an opportunity to look into alternative ways of disbursement of the subsidy like food coupons. Similarly, though there is an urgent need to undertake 100% metering to disburse power subsidy for irrigation pumpsets, consensus needs to be evolved to make any progress in the matter.

Conclusion

As has been mentioned in above, the State Government has been able to implement two critical reforms in the phasing out of the off budget borrowings, and the letter of credit system, and the implementation of the Zilla Panchayat Budget Control. It is necessary to consolidate upon these reforms. Therefore it is planned to link drawal of funds from treasuries to individual public works and implement Taluk Level Schemewise Budget Control in the Medium Term Fiscal Plan period. Similarly as mentioned in this paper, it is determined to move forward in the implementation of a budgetary screening process and the introduction of programme performance budgeting in the Medium Term Fiscal Plan period.

References

Ahluwalia, M.S. (2000), 'Economic Performance of States in the Post-Reform Period', *Economic and Political Weekly*, May, 1637-48.

Bagchi A, J.L Bajaj and W.A. Byrd (1992), *State Finances in India*, Vikas Publishing House, New Delhi.

Carlino, G and R Defina (1998), 'The Differential Regional Effects of Monetary Policy', *Review of Economics and Statistics*, 34: 572-87.

Chaudhuri, S. (2000), 'Economic Growth in the States-Four Decades-I', *ICRA Bulletin: Money and Finance*, October-December, 45-69.

Comment', *Journal of Regional Science*, 23: 249-61.

Conference of Indian Economic Association.

Dasgupta, D, P Maiti, R Mukherjee, S Sarkar and S Chakrabarti (2000), 'Growth and Inter-state Disparities in India', *Economic and Political Weekly*, July, 2413-22.

Financial Report of Karnataka Governament-2008

Garrison, C.B and J.R. Kort (1983), 'Regional Impact of Monetary and Fiscal Policy: A Jadhav, Narendra (1994): *Monetary Economics for India*, McMillan India.

Karnataka Economic Survey -2008

Karnataka State Budget 2009-10.

Kurian, N.J. (2000), 'Widening Regional Disparities in India: Some Indicators', *Economic and Political Weekly*, February, 538-50.

Rangarajan, C. (1988), 'Issues in Monetary Management', *Presidential Address*, 71st

Rao, M.G. (2002), 'State-Level Fiscal Reforms in India', Paper presented at the Conference on Comparative Economic Development, Cornell University.

Reddy, Y.V. (2002), 'Parameters of Monetary Policy in India', 88th Annual Conference of Indian Econometric Society.

Shand, R and S Bhide (2000), 'Sources of Economic Growth: Regional Dimensions of Reforms', *Economic and Political Weekly*, October, 3747-57.

8

SOCIO-ECONOMIC IMPACT OF RECESSION ON EMPLOYEE: AN ANLYTICAL STUDY

Amiya Kumar Mohapatra

Introduction

When the GDP growth rate is falling continuously for two or more consecutive quarters of a year then we call it as recessionary situation. Then it is followed by several quarters of slowdown to make it worst. This leads to fall in real income, visible in real GDP, employment, industrial production and growth, and wholesale-retail trade etc. During recession there is a fall in aggregate demand which in turn leads to fall in aggregate supply (Production). Fall in demand for goods and services give rise to unemployment and fall in price level and start bringing misfortune to the economy.

Recession mean '*recess is on in the growth processes*' which means the growth rate of GDP and employment is on a falling trend. Recession is further explained *as the re-assessment of the present economic scenario and plan accordingly for recovery and to stop the downfall. It provides sound ideas of getting prepared to fight against the meltdown.*

The current global economic recession has hardly left any country unaffected in the world. Developed countries like USA,

UK, Germany, Japan and Canada are most vulnerable to this economic tsunami. So there is nothing to surprise to know that our country is also getting upset from this global economic meltdown

Consequences of Recession on the Employee

During recession time cost cutting is done everywhere, so corporate sectors in India are doing cost cutting to minimize their loss as a weapon for survival. This is going to hit employees in India more badly as cost cutting in India will be severe. Corporate sector is reducing the salary and cut off the other perks' given to the employee. Sometime to make it more worst started doing employee reduction. Another problem could be for the people who are not effective and not hard working will lose job but this is going to affect the employee who are hardworking as they will be pressurized by the employee more severely with high target with less expenses. These people will work under more stress and has to face greater trauma and work load, as they will be having fear of losing job, salary reduction, and demotion.

This fear of losing the job will cause lot of mental, physical, social, economic problem and people will resort to various criminal and anti- social activities.

Economical Consequences: Impact on Economic Status

The financial positions get disturbed due to fall in income and employment. Indian people are extremely price sensitive and recession is having catastrophic effect on people. It is accompanied by reduction in personal disposable income which has worsened the financial situation. The after effect is that people are fully shattered and are committing various anti-social acts. It has further aggravated the situation. Some of the critical consequences are as follows:

- People are made work harder and paid proportionately less
- Salary gets reduced and price of good do not fall proportionately.

- Cut throat competition at work place makes ambience at work place pathetic
- Future planning is affected
- Reduction in perks and other benefits

Psychological Consequences: Impact on Mind and Health

Economic ups and down has 'deep brain stimulation', for the people. It became tough for people to adjust in this serious situation. People tend to over react and unable to handle the pressure easily. It is going tougher in the recessionary period. The return on investment and income is going downwards. People fail to maintain the kind of lifestyle they would like to do. They feel dejected and mental imbalance which leads various disorder and diseases. Family life and social life get crushed under socio economic pressure in recessionary period. The effect of recession on mind and health as follows:

- Excess of work load create pressure which affect mind and body
- Causes anxiety ,high & low BP, heart attack etc
- Career planning mind set is affected
- Weak body and mind due to low income
- Employer employee relation is affected
- Absentmindedness is caused
- Mental hazard due to job insecurity

Social Consequences: Impact on Social Life

A human is a social being and it can't live alone, he needs people to interact with, share it views. Every individual is deeply attached with the society. In recessionary period people neither have any job security nor have the adequate salary so this directly affects their value in society at large. They lose their job and feel shacked and isolated from the society as some of the major consequences are as follows:

- Loss of job leads to loss of prestige and goodwill in the society.

- Feel helpless and isolated from socializing
- Life style is get affected
- Get addicted to alcohol and drugs etc
- Gap between rich and poor is increasing, which again lead to vicious cycle of poverty

Other Impacts and Incidences of Recession

Besides these above consequences recession is also affecting the relation of employee with people and others

Employee to Employee

In recession situation lot of salary reduction made, people work hard and compete against the employees to stay in the job. Every employee wants to do well by hook or by crook, so they try all their skill in the working environment of organization. The common effects are as:

- Create cut throat competition
- Cordial relation is lost
- Working place becomes a knockout ring
- Moral values are lost
- Development suspicious and ill doing

Employee to Employer

Employee indulges themselves to tactics like impression management to impress their senior and to secure their position in company. This affects the cordial relationship between employer and employee. Some of the effects are as follows

- Mutual admiration is lost
- Belongingness towards firm is lost
- Work is taken as burden
- Healthy environment work place is lost
- Frequent argument at work place
- Lost of loyalties

Employee to Family

A family is very important part of the every individual and every individual wants to work hard for his family. In the recession it is difficult for the people to carry on the same life style and expenditure pattern which creates a lot of agitation and builds up frustration in the mind of bread earner.

India which is well known for its family system which considered as very strong, but this too is being affected by the contagious disease of recession. The bread getter is under intense pressure to juggle the both family burden and the workload burden. The major effects are as:

- Domestic violence increases
- Anger, anxiety and helplessness affect family ambience
- Low self esteem and self respect in family
- Indulgence in criminal activities like thefts etc
- Lack of care and support

Employee to Neighbourhood

It is seen that 'neighbors envy owners pride'. Recession affect the lifestyle of the people. The major effects are as:

- Person start reducing socializing
- Fear of losing job make person treason toward neighbour

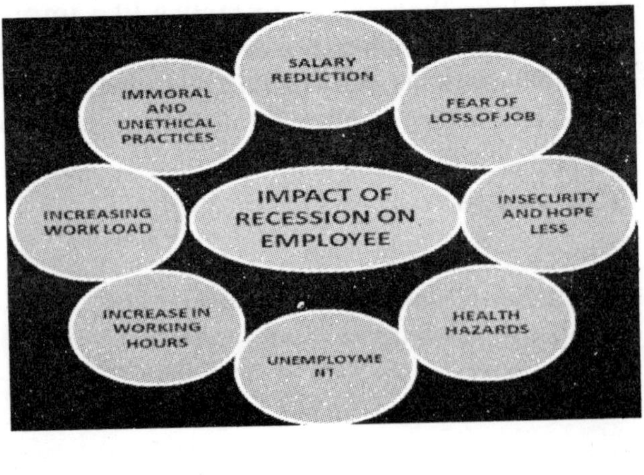

- Feeling of outcast creeps in the mind of employee
- Employee feel degraded among its friends
- Their belongingness to the society is lost

The above impacts of recession on working people are given in a chart format below.

Role of Government

Talking in today's context it is difficult to say whether the thoughts of Keynes which revived the world from the Great Depression era in the 1930's will work today. But Keynes talked of government intervention in the so called capitalist's economy. Keynes thoughts may not revive the economy at present from recession but what it would do is that it would restore confidence in the minds of people. And the intervention of government would be indicative of that. It would send out a message that the Government is there to help its people in times of need.

Certainly in this grim situation government has to play a vital role to bail out the firms and the people working in it. It is the duty of the government to take strong measure to help them out to face this situation. Government instead of giving its suggestion to corporate sector that firing people rather it should create new job opportunity for the people and boost the economy.

Role of the Corporate Heads and the Employee

Government is required to take a judicious effort to provide employment to the people so that further corrosion should not taken place and vicious circle of poverty would not be created. Firm and the employee has to understand each other situation and should react it accordingly.

An organization should communicate properly about their situation in recession and views of the employee have to taken into consideration so that a solution to the problem could be sorted out. Employee should understand that if any salary cut is there it is not for the sake of firm but for the existence of the firm and if firm do not exist then there will be no job and no salary.

Field Work and Finding of the Survey

A survey was conducted to asses the impact of recession on the people doing job and to evaluate extent to which they are affected.

On the basis of the survey and of 100 sample size of heterogeneous working population, I found that currently employed people are in great mental, social, emotional and psychological distress. They are under deep pressure to perform well in extreme conditions at a lower pay. They are under a constant fear that their jobs would be lost at any point of time and their families would suffer.

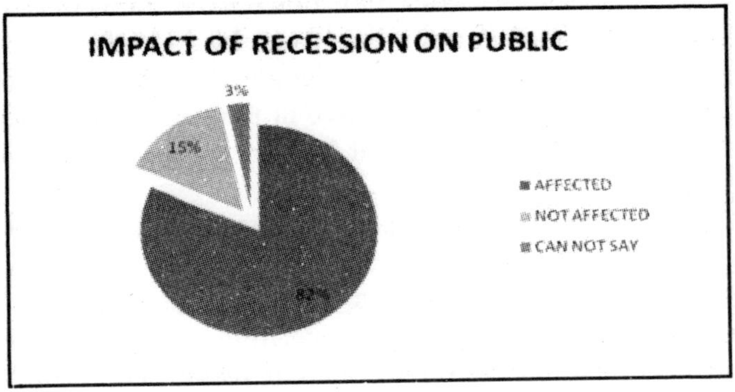

It is also found out from the survey that due to recession and instability, people are more inclined towards government jobs as compare to private jobs, because of job security, stability and fixed payments. People are now going for multi tasking to earn more to secure their future.

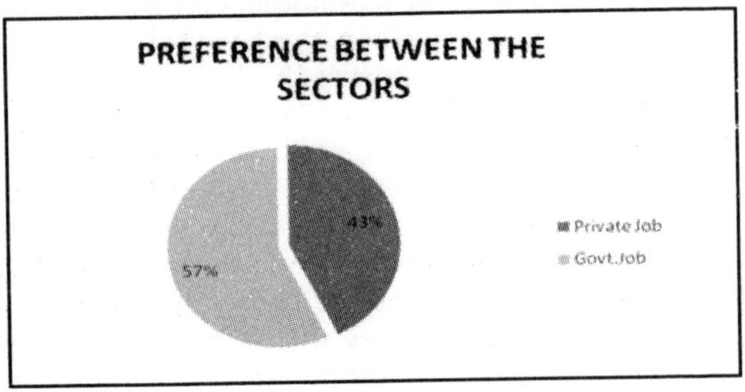

From the pie chart which is given below, it can be concluded that 50% of the respondents are of the opinion that family support & respect has a role to play in the socio-economic impact of recession on an employee whereas 40% of the respondents are opined the other way. 10% of the respondents haven't thought about it as a point of consideration.

So, from the below result it can thus be concluded that if we are to look the socio-economic impact of recession on an Employee then the role of family support cannot be neglected. At times during recession the employee may have constant pressure of losing his job but constant motivation from wife, children and other family members would ease that pressure off. Another aspect can be that during times of recession the other family members can take up the job if the head earning member looses out on his job to shoulder the burden

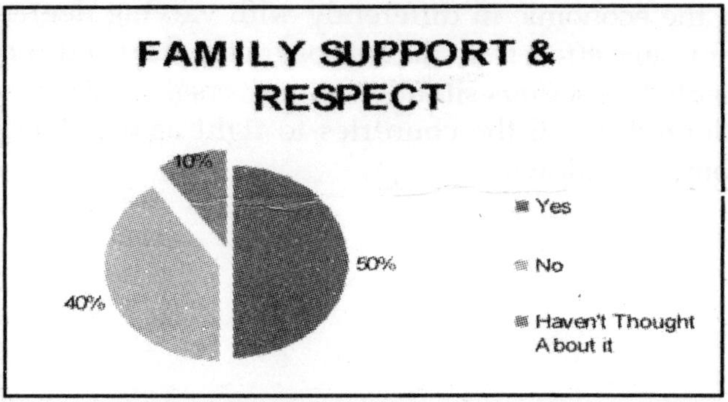

The results from the chart which is given below show that 55% of the respondents believe that an Employees Health does get affected during the time of recession. 30% of the respondents opine the other way i.e. they believe that Employees health does not get affected due to recession.15% of the respondent however does not consider this point to be relevant.

Analyzing the below results it can be interpreted that during times of recession it is believed that an employee's health does get affected. He suffers from mental pressures which come from the fear of losing the job. This pressure is so

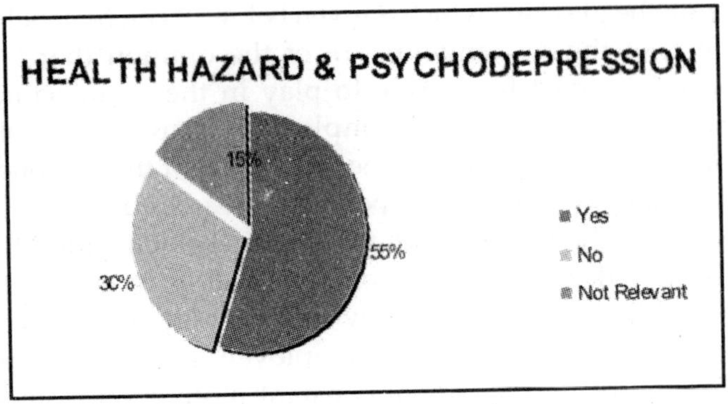

high that the employee ultimately suffers from mental depression.

As a concluding remark, right now we can't say how long this recession going to stay, but it is for sure that it is going to affect the economic in differently with varying degree. This calls for huge effort from the side of government and corporate to handle this serious situation. A universal approach should be adopted by all the countries to fight against the global economic meltdown

9

Global Financial Crisis and Impact of Indian Economy

A. Sangamithra, N. Savitha

Introduction

The turmoil in the international financial markets of advanced economies, that started around mid-2007, has exacerbated substantially since August 2008. The financial market crisis has led to the collapse of major financial institutions and is now beginning to impact the real economy in the advanced economies. As this crisis is unfolding, credit markets appear to be drying up in the developed world. While the overall policy approach has been able to mitigate the potential impact of the turmoil on domestic financial markets and the economy, with the increasing integration of the Indian economy and its financial markets with rest of the world, there is recognition that the country does face some downside risks from these international developments.

The First Network Crisis of the 21st Century

There is an increasing recognition that the nature of the cur-rent crisis is profoundly different in many ways and that radical approaches and tools will have to be used. The latest

International Monetary Fund (IMF) analysis (February 2009), for ex-ample, considers that the root causes of the current crisis lay in market failure... bred by a long period of high growth, low real interest rates and volatility and policy failures in financial regulation - which was not equipped to see the risk concentrations and flawed incentives behind the financial innovation boom; macroeconomic policies - which did not take into account building systemic risks in the financial system and in housing markets; and global architecture–where a fragmented surveillance system compounded the inability to see growing vulnerabilities and links. *(Andrew Sheng,2009)*

This is truly a momentous crisis of the network economy and globalisation. If the international architecture is not reformed and no equitable solution found on a democratic and legitimate basis, then the world will go through another round of protectionism and nationalism that plunged the world into the Great Depression. Globalisation has truly networked developed and developing markets alike, bound in their common interests, since emerging markets have much to lose from their savings in mature markets, just as mature markets benefit from trade and investments in the developing world. The risk is that if sound, transparent and effective regulation is not built into the international financial architecture to foster open trade in goods and services, emerging markets would neither have the confidence for investment abroad, nor would they have the confidence to open their markets to higher market volatility and contagion risks.

Global Crisis: Domestic Consequences

Though the decelerating phase of the Indian economy started way ahead of the US mortgage market meltdown, there can be little doubt that the global crisis has seriously aggravated the problem and made the task of reversing the domestic downturn much more difficult. Before examining how international economic developments might have affected the domestic economy since the outbreak of the crisis, it is useful to take stock of some of the striking features of the Indian macro economy during this period, especially of the sources and components of aggregate demand. First, the slowdown in GDP and industrial growth, which as already noted had started from the first quarter of 2007-08, became much more pronounced from the fourth quarter of 2007-08 and the first quarter of 2008-09, respectively. The proximate source of this was the sharper slowdown in both private consumption and aggregate investment from early January 2008. Second, over March-August 2008, export as well as import growth was significantly higher than in the pre-crisis period - something which cannot but be viewed as counter-intuitive in the context of the global economic woes. It was only from September 2008 that the crisis seems to have finally taken its toll of the country's trade flows. This combination of the sharper slowdown of demand driven primarily by domestic factors along with an acceleration of exports and imports 21 constitutes a veritable conundrum of the Indian economy during this period. Third and no less paradoxical, from June-August 2007-08, non-resident Indian (NRI) remittances zoomed, averaging a year of year growth of more than 38% between the second quarters of 2007-08 and 2008-09, and thereby belying the predictions of most pundits regarding the adverse impact of the world crisis on the inflow of such funds. Finally, with a much sharper deceleration of investment and private consumption and a steep downturn of export growth from the third quarter of 2008-09, the economy seems to have entered a new phase and been sucked into the maelstrom of the global crisis.

Financial Crisis and Impact on India

In the year 2007-08, three global crises viz., food, fuel and financial had impact on India. On the positive side, significant easing of international oil prices and softening of international food prices has helped in softening the inflationary pressure. Inflation has come down from 13% in the middle of 2008 to around 5% in January 2009. However, the unprecedented global financial crisis has been having severe adverse effect on Indian economy. The financial turmoil which started in the US financial system as a result of defaults of sub-prime mortgage loans has blown into an unprecedented financial crisis. It has affected the international money, credit, equity and foreign exchange markets. US households used to save 6% of their disposable income. But in recent years they went on a borrowing and spending spree and the household savings dropped to nearly zero. Corporations and financiers also were also having debts to buy houses, stocks and commodities. This created bubbles which exploded in 2008. There has been a massive choking of credit since then and a global crash in stock markets. The slowdown that was expected in the global economy became much worse with the US, Europe and Japan moving into recession. A crisis of this magnitude in industrialised countries is bound to have an impact on India. *(S.Mahendra Dev, 2009)*

The financial crisis originated in the US being transmitted to other countries through three principal channels.

- First, it has directly affected the financial institutions all over the world due to investments in mortgage-backed securities and their derivatives, which turned toxic following large-scale defaults in the US housing markets.
- Second, the financial crisis has created a liquidity problem. The US firms which needed liquid resources withdrew their funds from stocks and bonds had impact on local investors who pulled back from the market. This led to choking of credit all over the world.
- The third source of transmission is the impact on real sector. The financial crisis led to recession in the US. This led to decline in demand of goods from other countries in the US. As the contagion spread and job losses rose in the advanced industrial economies, confidence was eroded further and general consumer demand in both the US and other developed nations dropped. In consequence, emerging economies saw export markets contract. This has affected the exports and business confidence in developing countries.

While India has largely escaped the first transmission, it has not been able to avoid the other two channels. While the direct exposure of Indian banking system to the sub-prime market abroad is almost absent, there may be very limited investment by a few Indian banks in the collaterized debt obligations which had underlying entities with sub-prime exposures. The government ownership of banks has proved to be a big advantage in these troubled times. However, the indirect impact of the crisis, transmitted through capital flows, financial markets and trade (real sector) would affect India. The foreign exchange reserves have declined in India and created a liquidity problem due to global crisis as well as tightening of monetary policy earlier. The exports from India would also be affected. *(S.Mahendra Dev, 2009)*

The growth rate of GDP in India is expected to decline to around seven per cent in 2008-09 as compared to 9% growth in 2007-08. This is partly due to the financial crisis and partly due to the tight monetary policies which in turn was due to high inflation. The Economic Advisory Council indicated that growth could be around seven to 7.5% in 2009-10. But, other forecasts and international organisations showed that growth could be around six per cent in 2009-10. Lower growth may affect the employment prospects. It may have an adverse impact on social sector expenditures as tax/ GDP ratio may go down with lower growth.

The Impact of the Crisis on the Indian Economy

The effects of the global financial crisis have been more severe than initially forecast. The depth of the crisis in the United States and Europe, it was only to be expected that India too would be affected. But India's well-regulated banking system and adequate policy responses should ensure that the fallout, at least on the banking sector, will be contained.

Severity of the Present Crisis

The, "financial crisis" is a very broad term that covers a whole range of events, including crashes in the housing market, stock market, foreign exchange market, current accounts of nations and, of course, problems afflicting the banking sector. The International Monetary Fund (IMF) in 2008 surveyed 113 episodes of financial stress in 17 countries. Of these, 43 episodes were driven mainly by stress in the banking sector. In 17 episodes, stresses arising elsewhere in the financial system had a signifi-cant impact on the banking sector. Thus, a total of 60 episodes – or a little over half of all the episodes of financial stress – were banking-related. The IMF (2008) study found that "episodes of financial turmoil characterised by banking distress are more often associated with severe and protracted downturns than episodes of stress centred mainly in securities or foreign exchange markets". Of the 58 epi-sodes that were followed either by a slowdown or a recession, 35 (or 60%) were banking-related.

The present crisis of the global economy as something that flows inexorably from the imbalances created in the past several years. Two points are worth emphasising. First, while a correction was overdue, it need not have been as severe as it is turning out to be if the financial system had been better regulated. To put together all the adverse factors in the economic environment – current account imbalances, greedy bankers, excess reserves of Asian economies, low interest rates, housing bubbles and sub-prime loans – it does not follow that these must translate into a global financial crisis.

Impact on Emerging Markets

Views on how far the convulsions in the US economy will affect emerging markets, including India, have evolved with the unfolding of the crisis. In the initial stages, there was a fairly high degree of optimism about the capacity of at least some of the emerging markets, particularly leading lights such as China and India, to insulate themselves substantially from the crisis. Such optimism has since worn thin and, of late, one finds more doomsayers. Successive issues of the IMF's WEO report over the crisis period reflect this evolution. In the initial stages of the crisis, several reasons were put forward as to why the emerging markets might hope to get "decoupled" from the US and other advanced economies:

- the US slowdown was related to factors specific to the US economy, especially corrections in the housing sector, rather than to more generalised factors such as an oil shock or adverse equity market developments;

- trade linkages of the emerging economies with the US had diminished and trade among emerging markets had become more important than in the past;
- growth in some of the leading emerging markets was driven overwhelmingly by domestic demand;
- the emerging markets were net savers in the world economy, not borrowers; and
- over the past decade, the emerging markets had effected several economic reforms, as a result of which they had become more stable and efficient.

The IMF (2007) noted favourable factors such as the above and observed: the potential size of spillovers from the United States has increased with greater trade and financial integration, but that the importance of these links should not be overestimated... past episodes of highly synchronised growth declines across the globe were not primarily the result of developments specific to the United States, but rather were caused by factors that affected many countries at the same time. Examples of such episodes include the first oil price shock in 1974-75 and the bursting of the information technology (IT) bubble in 2000. Nevertheless, the IMF did distinguish between the effects of a moderate slowdown in the US and a sharp slowdown or recession in the US.

Overall, these factors suggest that most countries should be in a position to "decouple" from the US economy and sustain strong growth if the US slowdown remains as moderate as expected, although countries with strong trade linkages with the United States in specific sectors may experience some drag on their growth. However, if the US economy experienced a sharper slowdown because of a broader-than-expected impact of the housing sector difficulties, the spillover effects into other economies would be larger, and decoupling would be more difficult. *(T.T.Ram Mohan, 2009)*

The IMF provides an explanation that appears plausible. In a modest US slowdown, emerging markets (and also other economies) are affected mainly through the trade channel.

However, when the US economy runs into serious problems, the asset price channel gets activated. Financial flows to emerging markets are severely affected during a serious US recession and equity prices also tend to become highly correlated with those in the US market. Besides, there is a broader impact through undermining of confidence among consumers and investors.

A better way of judging the impact on an emerging market of a slowdown in the US economy, therefore, would be to take into account trade flows as well as financial flows. As the IMF (2007) puts it:

While export exposure to the United States appears to be an important determinant of the severity of the response to US recessions, "openness" in general seems to be more of a factor for emerging market economies. More open emerging market economies, in terms of both trade and financial openness ... consistently show larger declines in output gaps during US recessions.

Impact of Global Crisis on the Sectoral Level

The Impact on Manufacturing Sector

At sectoral level, manufacturing sector is the most affected sector. The credit crisis and decline in demand has adverse impact on several industries. Flow of funds to the corporate sector has declined by nearly Rs. 94,000 crore in the current financial year upto early January as all foreign sources of funding dried up. Despite expansion in bank credit, there has been a perception of non- availability. The RBI attributes this to reduced flow of funds from non- banking sources, mainly the stock market and External Commercial Borrowing (ECB) and short-term credit from abroad, which met more than 20 per cent of India's INC's credit needs in 2007-08 have contributed only 8.2 % of the financing needs. Increase in the bank credit has not been enough to plug the gap left by other sources.

Since the business confidence is low, in spite of monetary and fiscal measures, the banks are not able to deliver credit because of two reasons.

- First one is that credit demand is low.
- Second one is that the banks are also averse to lend at a time when economic growth is definitely slackening. The chances of even existing loans, leave alone new ones, turning bad are perceived to be high. Industrial activity decelerated during April-November 2008-09, with the year -on-year expansion in Index of Industrial Production (IIP) being 3.9 per cent as against 9.2 per cent during the corresponding period of the previous year reflecting slowdown in all the constituent sectors. The slowdown in manufacturing sector was largely on account of food, textiles and metals. The IIP output growth in October was reported to be (-) 1.2 per cent, from which it recovered slightly to a positive 2.4 per cent in November 2008. The sectors adversely affected are exports, real estate, housing and automobiles. A survey by the labour ministry indicates that already five lakh jobs are lost. In the export sector, most of the items particularly gems and jewellery, textiles would be affected adversely. The slow down in exports may have impact on 2 million workers.

The slowdown in industry would affect the growth of services. The remittances from abroad will go down including services in IT sector. The financial crisis would have impact on small and medium enterprises (SMEs). SMEs with investment less than Rs.five lakh employ 100 million people. They contribute 31% of GDP and spread over leather, coal, apparel, food processing and handicrafts. But they get only two per cent of net bank credit.

The Impact on Agricultural Sector

The impact of the financial crisis is likely to have negative effects on the agricultural sector and food security. Agriculture sector has been fortunate in having had five successive good monsoons and good harvests. In the last three years, the average growth in agriculture was 4.7 % per annum. The growth rate in 2008-09 is also expected to be three to four per cent. However, this good performance may not last if proper steps are not taken into account.

The pathways through which the agricultural sector will be affected are on both demand and supply sides. The slowing down of economic growth would affect demand for agricultural commodities. Prevailing uncertainty and consequent negative market expectations could further dampen demand. The falling demand may put further downward pressure on agricultural commodity markets. In general, lower food prices are good for consumers but reduce incentives for producers to make the necessary investments which would improve food security in the medium term. However, decline in food prices would not be sufficient to compensate the consumers from the reduction in household incomes due to recession, fall in employment and remittances from abroad.

On the supply side, reduction of agricultural prices may result in cutback in agricultural production. Although oil and fertilizer prices declined, in general, input prices can be sticky and would affect the supply of agricultural commodities. The financial crisis is likely to have negative impact on agricultural credit which is widely regarded as major constraint to agriculture in developing countries. Farmers who took advantage of rising agricultural prices to invest in raising production may find themselves unable to pay off their debts because of falling output prices. As banks cut lending because of financial crisis, it would be difficult for small farmers to make new investments. The financial crisis may reduce agricultural investment at macro level and cut back on social protection expenditures. The combination of falling agricultural prices, reduction in agricultural investment and access to credit may have negative effect on agricultural production. It would have serious implications for food security. Poverty reduction efforts may be stalled because of low employment and volatility in food prices. The negative impact on household income would affect the well being of women and children.

Impact on the Indian Economy and the Policy Response

India, like other emerging markets, has suffered a more severe impact than supposed earlier. The impact has been pronounced after the Lehman crisis and, as Reserve Bank of India (RBI) Governor D Subbarao (2009) has pointed out, it arises from three channels: the trade channel, the financial channel and the confidence channel.From the Lehman episode, it was assumed that the impact on India would be primarily through the trade channel. Since merchandise exports account for less than 15% of gross domestic product (GDP), the trade channel impact was assumed to be bearable – it would set back growth only by more than 1-1.5%.

One measure of financial integration, Subbarao points out, would be the ratio of total external transactions (gross current account flows plus gross capital flows) to GDP. This ratio has more than doubled from 46.8% in 1997-98 to 117.4% in 2007-08. In a time of global economic crisis, a higher level of financial integration impacts on the economy in three related ways: reducing Indian companies' access to overseas finance, lowering domestic liquidity and causing stock prices to fall.

Adverse global conditions have limited Indian firms' access to global finance in various forms: fresh international borrowings External Commercial Borrowings (ECBs) have become difficult and existing ones are not easily being rolled over; long-term finance for international acquisitions made earlier through bridge finance is not available; buyers' credit has become scarce for international transactions; Indian banks' overseas branches and subsidiaries find they are unable to access funds in the wholesale market and have had to be provided with dollar funds by their parents from out of India; and so on. There is a much broader impact on the Indian economy arising from foreign inflows in forms such as foreign direct investment (FDI) and foreign institutional investment (FII). These inflows had contributed to accretion of foreign exchange reserves. Any accretion to reserves enhances domestic liquidity; any decline in reserves constitutes a reduction in liquidity. The gap between domestic investment and savings or the current account deficit - of around 1.5% of GDP - in recent years understates the potential impact on the Indian economy of foreign inflows.

The impact on investment and economic growth is greater than is suggested by the current account deficit gap of 1.5% of GDP. If the impact was only of this order, then economic growth should not decline by more than 0.5-1%. Most projections place economic growth for 2008-09 at around 7% and even lower for 2009-10, which indicates that financial integration exacts a much higher price in adverse conditions. (The prime minister's Economic Advisory Council is among the few exceptions: it estimates a growth of 7-7.5% in 2009-10.)

The fall in domestic stock prices is another aspect of financial integration, reflecting as much the impact of net sales by FIIs as sentiment about prospects for global and domestic economic growth. (FII inflows were - $6.6 billion in April-September 2008-09 compared to $15.5 billion in the same period in 2007-08.) At a time of low share prices, firms are reluctant to tap the capital market. Unless bank finance can substitute adequately for the capital markets, firms' investment plans are bound to be hit. In a time of global crisis, consumers and investors are both bound to cut back on spending because of the general setback to confidence or "animal spirits". Job losses accentuate the impact on consumer spending. Not least, there is pronounced risk aversion among banks. Banks are either averse to lending altogether (especially to risky areas such as real estate) and would like to hoard capital or will lend only at a steep price. All these effects have been in evidence in recent months in the Indian economy. *(T .T .Ram Mohan 2009)*

The monetary response to the financial crisis has been activated primarily since September 2008 following the Lehman collapse. Prior to that, the RBI had focused on fighting inflation and had adopted measures that contributed to tightening rather than relaxation. The flight of capital from India as well as the drying up of dollar credit abroad meant that both rupee and dollar liquidity were tightly squeezed. The sharp depreciation of the rupee with respect to the dollar required the RBI to intervene with dollar sales and this also impacted negatively on rupee liquidity.

Impact on the Banking System

India's banking system has been considerably less affected by the ongoing crisis than banking systems in the US and Europe. This is because the causes of the crisis in India are quite different from those elsewhere. In the advanced economies, the banking system suffered huge losses, this led to a collapse in the flow of credit and in confidence and dragged down the real economy. In India, it is the real economy that has been affected through various channels and banks are feeling the effects of a slowing down of the economy. There are three key issues with respect to the banking system: the volume of credit; the price of credit; and the performance of the banking system in today's stressed conditions.

Volume of Credit: Much has been said and written about the credit squeeze faced by industry in recent months. Commercial credit had grown by 24% year on year up to 2 January 2000. In the corresponding period last year, it grew by 22%. Even after adjusting for credit extended to cash-strapped oil and fertiliser companies, commercial credit growth has been 22%. This year's credit growth has happened in the face of a deceleration in economic growth in the second half of Financial Year 2008-09. Industry contends that bank credit growth has not been adequate in light of the drying up of credit from a variety of sources.

Cost of Credit: There is also a clamour for a steep reduction in policy rates to facilitate a sharper decline in lending rates. Policy rates have been falling steeply since October 2008 as outlined above. But lending rates have not followed suit. While the repo rate has declined by 350 basis points, the prime lending rate at public sector banks (PSBs) has declined only by a maximum of 150 basis points and that at private banks by 50 basis points. Private banks are said to be market savvy while PSBs' lending decisions are said to be subject to political direction.

There are sound reasons for lending rates not declining as much as expected and the RBI has spelt out these in its macroeconomic review of January 2009:

- banks face competition for savings from small savings schemes whose rates are administered and relatively inflexible;
- banks would have mobilised term deposits at higher rates and would face higher cost of funds until such time as the deposits come up for renewal;
- banks have to raise wholesale deposits in order to meet high demand for credit and such deposits are more expensive than retail deposits;
- market borrowings of government are high and will be even higher in light of the fiscal stimuli announced; and
- there is heightened risk aversion and banks will expect higher spreads over the risk-free rate in today's conditions.

There is a more fundamental reason why lending rates will not decline when policy rates are cut. These rate reductions are quickly transmitted to the government securities market and result in capital gains on banks' investment portfolios. The total return on government securities (interest plus capital gains) could be in excess of 8%, especially on older securities.

Outlook for the Indian Banking Sector: India's banking sector is in far better shape than its counterparts in the advanced economies. There is a heightened appreciation today–even among long-standing detractors of the RBI–that the bias towards caution in matters regulatory has stood India in good stead.

Important features of regulation in recent years have been: a gradualist approach towards capital account convertibility; prudence in opening up the sector to private and foreign banks; stringent norms on exposure to sensitive sectors; pre-emptive action in respect of housing, real estate and consumer credit; stricter norms for securitisation; prudential limits on inter-bank borrowing; and tighter regulation of NBFCs. It is unlikely that there will any major departure from these in the near future and we can expect additional regulations based on the lessons drawn from the sub-prime crisis.

- A deceleration in commercial credit growth to 15-20%, although the RBI has revised its target to 24%.
- A decline in the net interest margin consequent to the decline in interest rates. But the margin in India of 2.4% is still on the higher side despite the decline we have seen since 2006-07.
- An increase in the level of non-performing assets, thanks to stresses among corporates, especially small and medium enterprises, and also in retail credit.

However, the Indian banking system is well placed to withstand these adverse conditions because of a whole set of favourable factors created over a decade and a half of reforms and five years of buoyant economic conditions.

- Capital adequacy averages 13%.
- The level of non-performing assets (NPAs) to net advances has been brought down to 1%; and
- Return on assets is 1%, which constitutes a benchmark for performance for banks worldwide.

American and European banks have been undone by problems originating in the housing sector and compounded by investments backed by housing loans. There is as yet no sign of a serious collapse in housing prices in India. Even if it happened, the impact on the banking sector would be limited because housing loans constitute only around 10% of all advances.

Impact on Banks and Financial System

According to RBI, none of the Indian banks had any direct exposure to the sub- prime markets in the USA or other markets. However, a few Indian banks had invested in the collateralised debt obligations (CDOs) which had a few underlying entities with sub-prime exposures. The financial sector, especially banks is subject to prudential regulations, both in regard to capital and liquidity (Rakesh Mohan, 2007). Indian banks, both in the public and private sectors, are financially sound, well capitalised and well regulated. At time when the financial system across the globe is engulfed in a deep crisis, the Indian banking system continuous to show resilience.

Table 1
Trends in Capital Flows (Figures in $ million)

Components	*Period*	*2007-08*	*2008-09*
FDI	April-August	8,536	16,733
FII	April-September	15,508	-6421
ECB	*April-June	6,990	1,559
STC	** April-June	[[[[[[1,804	2,173
ECB (approvals)	April-August	13,375	8,127
Forex (variations)	April-September	48,583	-17,904

Source: RBI * External Commercial Borrowing **Short Term Trade.

Our financial markets, equity markets money market and credit market all have come under pressure mainly because of what we have begun to call 'the substitution effect' of

(i) Drying up of overseas financing for Indian banks and Indian corporate;

(ii) Constraints in raising funds in a bearish domestic capital market;

(iii) Decline in the internal accruals of the corporate all these factors are responsible for pressure on the domestic credit market. Simultaneously, the reversal of capital flows, caused by the de-leveraging process has put pressure on our forex market. The Indian financial system has not been affected in the same way the financial system abroad has been affected.

However there is the impact of the drying up of liquidity because of the fall in reserve. The strong inflow of over $100 billion last year, this year may not see any net increase in capital flows. Portfolio has already turned negative, with a significant impact on the stock market. Indian firms may also experience difficulties in raising money abroad. All this will impact on exchange rate. However, draw down of reserves would moderate the impact.

Conclusion

The world is in the midst of a severe financial crisis, meaning a crisis that will exact a huge cost in terms of lost economic growth. It is not true, however, that all financial crises are severe. There is a high probability of a financial crisis having an impact on the real economy when there is disruption of the banking sector. Second, the severity of the crisis is not independent of the policy response. An appropriate policy response does help contain the depth and period of an economic downturn.

India will not escape unscathed in the present crisis because its economy has become more integrated with the rest of the world over the past decade and a half. Overseas finance has become increasingly important for Indian corporates and the drying up of such finance is bound to tell on their fortunes. There is also a broader impact arising from tighter liquidity conditions and a decline in stock prices. India's authorities have responded to the crisis with both fiscal and monetary stimuli although the scope for the former appears somewhat limited given India's fiscal position. The Indian banking sector is well placed to weather the storm because it is not directly exposed to the financial crisis. It faces secondary effects arising from the slowdown of the economy.

References

Abheek Barua (2008), Anatomy of a Crisis, Times of India, October 12.

Ajay Dua (2008), The Impact of Slowdown on India Times of India, November 21, 2008.

G. Rangarajan (2009), Financial Crisis Impact on India, January 4,2009.

C.P. Chandrashekhar and Jayanti Ghose India and the Global Financial Crisis Business Line, October, 15, 2008.

Dr. Subbarao, Governer, RBI Speech at the Bankers Club, December 10, 2008.

Rakesh Joshi and Lancelot Joseph (2008), Global Storm Sweep India, Business India, November 2.

Rajat Guha (2008), 30 FDI-Boosting Proposal Economic Times, November 7.

Rakesh Mohan (2008), Global Financial Crisis and Key Risk: Impact on India and Asia, Speech at IMF, Washington, October 9, 2008.

Rakesh Mohan (2007), Indias Financial Sector Reforms: Fostering Growth While Containing Risk, RBI Bulletin, December.

T.T. Ram Mohan (2009), The Impact of the Crisis on the Indian Economy, Economic & Political Weekly, March 28, 2009 Vol. XLIV No. 13.

Andrew Sheng (2009), The First Network Crisis of the 21st Century: A Regulatory Post-Mortem, Economic & Political Weekly, March 28, 2009 Vol. XLIV No. 13.

10

The Impact of Global Slowdown on India Economy With Special Reference to Agriculture Sector

Jitendra Ahirrao, Shankar Ambhore

Introduction

In economics, 'a recession is a general slowdown in economic activity over a sustained period of time, or a business cycle contraction. Production as measured by Gross Domestic Product (GDP), employment, investment spending, capacity utilization, household incomes and business profits all fall during recessions.' Now this is recession only by definition. Although India has not been directly impacted by the global financial crisis, we should be cautious about the indirect knock-on effect of the global crisis. According to the GET report, over 50 million could lose their jobs by 2009 worldwide. The one thing is that as we live in an agrarian economy where the unemployment rate is already high and 60 per cent of the population is still dependent on agriculture, the rate of unemployment is rising further due to these worldwide lay-offs.

About 60-65 per cent of India's population and workforce depend on agriculture. It is the known fact that the agriculture sector will continue to provide support to our economy. Indian agriculture has not much impacted by global economy crises, except some export oriented crops. Country's agriculture sector will save the India from the huge impact of the global economic recession. Right now agriculture is the key for Indian growth in this difficult time. Agriculture is an absolute necessary, producing the basic human needs of food and clothing. An Investment in agriculture is considered as a conservative and tangible Investment with consistent returns. Agriculture is the best solutions to maintain economic growth this year. Even in down markets agriculture companies performed very well in 2008 and will do the same in 2009.

India has always been a land of *'Rishi'* and *'Krishi'*. We forgot this aspect of India. We still have not done much for the farmers of this nation. We know for sure that 18 percent of the GDP (agriculture) supports 60 per cent of the population. What we need is value addition to agriculture and connecting the value chain of agriculture business to farmers at the place of produce. We need to think more about farmers producing cash crops besides staple crop. We need to increase the value of 18 per cent. We must note that 80 per cent farms in India are smaller than 5 acres. From 1971-96, the average size of the farms has reduced from 2.3 to 1.4 acres. Whilst, in the developing countries the average farm size has decreased, same has increased in developed world.

Impact of Global Slowdown

The impact of global slowdown on India's economy is impacting the employment scenario. In fact the rising joblessness in India has assumed worrisome proportions. With overall economic growth sharply slowing down, the ranks of those without work are growing by the day. Many people were rendered jobless in 2008-09, according to a survey conducted by the Ministry of Labour and Employment. India could lose up to 1.5 million jobs during the period.

A disturbing trend of India's economic performance is a deceleration in employment growth to 1.92 per cent per annum from 1993-94 to 2006-07 from 2.61 per cent between 1983-1993-94 although growth in terms of gross domestic product (GDP) was rapid. Clearly, there has been a decline in employment per unit of GDP growth or employment elasticity to 0.28 from 1993-94 to 2006-07 from 0.52 over the years 1983 to 1993-94. Applying this elasticity to the likely GDP growth of 7 per cent in 2008-09 and 5 per cent in 2009-10 to project the generation of employment provides an aver age of 8 million work opportunities this year and 6 million the next. This is much short of the 10 million opportunities generated during each of the last five years. In other words, there will be 2 million fewer jobs than before this year and 4 million fewer jobs next year.

Official number crunchers might suggest that a better measure is to focus only on non-agriculture. Even on this basis, the economy would turn out 1 million fewer non-agricultural opportunities this year and 2 million fewer the next than the average of 5.6 million jobs per annum during the growth boom of the last five years. This striking shrinkage of employment opportunities when 9 to 10 million people join the labour force each year looking for work will certainly result in a spike upwards in unemployment and exacerbate social tensions. Interestingly, more up-to-date economy wide estimates of unemployment—based on extrapolations from recent trends—are consistent with the above numbers for job losses this year as growth is likely to decline to 7 per cent as compared to 8.8 per cent per annum during the last five years. But with India's growth expected to plunge to 5 per cent next year, the incidence of joblessness will be more severe than before.

The global recession has impacted only the urban India. But rural India, which depends mainly on agriculture which grew by 2.7 per cent in the last quarter of 2008-2009 (compared to -1.4 in manufacturing), has a lesser impact due to global slowdown. Because of buying power of the rural India, the Economy in the fourth quarter of the fiscal year (January-March 2009), the economy grew 5.8 per cent against expectations of less than 5 per cent. Is rural India's growth a short term anomaly or a secular trend that is going to aid India's long term growth? Let's look at some numbers. 12.2 per cent of the world's consumers live in India and rural households form 72 per cent of the total households. This puts the rural market at roughly 720million customers. According to the Wharton article, total income in rural India (about 43 per cent of total national income) is expected to increase from around US$220 billion in 2004-2005 to US$425 billion by2010-2011, a CAGR (Compounded annual growth rate) of 12 per cent.

Global Recession and Agriculture Sector

India is dependent on USA and other developed nations for its trade. Eventually developing nation's economy affected by recession due to globalization. Recession will have its plus point and minus points. The minus points are that, there will be job scarcity; retrenchment will be all time high, liquidity in the market will be low; export market will be severely hit etc. The plus point is that cost of living will come down. Things we were exporting will be forced to be sold locally, bringing the price of products down. Real estate which was out of reach for the common man will be within his reach. Every one has to think global recession is a challenge posed to the nation and work accordingly keeping agriculture at the centre-stage. The country has to lay more focus on agriculture sector. Agriculture Sector of India shows Strong resistance against recession. The agricultural sector will also have to contend with the rising challenges of growing water scarcity and rising temperatures from global warming also.

The agriculture sector is performing well compared too other industries in recession owing to high food demand, emerging bio-fuel markets and economic recovery. According to the Annual Agriculture Outlook report prepared by the Organization for Economic Cooperation and Development (OECD) and the Food and Agriculture Organization of the United Nations (FAO), there is no impact of global economic crisis on agriculture as compared to other sectors. The report also says that the underperforming sectors are still facing a number of difficulties like credit access, low liquidity and constricted trade finance, but the agriculture sectors has shown remarkable resistance against the global recession.

The average prices of agricultural products in the next 10 years are projected to stay at or cross the levels of the decade before 2007-08 peaks. Vegetable oils prices are expected to surge by nearly 30 per cent, while crops prices rise by 10-20 per cent. Although diary products prices will see slight gain in coming years. The projected increase in agricultural products prices is likely to stem from economic recovery, emerging bio-fuel markets and food demand from developing markets. A number of companies are seeking ways to enhance the crop production to meet the continuously rising food demand. While the scenario varies in terms of commodity, the overall sector is expected to perform better on account of the recent period of high incomes and demand for food.

According to a Research Analyst at RNCOS, "The agriculture sector is showing strong resistance against the global economic crisis compared to other industries due to consistent strong demand for food products. However, food security is the main issue that needs to be addressed at present because it not only solves the urgency in short time period but also helps in dealing with long-term issues such as poverty alleviation and economic growth. Rise in food prices in coming years is likely to be driven by the recovery of global economy. According to the study, the food prices have substantially dipped after touching the peak level in 2008. Given the downturn in food prices, the pressure is shifted to consumers who have lesser money to spend on. Despite this, many developing countries continued to be battered by high food prices.

Government's Efforts Through Budget

Poverty in India is predominantly a rural phenomenon. About 70 per cent of the population, and about 75 per cent of the poor, live in rural areas and agriculture provides livelihood to 60 per cent of the rural people. But Indian agricultural will take a direct hit from the poor monsoons this year. India's rural economy has received more attention and resource commitments in the government's latest budget proposals than in recent years.

The budget's pro-poor and pro-rural biases are not surprising. Huge funds have been allocated for rural programs that involve rural job guarantees, food subsidies and farm lending. At first site, budget is generously shown in favor of rural India. For instance, the budget provides for a 144 per cent funding increase over last year's estimates for programs under the National Rural Employment Guarantee Act, to Rs. 39,100 crore. This covers higher unemployment payments and an expanded scope of the program. Another program for the 2009-2010 year ensures that every poor family will get 25 kg of rice monthly at Rs 3 each. In addition, the Pradhan Mantri Gram Sadak Yojana, a high-profile program that aims to connect every village with a motorable road, has been given a 59 per cent higher allocation in the budget over that of 2008-2009 at Rs. 12,000 crore. A rural housing program (Indira Awaas Yojana) is 63 per cent richer compared to last year, with an allocation of Rs. 8,800 crore. Other programs promise to bring integrated development to combat caste-based discrimination in villages, housing subsidies for the poor and other poverty eradication measures. Prime Minister Manmohan Singh said the Union Budget 2009-10 is aimed at minimizing the impact of the global recession and achieving 8 to 9 per cent growth in the medium term.

Focus on Agricultural During the Recession Period

- Greater investment in rural infrastructure in the form of road connectivity and much better water management is absolutely crucial.
- There has to be much greater emphasis on commercially applicable Research and Development in agriculture for both crop agriculture and animal husbandry.
- Improvement in primary education and health will continue to bring high returns in terms of agricultural productivity. Such improvements are urgently required for their own sake.
- There are many shortcomings are pointing out in our present rural credit delivery system which need to be urgently improved.

- Public spending in support of agriculture continues to be excessively dominated by input subsidies for fertilizer, power and irrigation. The returns to these massive subsidies is much less than if the same resources were used to improve rural road network, organized better water management systems and support much stronger R & D and agricultural extension.
- We need to focus and take immediate steps for setting up Agri and processed foods SEZ on an urgent basis. Agriculture and food processing SEZ must be established near ports and in every state.
- The government in support of the local villages should concentrate on the sectors like diary cooperatives, horticulture, this will sustain and help in growing the livelihood of villages and make them self reliant. For this, corporate have to come forward to adopt villages and make them self reliant.

Conclusion

Recession is equally big an opportunity as robust economic growth. The global economic crisis has definitely taken a toll of India's economic performance. It has also reduced our potential for economic development in the next 2 or 3 years. Despite the severity of the global crisis, India's economy has demonstrated considerable resilience due to agricultural sector. We were managed the crisis of the 90's but how we manage global recession 09. That time, we were alone in the crisis and now it is a Global crisis. With sound and determined economic policies we should be able to recover a growth momentum of 7-8 per cent in a year or next another one year. The challenge for our policies and programmes is to convert this potential into performance.

References

Dr. Shankar Acharya–Global Crisis India and Agricultural–9th Convocation Address of Rajastan Agricultural University, Rajastam.

http://www.foodsectornews.com

http://rajendrasays.blogspot.com

http://www.indianexpress.com/news/budget.

http://theviewspaper.net

http://indianeconomy.org

http://hubpages.com

http://www.thaindian.com

11

Global Recession and Indian Financial System

M.S. Gupta, Asha Singh

Introduction

The economic slowdown of the advanced countries which started around mid-2007, as a result of the sub prime crisis in the USA, led to the spread of economic crisis across the globe resulting into significant changes in the global financial landscape. Several large global financial institutions have either failed or have had to be restructured to avoid failure. The recent financial market turbulence has brought into sharp focus the issue of financial stability to the forefront of policy discussions. The turmoil was fallout of an exceptional credit boom and leverage in the financial system. On a hindsight, the present crisis appears to be a result of a macroeconomic environment with a prolonged period of low interest rates, high liquidity and low volatility, which led financial institutions to underestimate risks, a breakdown of credit and risk management practices in many financial institutions, and shortcomings in financial regulation and supervision. A slowdown in the US real estate market triggered a series of defaults and this snowballed into accumulated losses, especially in the case of complex structured securities. The US sub-prime crisis has led to both the strained conditions of financial markets and the slowdown of the broader economy. The US economy continues to confront substantial challenges, including stresses in financial markets, a weakening labour market and deteriorating economic activity.

The ongoing financial turmoil took a serious turn when major financial institutions started experiencing extreme degrees of difficulty. Bear Stearns was the big first Wall Street investment banks of the five to collapse in March 2008, followed by the filing of chapter 11 bankruptcy petitions by Lehman Brothers Holdings inc. and the sale of Merrill Lynch to Bank of America in September 2008. The remaining two, Goldman Sachs and Morgan Stanley, have abandoned their once-cherished investment bank business model to become bank holding companies to secure greater Fed protection and to soothe negative market sentiments. This was soon followed by the takeover of the sixth largest bank, Wachovia, by the Citi Group. The recent turn of events prompted the US Government to come out with a $700 billion bail out package for banks to buy the distressed assets. Full prudential supervision and regulation at the hands of the central bank and the Federal Deposit Insurance Corporation would provide them access to permanent liquidity and funding by the Fed. Though the Fed had allowed investment banks to access discount window financing since Bear Stearns crumbled, this source was set to close at an unspecified point in 2009. The Securities and Exchanges Commission (SEC) was previously responsible for the supervision of the investment banks under the voluntary consolidated supervised enterprises regime. Lighter regulation of investment banks had enabled the industry reap greater rewards than their commercial banks counterparts in the boom preceding the credit crisis. But the crunch has revealed the drawbacks of the industry's high-risk strategy. The shocks in the US financial system have reverberated in some European countries as well such as the UK, Switzerland and Germany. Though the direct impact on India and other Asian emerging market economies (EMEs) was muted, the indirect impact has been significant.

Global Financial Contagion in India

The multi-pronged approach followed for strengthening and developing financial institutions, markets, payment systems and infrastructure have had a positive impact on the Indian financial system. The assessment of developments during 2007-08 and 2008-09 so far suggests that financial institutions, especially scheduled commercial banks, are on a sound footing. Domestic financial markets have been constantly developing, and functioning normally, despite some indirect knock on effects of global developments. Financial infrastructure now is much more robust than it was a few years ago. While the financial system on the whole is quite robust, which augurs well for financial stability, there is also a need to be aware of some downside risks in certain areas that could have a bearing on the stability of the financial sector in the near future.

The initial impact of global financial contagion in India, however, has been limited for a variety of reasons. India's growth process has been largely domestic demand driven and its reliance on foreign savings has remained around 1.5 per cent of GDP in the recent period. It also has a comfortable level of forex reserves. The credit derivatives market is in an embryonic stage; the originate-to-distribute model in India is not comparable to the ones prevailing in advanced markets and there are restrictions on investments by residents in such products issued abroad. Regulatory guidelines on securitization do not permit immediate profit recognition. However, some impact has been felt through the credit, equity and the foreign exchange markets. Risk aversion, deleveraging and frozen money markets have not only raised the cost of funds for Indian corporates, but also its availability in the international markets. This additional demand for funds spilled over to the domestic credit market. Reduced investor interest in emerging economies has led to reversal of portfolio flows affecting the equity and the foreign exchange markets. The impending recession in the US and other advanced economies would also impact Indian exports and the growth momentum. Several measures have been initiated to mitigate the impact of global financial crisis on the domestic financial markets and its spillover impact on the real economy.

Financial Turmoil

The global financial turmoil has reinforced the importance of putting special emphasis on preserving financial stability. Financial stability in India has been achieved through perseverance of prudential policies which prevent institutions from excessive risk taking and financial markets from becoming extremely volatile and turbulent. With increasing priority being given to financial stability, the central task for the conduct of monetary policy has become more complex and challenging than before. The current challenge is to strike an optimal balance between preserving financial stability, maintaining price stability, anchoring inflation expectations, and sustaining the growth momentum. The relative emphasis between these objectives has varied from time to time, depending on the underlying macroeconomic conditions.

The recent developments in the global financial markets have been closely followed by market participants, central bankers, supervisors, multilateral institutions, political leaders, analysts, academicians, and also the general public. The ongoing debates cover several stability issues in the areas of regulation and supervision of institutions and markets, risk management strategies and practices of institutions, safety net and liquidity backstops. Simultaneously, the vexed issue of light versus tight regulation has also been receiving considerable attention. Financial stability in the current context is also being viewed in terms of a trade-off between risk and innovation/return. A financial system that is heavily regulated and supervised may be very stable and not prone to experiencing financial crises in contrast to a financial system that is very free and innovative and which is lightly regulated and supervised. A controlled system to its disadvantage could have lower financial development and innovation compared with a free and innovative system that increases returns, diversifies risks, and better allocates resources to the highest-return investments. The latter, however, may eventually become unstable and trigger credit booms and asset bubbles that could severely affect growth, returns and welfare. Though there is some trade-off between the stability of the financial system and its degree of innovation and sophistication, financial stability remains an important input in the process of financial development.

Adverse International Developments

Developments in the global financial system have heightened the uncertainty in the global economy. The credit markets in the western world, especially in the US, have, in the recent past, witnessed considerable turmoil and significant loss of market liquidity leading to financial distress in a few institutions and considerable financial damage to several others, prompting some of the major central banks to inject liquidity into the markets. There was a collective failure to appreciate the extent of leverage taken on by a wide range of institutions - banks, monocline insurers, government-sponsored entities, hedge funds and the associated risks of a disorderly unwinding. Private sector risk management, disclosure, financial sector supervision, and regulation all lagged behind the rapid innovation and shifts in business models, leaving scope for excessive risk-taking, weak underwriting, maturity mismatches, and asset price inflation. The transfer of risks off bank balance sheets was underestimated. As risks have materialised, this has placed enormous pressures back on the balance sheets of banks. Notwithstanding unprecedented intervention by major central banks, financial markets remain under considerable strain, now compounded by a more worrisome macroeconomic environment, weakly capitalised institutions, and broad-based deleveraging.

The exact extent of losses and exposures is not known as yet and perceptions of a pronounced increase in default risk continues to prevail as was evident in high credit default swap (CDS) spreads. Money markets remain dislocated and, despite central bank liquidity injections alleviating pressures, uncertainty about future liquidity supply and counterparty risk persists. Global equity markets have fallen considerably in 2008 with an increase in volatility, decline in investors' risk tolerance, the worsening of the macroeconomic outlook and renewed credit related concerns. Bond yields, which stabilised since mid-March, 2008 have started to recover in developed economies and a flight to safety is leading up to a shortage of paper. Longer term real yields have declined sharply on recession fears. In the foreign exchange market, the US dollar and the pound sterling depreciated in effective terms whereas the euro, the yen and the Swiss franc appreciated along with several Asian currencies. Concerns about a more widespread slowdown, and perceptions of overvaluation have been weighing on emerging market asset classes in 2008 with spreads on sovereign debt widening. The outlook is highly unclear and the prospects of resolution of the multiple disequilibria embedded in global developments are fraught with uncertainty.

The financial market crisis with US at its epicentre has started to spread across markets, and across nations. The US slowdown is spreading *via* the trade and financial channels. The significant slowdown in the projected global growth from 5.0 per cent in 2007 to 3.7 per cent in 2008, and to just over 2.0 per cent in 2009, is likely to have implications for every economy. In view of strong international linkages among economies, macroeconomic prospects for the EMEs, which till very recently remained relatively insulated, face the downside risks from lagged effects of the downturn. As the notion of 'decoupling' of emerging market countries from mature markets has turned out to be incorrect, emerging market policymakers would have to cope with a global growth slowdown, and reversal of capital flows.

Economic Integration and Decoupling of the Emerging Economies

In recent years with rapid increase in trade and financial linkages across countries, emerging market economies have emerged as major players in the global economy. Decoupling holds that emerging European and Asian economies have broadened and deepened to the point that they no longer depend on the US for growth. This has generated a debate about possible changes in the generally observed patterns of international business cycle co-movement.

The major channels of coupling include: (i) integration between economies and rise in internationally integrated production; (ii) the international movement of workers leading to remittances; (iii) growth in international linkages in financial services through increased cross-listings of stocks and more cross-border ownership and control of exchanges, banks, and securities settlement systems; (iv) spillover through commodity prices and through financial variables such as short and long-term interest rates and equity prices.

Empirical research shows convergence of business cycles among a larger group of industrial economies and among emerging market economies over time, but there has also been a simultaneous decoupling of business cycles between these two sets of countries. The authors cautioned that although the results suggested emerging markets as a group are becoming an independent driver of global growth, their decoupling potential would still depend on the duration and severity of a US downturn. However, their analysis includes linkages through real macroeconomic aggregates but does not account for financial ones.

So long as the US slowdown was attributed to US specific developments - primarily in housing and manufacturing, the spillover effects to other economies was Considered modest. However, as the transmission began to involve asset price spillovers or confidence channels, the impact became much larger. The influence of the U.S. economy on other economies does not appear to have diminished. On the contrary, indications are that the magnitude of spillovers has increased over time, particularly in neighboring countries and regions, which is consistent with the notion that greater trade and financial integration tends to magnify the cross-border effects of disturbances. Stock prices in the emerging market economies moved downward during acute periods of US financial stress over the past year. The IMF in a recent study confirms that global factors are as important in explaining the movement in emerging markets equity prices as their domestic fundamentals. Using various measures of correlation, it is also found that the scope for spillovers to emerging equity markets has risen, suggesting a growing transmission channel for equity price movements. This could, in turn, affect consumption and investment in emerging markets, although such macro financial linkages are found to be small and they tend to play out gradually.

In the context of effect of financial crisis on developed countries, it is argued that financial innovations like growth of non-bank intermediaries such as private equity firms and hedge funds, deepening of resale markets for capital, and sophisticated products and contracts, among others, might have made these economies less vulnerable to crises by widening the access to liquidity and allowing assets to be traded more easily during periods of stress. Though the developed economies are able to tide over mild and less severe shocks, in case of extremely severe shocks, a crisis is inevitable, regardless of the ex ante beliefs. In the crisis situation, such financial innovations could impact more severely by way of relaxing the financial constraints facing borrowers with the result that asset prices are driven down to such an extent that all intermediaries and firms are forced to liquidate all of their assets, intermediaries shut down, and the closure of firms means that there are no investment opportunities in the more-productive sectors of the economy. It is also argued that crises in emerging market economies are more frequent but less severe than in developed countries.

As per the WEO update of November 2008, growth in emerging economies would decelerate from 8.0 per cent in 2007 to 6.6 per cent in 2008 and further to 5.1 per cent in 2009. There is a risk that the confluence of circumstances emerging out of the financial turmoil could accelerate a downturn in the credit cycle in some emerging market economies.

Indian Banking Sector and US Sub-prime Market

The banking sector in India does not have any direct exposure to the US sub-prime market. Some banks in India, however, have indirect exposure through their overseas branches and subsidiaries to the US sub-prime markets in the form of structured products, such as collateralised debt obligations (CDOs) and other investments. However, such exposure is not very significant, and banks have made adequate provisions to meet mark-to-market losses on such investments. Besides, banks also maintain high level of capital adequacy ratio. Thus, the risks in the banking sector appear limited and manageable.

There is, however, apprehension that current market conditions, may lead to recession in the US having significant impact on other economies. In this context, it may be noted that India is largely a domestic demand driven economy and exports constitute a relatively smaller portion of India's GDP, as compared to many other economies. In recent years, India's export basket has also become more diversified, although the US continues to be one of the major trading partners. While strong regional sources of growth within EMEs may be a mitigating factor, weakening of economic activity in the US would impact India's economy through the trade channel. There are indications that the current crisis has implications in terms of higher funding costs and difficulties in raising external finance, particularly, for lower rated firms.

Portfolio Investment by Foreign Institutional Investors

The main impact of the global financial turmoil in India has emanated from the significant change experienced in the capital account in 2008-09 so far, relative to the previous year. Total net capital flows declined from US $17.3 billion in April-June 2007 to US $13.2 billion in April-June 2008. Capital flows are expected to be lower in the current fiscal year 2008-09 as compared with the previous year. While foreign direct investment (FDI) inflows have continued to exhibit accelerated growth (US $ 19.3 billion during April-September 2008 as compared with US $ 9.2 billion in the corresponding period of 2007), portfolio investments by foreign institutional investors (FIIs) witnessed a net outflow of about US $ 11.9 billion in April-October 2008 as compared with a net inflow of US $ 22.3 billion in the corresponding period of the previous year.

Indian Economy and Inflation

In India, inflation based on year-on-year variations in the wholesale price index (WPI) increased to 7.7 per cent in 2007-08 compared with 5.9 per cent in 2006-07. Consistent with the stance of monetary policy, the evolving liquidity situations and on the basis of incoming information on domestic and global macroeconomic and financial developments, it was decided to increase the CRR by 25 basis points each on May 10, 2008 and May 24, 2008 to 8.25 per cent. Furthermore, the repo rate under the LAF was increased from 7.75 per cent to 8.00 per cent on June 12, 2008 and further to 8.50 per cent with effect from June 25, 2008. The CRR was again increased by 50 basis points to 8.75 per cent in two stages from July 5, 2008 and July 19, 2008 by 25 basis points each.

Inflation, in terms of the WPI, softened steadily from the level of 12.9 per cent on August 9, 2008 and has declined to 8.4 per cent for the week-ended November 22, 2008, reflecting decline in prices of freely priced petroleum products (in the range of 15-22 per cent) in line with decline in international crude oil prices (by 45 per cent since July 2008) as well as easing in other commodity prices such as oilseeds/edible oils/oil cakes, raw cotton and cotton textiles following global trends. Globally, pressures from commodity prices, including crude, appear to be abating. The international crude prices which hardened from an average level of US $ 57 per barrel at end-2005 to an average level of US $ 73 per barrel by July 2006, and thereafter rose sharply to reach a historic high of US $ 145.3 per barrel by early July 2008, eased significantly to around US $ 44 per barrel by December 10, 2008 reflecting decline in demand in OECD countries and improved near-term supply prospects in non-OPEC countries. The moderation in key global commodity prices, if sustained, would further reduce inflationary pressures.

Conclusion

The ongoing financial crisis has had a deep impact on the existing framework for measuring, assessing and maintaining financial stability. The crisis has become more widespread. Although international financial markets had started showing some signs of improvements by mid-2008 in response to the co-ordinated policy responses, developments since September 2008 further precipitated the crisis. Emerging markets, which had earlier escaped the direct impact of the financial turmoil, increasingly became vulnerable to the international financial contagion. With the crisis extending to new areas and instruments, it has become extremely difficult to gauge its magnitude and implications, thereby rendering any assessment of financial stability extremely difficult at the current juncture.

India's financial sector is stable and healthy and capable of withstanding the global stock, perhaps somewhat bruised but definitely not battered. Financial strength indicators such as capital adequacy and return on assets of commercial banks continue to be robust. A major challenge is how to meet the credit demand without impairing credit quality. Banks have to monitor their credit portfolios closely in the context of persisting high growth in bank credit at the system level and take corrective action as appropriate in order to prevent undue asset-liability mismatches or deterioration in the quality of credit, recognising the reality of business cycles and counter-cyclical monetary policy measures. The Reserve Bank has been monitoring the functioning of systemically important NBFCs and banks' exposure to them. In the light of international developments and increasing exposure of banks to these systemically important NBFCs, more stringent regulations in respect of capital adequacy, liquidity and disclosure norms for these entities were issued in August 2008.

Though emerging market economies, including India, do not have direct or significant exposure to stressed financial instruments and troubled financial institutions, they are facing significant indirect impact of the financial crisis. There are a number of lessons that can be drawn from the crisis. One, financial supervision should not lag behind financial innovations and emerging new business models. However, it needs to be ensured that in the process of staying ahead of innovation through continually upgrading skills and instruments for financial regulation and supervision, innovations should not be stifled. A second lesson relates to inter-agency coordination. The origins of the current crisis can be traced to both the build up of macro-global imbalances as well as the mis-pricing of risks in the financial system, which in turn, was encouraged by excess liquidity. The respective roles of central banks, regulators, supervisors and fiscal authorities regarding financial stability need to be revisited such that central banks have the necessary informational base to play a central and effective role in maintaining financial stability. The third lesson is that the large scale bailout packages would have implications for the regulatory architecture of the financial system and for the fiscal condition of countries. A relevant issue in this context is the efficacy and coverage of deposit insurance. Fourth, the unfolding crisis has revealed the weaknesses of structured products and derivatives in the credit markets, including the "originate-to-distribute" model, which need to be addressed. Also, the near meltdown of the US financial sector should not be construed as evidence that markets and competition do not work. The right lesson is that markets and institutions occasionally succumb to excesses, so that regulators have to be vigilant, constantly finding the right balance between attenuating risk-taking and inhibiting growth. Further, inasmuch as emerging and developing economies are likely to be increasingly impacted by the crisis, going forward, two issues become important. First, in managing the crisis, the implications of that management for emerging and developing economies should be explicitly factored in. Second, in terms of global financial architecture, emerging and developing economies should be taken into confidence for policies and actions of the developed countries that have significant implications for them.

There is a need to deliberate on the issue of coping with liquidity stresses under unusual circumstances. The role of 'pro-cyclicality' of capital requirements needs to be examined as a factor that escalates the impact of booms and busts. The role of non-banks in the financial system also needs to be examined from a regulatory perspective. It also needs to be assessed whether institutions should be allowed to become so big and so complex that their problems could have system-wide repercussions.

The Reserve Bank accords considerable importance to financial stability which is also recognised as one of the objectives of monetary policy. The Reserve Bank has been keenly observing the latest developments in regulation and supervision and would continue to adapt institutional best practices to domestic conditions. Banks, on their part, would need to ensure that their business strategies and decisions are guided by the longer-term perspective of systemic and macroeconomic developments and are not unduly influenced by the current stream of exceptional events. It needs to be recognized that as banks have a key role in successfully countering the adverse impact of the recent developments, their continued safety and soundness and financial health would be of utmost importance for preserving financial stability so that the momentum of growth could be maintained.

The global economic environment continues to remain uncertain, although the rate of contraction in economic activities and the extent of pressures on financial system eased in the first quarter of 2009-10.Yet it is not possible to clearly see the path of crisis and its resolution over the coming months. In this sense, India is not unique as almost every country, whether or not directly affected, has to manage the current economic crisis under uncertainty. In the words of Dr. Rakesh Mohan, former Deputy Governor of RBI "As the monetary and fiscal stimuli work their way through and, if calm and confidence are restored in the global markets, we can see economic turnaround later this year. Once calm and confidence are restored in the global markets, economic activity in India will recover sharply. Yet there will be a period of painful adjustment which is inevitable".

References

Strauss-Kahn, Dominique (2008), Lessons from the Financial Market Crisis: Priorities for the World and for the IMF, at Indian Council for Research on International Economic Research (ICRIER), New Delhi, February, 13.

Mohan, R. (2008), Global Financial Crisis and Key Risks: Impact on India and Asia, remarks at the IMF-FSF High-Level meeting on the Recent Financial Turmoil and Policy Responses, Washington D.C., October 9.

Governor (RBI), Dr. D. Subbarao's Press Statement on Stance of Monetary Policy for the Remaining Period of 2008-09, October, 24, 2008.

The Financial Development Report (2008), World Economic Forum.

Bayoumi, Tamim and Andrew Swiston (2007), "Foreign Entanglements: Estimating the Source and Size of Spillovers Across Industrial Countries." IMF Working Paper 07/182, Washington: International Monetary Fund, July.

World Economic Outlook (2007), "Decoupling the Train? Spillovers and Cycles in the Global Economy", International Monetary Fund, April.

Kose. M. Ayhan, Christopher Otrok and Eswar Prasad (2008), "Global Business Cycles: Convergence or Decoupling?" IZA Discussion Paper No. 3442, April.

Gai, Prasanna, Sujit Kapadia, Stephen Millard and Ander Perez (2008), "Financial Innovation, Macroeconomic Stability and Systemic Crises" Bank of England Working Paper No. 340, February.

Kohn, Donald L. (2008), "Global Economic Integration and Decoupling" at the International Research Forum on Monetary Policy, Frankfurt, Germany, June 26.

RBI (2007-08), Report on Trend and Progress of Banking in India.

www.finmin.nic.in

12

Global Recession and Resilience of India's Economy: Monetary Policy Perspectives

S.K. Sharma

Introduction (Start of Recession)

When 158 year old American firm the Lehman Brothers went bankrupt on 13thSeptember, 2008 the Global Recession started. It filed for protection against bankruptcy on the 15th September to the US treasury. The Federal Reserve extended $138 billion loan to help unwind Lehman in an orderly fashion. Prior to its bankruptcy, the LB was the fourth largest investment bank of the world. It suffered a loss of $639 billion owing largely to wrong policy measures. Founded in 1850, the LB is a global financial services firm. It does business in investment banking, equity and fixed income sales, research and trading, investment management, private equity, and private banking. It has been a primary dealer in the U.S. Treasury Securities Market. The firm has headquarters in London, Tokyo, as well as offices located throughout the world including India. The LB lost 50% of their asset within three days of asking for protection. As a follow up of the fall of LB., the UBI shares tumbled $300 million due to its exposure to LB (cost of closing).

In addition to LB, the other giant firm, the AIG (American Insurance Group) which operates in approximately 130 countries ran in deeper financial crisis. Its jurisdiction offers auto insurance, life insurance, commercial insurance. In addition, AIG companies are leading providers of retirement services, financial services, and asset management in the world. Its common stock is listed on the New York Stock Exchange in Paris and Tokyo. It decided to sell wholly owned HSB group (Hart Ford Steam Boiler Inspection and Insurance Company) in $742 million. On September 17, 2009, the Federal Reserve announced AIG bail out package of a loan between $85 billion to $106 billion. The US Government has now 80% stake in the insurer and right to veto the payment of dividends to shareholders. The AIG will sell assets to repay the loan in two years. The AIG has been the early household name from US to Kolbe in Japan to Kolkata in India. It has been the biggest insurer in Japan and China (40% of $54 billion revenue). The AIG had the reputation of prudence and reliability. But with its fall its share plunged on the Wall Street.

The other two firms that filed for bankruptcy were Merrill Lynch and Goldman Sachs. The Bank of America, the largest Bank in the US with $154 billion bought Merrill Lynch in $46 billion. After merger and acquisition of ML, the BOA has become the world's biggest bank. The BOA valued to pay $25-30 a share of ML which closed at $17 on Friday night with region of $38-46 billion on 14th September, 2008.

The Goldman Sachs was ranked first in the investment banking and it housed some of the World's biggest private equity and hedge funds. Its investment bankers were the smartest; its traders, the best. In 2007, when two of its competitors Merrill Lynch and City group underwent losses, the Goldman Sachs booked record revenue and earnings, and paid its CEO $627 million, the most ever for a Wall Street CEO. But in September, 2008 due to its overexposure to the AIG the company suffered most to the tune of $2.12 billion. On 21st September, 2008, it announced its merger and acquisition for the status of a bank only. The US Federal Reserve supported this with a bailout package of $10 billion. Now, Goldman Sachs would look much like a commercial bank, with significantly tighter regulation, and much closer supervision by bank examiners from several government agencies.

In addition to the above four, the case of Morgan Stanley security firm is also the same which was supported by the Federal Reserve by a loan of $10 billion.

Financial Implications

The financial implications of this global recession is widespread, and it has its impact on all the countries which are linked to the US. It is still very difficult to gauge the impact in financial term, but it has started eroding the development works; it has started throwing people out of their jobs; it has made people overnight bankrupt thereby leading to social unrest and breaking of family ties. The immediate impact of this recession may be summarized as follows.

The unemployment rate in the US has risen to all time high above 7.4% as it was 6.5% in October, 2008. The US GDP will fall by 2.8% in first quarter of 2009. Already 20,000 people have been laid off in the US. Around 25,000 Lehman employees in India are feared to get the pink slip. The Wall Street has lost its glory in world business. Three of five Wall Street's major independent brokers have disappeared. Only Goldman Sachs and Morgan Stanley left. The economists expect contraction in the Japanese, the British, and European economies in 2009. The consensus suggests that the current recession will be deeper and shall last longer than those of 2001 and 1990-91. The monetary loss is over trillions of dollar in the US and any effort by the new US President has to be tested on sound economic parameters. The Bush administration $700 billion package is too small to have its impact on building confidence measures in the US economy. There are already more than $1 trillion worth of sub-prime collaterized mortgage- backed securities. With the tightening of credit and rising interest, the people are finding the housing sector less profitable, and it is no more sufficient to pay off their debts as it was the case earlier. As an offshoot of global recession, the share prices in Tokyo, London, China, India and Euro-zone have undergone a free fall. There has been a big loss to Indian software companies. India's share prices of BSE have fallen from a high of 21,000 to below 9,000 during the last six months thereby eroding the confidence of small and medium investors. Even, in the US, there have been suicide cases among bankrupt people who could not find a way out of this recession. According to one estimate, the housing market in the US would not revive until 2010.

In case of India, rupee slid 19.2% in 2008 which was the worst annual performance since 1991, and second worst among 10 most active Asian currencies excluding Japan. The inflation rate rose to more than 11% nearing 12% in September, 2008. Growth rate in real sectors came down.

Genesis of the Crisis

The US is the World's biggest consumer. So, a slow down in the US means a slow down everywhere. The genesis of the crisis is due to the mortgage crisis that started in September, 2007 in the US. The present mortgage crisis is due to decline in prices of real estates. As a result, housing loans made by the banks to people with little support made these loans very risky, and when interest rates were raised by these banks, these borrowers could no more repay Lehman. This led to huge losses for Lehman. It caused $60 billion loss in bad real estate loan for the Lehman Brothers. Among others, one of the main reasons for its downfall was its poor relation with top banks of the US. They refused to do business with the LB due to over confidence of its CEO over the Lehman financial assets. And after big debt of $639 billion, when Lehman asked Barclays and Bank of America for acquisition, they simply rejected the offer.

Earlier, people with good credit were regarded as bulwark against the economic strain posed by the rising defaulters among borrowers with blemished or sub-prime credit- like sub-prime mortgages many prime loans made in the US in recent years allowed borrowers to pay less initially and face higher adjustable payments a few years later. As long as home prices were rising, these borrowers could refinance their loans or sell their properties to pay off their mortgages. But, now with prices falling and lenders clamping down home owners with solid credit are starting to come to the same financial stress as those with sub-prime credit. Naturally, this crisis has led to steep losses across the US financial industry.

According to AIG reporting by the auditors, it may have understated losses on complex financial instruments linked to mortgage and corporate loans. There is overriding fear that some hedge funds may run into trouble. According to the Mortgage Bankers Association, based in Washington at the end of September 2008, nearly 4% of prime mortgages were past due or foreclosing. This was the highest rate since the group started tracking prime and sub-prime mortgages separately in 1998.

Unlike sub-prime borrowers, who tend to have lower income and fewer assets, prime borrowers have greater means to restructure their debts if they lose jobs or encounter other financial challenges. The recent reductions in short-term interest rates by the Federal Reserve should also help the borrowers by reducing the real rate for adjustable loans. Still economists are of the view that the rates cut and the $168 billion fiscal stimulus package are unlikely to make a significant dent in the large debts weighing on many Americans because banks have tightened lending standards, and expected rebates from government will not cover most house payments.

The problem of mortgage crisis is most acute in areas that experienced big boom in housing in California, the South west, Florida and other coastal markets— — and in the Midwest, which is suffering from job losses in the manufacturing sector.

During the 1970s, the US economy was afflicted wit stagflation, crippling inflation coupled with stagnant economic growth and high unemployment. But, this housing mortgage crisis has been the worst housing recession in more than 15 years.

Futuristic Outlook

Rex Nutting in the "Market Watch" on Nov. 10, 2008 observed that US economy was expected to shrink 0.4% in 2009 compared with 2008. It was a survey by 49 economists. These economists also expect contraction in the Japanese, British and Euro-zone economies in 2009. The US GDP will fall by 2.8% in first three months in 2008 and by 1.5% in the first quarter of 2009. "The consensus strongly suggests that the current recession will be deeper and last longer than those of 2001 and 1990-91," said Blue Chip editor Randel Moore in his commentary. The projected unemployment rate in 2009 is 7.4% as compared to 6.5% in October, 2006. The Federal Bank has further cut the interest rate by 0.5%. There is also a growing consensus that $700 billion bail out package given by the erstwhile President George Bush shall fail US Tax payer. This is the observation by Shah Gilani, contributing editor, Money Morning. The US bail out package of $700 billion was regarded as the "Emergency Economic Stabilization Act of 2008." Why the bail out package shall fail is substantiated by the following reasons:

- There are more than $1 trillion worth of sub prime collaterized mortgage-backed securities – and that is just one type of problematic derivative security. Hence, $700 billion is not enough.
- The purchase plan is not limited to just resident mortgage- backed securities.
- Who is going to fight off the Lobbying group out to influence the managers that Treasury Departments hires to direct money to their masters?
- The government plan is even more under funded than the people realize.
- Treasury is going to hire banking industry managers to manage the process. Those managers are more likely to serve themselves as they did earlier.
- There is no defined mechanism to determine which price the Treasury Department will pay for what it buys.
- Since treasury can't buy all the problem securities, if it prices what it is going to buy too low, all remaining

holders will have to work down their holdings and take more write-downs and losses— —. This will not create confidence in providing liquidity.

– If the treasury department prices the securities too high, several problems quickly emerge. Hedge funds will rust to sell their current holdings, and may very well speculate by buying up more securities to sell them at higher prices (profit) to Treasury, meaning that the Treasury Department Plan won't necessarily be helping banks directly. What is more, if those securities are priced too high, and the market for them continues to fall, taxpayers will eat the losses—a reality that likely will lead to an end to further program. The 'Head I win, Tails you lose' Bargain.

Immediately after taking charge of US presidency, Barak Obama gave another bail out package of $838 billion on 10th February, 2009. It was stated that a mix of tax cuts and spending was needed to check the global recession. According to one estimate, if we add up all the bail out packages of Bush, Obama and all that were provided to safeguard the LB, the AIG, Merril Lynch , Goldman Sachs, etc; the sum total would be more than $8 trillion — — — —. Will it really bail out the US recession in a very short period of time? Definitely, not. The experts are of the view that the global recession will continue for two to three years having its impact on each and every corner of global economy which are linked by the international investment institution. A more rigorous bail out package need be carried out to provide relief to all the victims. The Federal Reserve Chairman Bernanke has cautioned more cuts for the multinational financial institutions to avoid the deepening of global melt down crisis. These conglomerates must be kept alive to avoid bigger collapse of the financial system. There is need to isolate bad assets. A bad bank anywhere can affect a good bank anywhere. Paul Volcker chairman of Obama Advisory board, and also former Federal chairman has also advocated controlling risk-taking by systematically vital institutions.

The Case of India

Considering the fact that the crisis is global and it has its impact on all the countries that were outward oriented, shall India's economy cope up with this recession. Does India's economy has enough strength to be resilient enough to bear all the shocks which are witnessed owing to our exposure to multinational financial institutions. To summarise the Indian scenario as an offshoot of global recession, we have witnessed the fall of share market in India from 21,000 of BSE to below 9,000. India's rupee slid 19.2 % in 2008, which was the worst annual performance since 1991, and second worst among 10 most active Asian currencies excluding Japan. Inflation reached more than 11% and it was nearing 12% by the end of 2008. The growth rates in real sectors have come down. The housing sector, the automobile sector and software industries suffered.

In the very first quarter since the start of global recession in September, 2008, the confidence of India's economy was shaken and it appeared that this recession will take its toll on each sector of our economy. Many of private sector companies have already reduced the wages of their employees. The TCS for example has already cut the variable pay. The employees will have to work more from 40 hrs to 45 hrs in a week. The TCS may also defer absorbing 24,000 campus recruits, scheduled to join in June 2009. There has also been slowdown in placements reduced to 50% at IIMs. The salary also has gone down accordingly.

But the overall impact of global recession on India's economy would have been much deeper had the government not acted promptly to overcome the recession. The government resorted to both fiscal and monetary measures to increase demand, boost employment and yet check the price rise.

Macro-economic Strength of India's Economy

The inflation rate has come down from nearly 12% to 3.92% by 17th February, 2009. It has been further brought down to 3% by the end of February, 2009. Although, the growth rate has been scaled down to 7.1% in 2008-09, it is still the second highest in the world, the first being China having growth rate of 8.5% in 2008-09.

Although, there has been flight of capital to the tune of billions of dollar from India, yet India has a substantive amount of foreign exchange reserves. The foreign exchange reserve as on 16th January, 2009 stood at $242.85 billion. Let us compare this against the foreign exchange reserve in June 1991 which stood in the range of Rs. 2000 crore (equivalent to $0.5 billion) only. This is very powerful indicator which India has sustained after its emergence in liberalization, privatization and globalization in 1991.

India's economy achieved a sustained growth of 9% during the last three years 2004-05 to 2007-08. PCI (Per Capita Income) has grown at 7.4% per annum during the last four years. The fiscal deficit came down from 4.5% in 2003-04 to 2.7% in 2007-08. Revenue deficit declined from 3.6% to 1.17%, Domestic Investment Rate as a proportion of GDP increased from 27.6% in 2003-04 to over39% in 2007-08. Domestic Saving Rate as a proportion of GDP increased from 29.8% to 37.7% during this period. Agriculture as a proportion of GDP improved from 11.1% in 2003-04 to 14.2% in 2007-08. Growth in agriculture has reached to nearly 4% and food-grains reserve has reached 230 million tons. Social sector reforms have been introduced heralding *NAREGA, Sarva Siksha Abhiyan, Rajiv Gandhi* Potable Water Provision Schemes etc.

Fiscal Measures by the Government

So far the government has given three packages, one on December 7, 2008, the second on January 7, 2009, and the third on February 24, 2009. These packages provided tax relief to boost demand. It aimed at increasing expenditure on public projects to create employment and public assets. The government reviewed infrastructure investment. During August 2008 to January, 2009 Government approved 37 infrastructure projects worth Rs. 70,000 crores. Through PPP (Public Private Partnership) the government opened means for public sector investments. IIFCL (India Infra-structure Finance Company Limited) will refinance 60% of commercial bank loans for PPT projects in critical areas over the next 18 months. IIFCL will raise Rs. 10,000 crore in the market by March 2009. If required, additional Rs. 30,000 crore can be raised.

By the third stimulus package announced on February 24, 2009, the government reduced the Excise duty and service tax from 10% to 8% and 12 per cent to 10 per cent respectively. The existing duty cut was extended beyond 31st March, 2009. States have been allowed an additional fiscal deficit of 0.5 per cent in next fiscal too. It would lead to revenue loss of Rs. 29,100 crore, thereby raising the fiscal deficit by 0.4 per cent of GDP. The resultant fiscal deficit as per cent of GDP will be 6 per cent. This is alarming; but perhaps it has been done to accelerate growth in the economy by increasing investment in the critical sectors.

Monetary Measures by the RBI

RBI has also worked in tandem with the government in fighting the global recession ever since 15th September, 2008. The prime responsibility of the RBI is to regulate the supply of money so as to check the price rise and yet generate demand for long term investment in the economy for increasing employment. Therefore, in order to check recession and provide liquidity the market for employment generation and long term investment for development activities, the RBI resorted to take measures since 15th September 2008. By 27th January, 2009, the SLR has been reduced to 24.00 per cent from 25 per cent. The CRR was reduced from 9.00 per cent to 5.00 per cent, the Repo Rate was reduced from 9 per cent to 5.5 per cent, and the Reverse Repo Rate was reduced from 6.00 per cent to 4.00 per cent. But, during the period of 15th September 2008 to 27th January 2009, the Bank Rate remained at 6.00 per cent. By reducing the above rates, the RBI has provided enough liquidity in the economy. Earlier, by tightening the monetary policy with the mix of fiscal policy measures by the government, the price rise was brought down by the end of December, 2008. And later by reducing the SLR, CRR and Repo Rates, the RBI encouraged the commercial banks to lower down the rates in respect of housing, personal loan etc.

Confidence in share market remained shaky and it could not cross 9,000 ever since it fell from 21,000 in September 2008. Owing to over exposure to the MNCs and weakening of demand in most developed economies, the foreign institutional investors want to liquidate their money from the Indian share market. Naturally, every time there is some upsurge in share market, it falls immediately. But, the share market has already come to a level, which is almost equal to the minimum after the fall of price of most of issues. Naturally, this volatility would continue in near future till confidence for long term investment is ensured among investors.

For the first time in the first quarter of 2009, banks' investments in statutory liquidity ratio (SLR) fell below incremental credit flow during a fortnight. This is a healthy sign as banks are now lending to retail, housing and automobile sectors where earlier they were reluctant to enter. But, these commercial banks are still reluctant to few sectors like non-banking finance companies and real estate.

The RBI has also introduced advanced level BASEL II accord to check the susceptibility of commercial banks to go bankrupt due to over exposure of their businesses. In order to check recession, Basel II recommendations are very relevant. The RBI has asked all banks to graduate from the simpler approaches of Basel II framework to move to more advanced ones. It set up rigorous task and capital management requirement aimed to ensure that a bank holds reserves appropriate to the risk it exposes itself through lending and investment practices. Since March 2008, foreign anks working in India including Indian banks working outside India have already migrated to simpler approaches under Basel II framework. Other commercial banks were requested to migrate to these norms by March 31, 2009.

This framework includes standardized approach for credit risk arising from default by borrowers. It has basic indicator approach - sealing against robbery, or power loss. It also has standardized duration approach for market risk arising from fluctuation in interest rates and share prices which affect the investment and market portfolio of the bank while the banks have the discretion tc adopt the advance approaches, they need to seek prior approval from the RBI.

Under the standardized approach banks activities are divided into eight businesses viz. (i) corporate finance, (ii) trading & sales, (iii) retail banking, (iv) commercial banking, (v) payment and settlement, (vi) agency services, (vii) asset management, and (viii) retail brokerage. Within each income, there is a broad indicator for the scale of business operations, and so is the scale of operational risk exposure within each of these business lines. The capital charge for each business is calculated by multiplying gross income by a factor.

Currently, banks are using the basic indicator approach as per which the banks are required to hold capital for operational risk equal to the average over the previous three years of a fixed percentage of positive annual gross income.

Naturally, with the adoption of the advanced level Basel II accord, the commercial banks shall overcome the risks of any type of businesses, and they would be aloof fro the melt down effect of the global recession.

In spite of the best efforts taken by the government and the RBI we observe that the confidence of stock market has not been stored. Unless the prices of stock market is stabilizes one cannot think of investing in the volatile market. The whole sale prices have come down owing largely due to cut in fuel and metal prices. But the consumer price index has not come down. Still, the prices of essential commodities like vegetable and pulses are ruling high. The prices of real estate viz. bricks, cement, and constructed materials are again ruling high. Unless, the falling CRR and Repo- Rate do not get translated into lowering of interest rates, the demand for liquidity for investments in real sector will not rise. Due to global recession and sudden shrinkage of aggregate demand, there are sudden loss in sectors like information technology, travel and tourism, real estate, motor vehicles, domestic airlines and some of our financial institutions.

Conclusion

As Keynes would put it, the problem of global recession is due to the fall in effective demand, which again is dependent upon how the growth in national income is distributed in favour of common people, who constitute a sizable percentage in consumption. Unless the income of people of mass consumption is not raised, the aggregate demand shall not rise in respect of commodities and services whose demand has sharply declined. Therefore, the government must resort to the welfare and employment generating programmes. The basic *Bharat Nirman Yojana* programmes of road construction, *NREGA*, provision of irrigation facilities and linking of our villages by potable water and minimum health services must be supplanted by an efficient administrative system,

As already discussed, India has high growth potential. Growth need to be widely spread so that its benefits in terms of income and employment, reaches to the common man, especially, the socially weaker sections viz. SC/ST/OBCs and minorities. In the very foreward of the XIth Plan by the Prime Minister, there is thrust on the inclusive growth, which is reflected in most programmes especially the flagship programmes. The pace of decline in absolute poverty in terms of population without access to essential services or in terms of consumption, is slower than it should be. Although, the expected growth target by 2011 is 9 per cent, it will depend mainly on how our economy is integrated into the world economy. Since the initiation of liberalization, privatization, and globalization in 1991, India has moved much ahead in this process of incorporating reforms in production process, and also reforms in social and legal institutions. Both public and private entrepreneurship have responded magnificently to new opportunities opened up by the economic reforms.

Unlike the US, where the global recession has its roots in sub-prime lending in the housing sector, India must avoid this. In recent times, there has been a move to attract the borrowers at lower rate of interest in the first year, and thereafter a higher rate of interest. As the oil prices are rising followed by the fall in the monsoon, there would be rise in inflation, which might aggravate the housing sector. This may follow tightening of monetary policy and hence further rise in interest rates. But unlike the Asian countries, India's economy is less dependent on global demand. Our trade to the US is limited to around 20 per cent which is gradually on the decline over the Xth. plan period. On the contrary, our export to Asian countries is around 50 per cent, and it is on the rising trend. The BPO companies like the TCS, Infosys, WIPRO and others have already gone through the structural changes to diffuse the impact of global recession. Naturally, India has the resilience to cope up with the global recession.

References

Business Standard, Tuesday, 10 February, 2009.

Economic Survey (2007-08), Government of India, Oxford University Press.

Economic Survey (2008-09), Government of India.

Interim Budget (2009-10), Government of India, 16 February, 2009.

Keynes, J.M. (1936), "The Theory of Employment Interest and Money"

Macro-economic Indicators, EPW, Mumbai.

Miller, Don., "Outlook 2009" in 'Money Morning'. 15/01/2009.

New York Times, Thursday, 12 February, 2009.

Nutting, Rex., Market Watch, November 10, 2008.

RBI's Quarterly Reviews

Union Budget (2009-10), Government of India.

Times of India, Friday, February 6, 2009.

Vaidyanathan, A. (2009), "Reviving the Economy: Problems and Prospects", Economic and Political Weekly, February 7.

XIth Five Year Plan (2007-12), Oxford University Press

http://federalreserve.gov/boarddocs/speeches/

http://moneymorning.com

http://en.wikipedia.org/wiki/Money_supply

13

The Global Crisis: Impact on Indian Economy

Manjushri Gupta, Parul Saxena, Anjila Gupta

Introduction

The concept of financial crisis is applied broadly to a variety of situations in which some financial institutions or assets suddenly lose a large part of their value. In the 19th and early 20th centuries, many financial crisis were associated with banking panics, stock market crashes and the bursting of other financial bubbles, currency crises, and sovereign defaults.

The turmoil in the international financial markets of advanced economies that started around mid-2007 has exacerbated substantially since August 2008. The financial market crisis has led to the collapse of major financial institutions and is now beginning to impact the real economy in the advanced economies. As this crisis is unfolding, credit markets appear to be drying up in the developed world.

USA is a dominant force in world economy and as per data it represents 21 percent of the world economy. The worst global financial crisis since the Great Depression has witnessed failures and collapses of major financial institutions in the United States (US) and several European countries. With the spread of the US subprime mortgage crisis to the rest of the

US financial system and other industrialized countries' financial markets, a significant slowdown in economic growth has taken place in the US, Europe, and Japan. A squeeze on credit falls in house prices and tumbling stock markets are all reinforcing a slump in consumer confidence, consumption and investment.

Many economists are predicting that this 'Great Recession' of 2008/09 will be the worst global recession since the 1930s.World growth is projected to slow from 5 percent in 2007 to 3.75 percent in 2008 and to just over 2 percent in 2009, with the downturn led by advanced economies. Weakening global demand is depressing commodity prices. Oil prices have now declined by over 70 percent from a record USD 147 a barrel in July 2007, reflecting the major global downturn, the strengthening of the US dollar, and the financial crisis. Similarly, metals and food prices have fallen from their recent peaks. While this eases the burden on households in advanced economics and emerging economies in Europe and Asia, it lowers growth prospects too.

Table 1
A Short List of Some Major Financial Crisis Since 1980

1980s	Latin American debt crisis, beginning in Mexico
1989-91	United States savings and loan crisis
1990s	Collapse of Japanese asset price bubble
1992-93	Speculative attacks on currencies in the European Exchange Rate Mechanism
1994-95	1994 economic crisis in Mexico: speculative attack and default on Mexican debt
1997-98	Asian financial crisis: devaluations and banking crisis across Asia
1998	Russian financial crisis: devaluation of the Rouble and default on Russian debt
2001-02	Argentine economic crisis (1999-2002): breakdown of banking system
2008	USA, Europe: spread of the sub prime mortgage crisis

Source: www.Nytimes.com

The UK's Overseas Development Institute (ODI) notes two possible transmission mechanisms:

1. Through financial contagion across stock markets: as capital has been withdrawn from emerging country stock markets, equity value has fallen and the interest paid by firms for borrowing through the stock market has increased. As of mid-October, developing country equity markets had given up all of their gains in 2008 and initial public offerings had disappeared.
2. The financial crisis has resulted in an economic downturn in developed countries which may impact developing countries in three important ways:
   - Remittances to developing countries will fall: Although the impact on each country will depend on exchange rates, aggregate world remittances will fall in 2009. In fact, they have already slowed down in the second half of 2008. Also, the economic slowdown will especially reduce employment opportunities in the developed world in the sectors with a high concentration of migrants, such as construction, retail or catering.
   - Fall in trade volumes: World trade volumes may fall for the first time since the 1982 recession, led by the pulling back of international bank lending.
   - Foreign direct investment will come under pressure: Private flows into developing countries are projected to decline from $1 trillion in 2007 to around $250 billion in 2009 (or from 7.7% to 3.0% of the developing country GDP). Additionally, aid commitments are likely to come under pressure too.

Factors Leading to U.S. Recession

The crisis emerged as a crisis of securitisation. Securitisation is an old and tested technique used to refinance a range of loans, got used extensively in certain unstable financial structures, which were financing short-term assets that were illiquid, complex, and whose value proved to be uncertain. The instability of such structures was therefore largely masked. Indeed, cheap money allowed easy refinancing of poor quality debt and of assets with uncertain value. Favorable ratings and credit enhancements artificially boosted the quality of loans underlying such structured products. The rise in defaults on such loans, first on sub-prime mortgages, followed by others, triggered a chain of reactions whose consequences are still unfolding.

Sub Prime Crisis

Based on the assumption that sub prime lending precipitated the crisis, house prices fell by 20 to 30 percent from their peak, wiping out between $4000bn and $6000bn in household wealth. The falling property rates compelled lot of people who had taken loans at high interest rates to default on repayment. When borrowers defaulted on loans, CDOs became worthless and the investors lost their money. Banks also had no money to lend. This compounded the problem further. This is known as the Subprime Mortgage Crisis. The bursting of housing bubble plunged the US into an economic crisis that had far-reaching effects across the globe.

Over-Leveraging, Credit Default Swaps and Collateralized Debt Obligations

Another probable cause of the crisis was widespread miscalculation by banks and investors of the level of risk inherent in the unregulated Collateralized debt obligation and Credit Default Swap markets. Under this theory, banks and investors systematized the risk by taking advantage of low interest rates to borrow tremendous sums of money that they could only pay back if the housing market continued to increase in value.

The pricing model for CDOs clearly did not reflect the level of risk they introduced into the system. The massive, practically unthinkable, losses have dramatically impacted the balance sheets of banks across the globe, leaving them with very little capital to continue operations.

Bankruptcy of Large Banks

In many developed countries, Banks have ceased to trust each other's creditworthiness and Liquidity has dried up.

Governments and Central Banks have moved aggressively to support banks' solvency and resilience by infusing capital in the form of bailout packages . Some cases that are already in public domain include such big names as Citigroup, Bear Stearns, Merrill Lynch, Goldman Sachs, AIG, Lehman Brothers, Freddie Mac, Fannie Mae, RBS, ING Fortis, Deutsche, Barclays, BNP Paribas, Soc Gen, and Swiss Re.

U.S. Consumer Spending

The sudden weakness in US consumer spending has an obvious reason. The spending bubble on consumer durables-that is, on autos and housing durables-is going bust. It was largely spending borrowed from the future to be implicitly followed by payback time. For the US, this rapid, steep decline in the growth of consumer spending is the first decisive consideration to expect in the United States' impending serious recession; and remarkably, this is happening with record credit growth and even before the housing bubble is truly bursting.

This sharp slowdown in consumer spending strikingly conforms to the downward shift in the growth of real disposable personal incomes. Under these miserable US income conditions, the strength of future consumer spending manifestly depends on the possibilities of ever-higher cash-out mortgage refinancing against rising house prices.

Current Credit Expansion

The Austrian School of Economics proposes that the crisis is an excellent example of the Austrian Business Cycle Theory, in which credit created through the policies of central banking gives rise to an artificial boom, which is inevitably followed by a bust. This perspective argues that the monetary policy of central banks creates excessive quantities of cheap credit by setting interest rates below where they would be set by a free market. This easy availability of credit inspires a bundle of malinvestments, particularly on long-term projects such as housing and capital assets, and also spurs a consumption boom as incentives to save are diminished. Thus an unsustainable boom arises, characterized by malinvestments and over-consumption.

But the created credit is not backed by any real savings nor is in response to any change in the real economy. The bust occurs when investors collectively realize their mistake. This happens usually some time after interest rates rise again. The liquidation of the malinvestments and the consequent reduction in consumption throw the economy into a recession, whose severity mirrors the scale of the boom's excesses.

The central bank of the United States, led by Federal Reserve Chairman Alan Greenspan, kept interest rates very low for a long period of time to blunt the recession of the early 2000s. The resulting malinvestment and overconsumption of investors and consumers prompted the development of a housing bubble that ultimately burst, precipitating the financial crisis. This crisis, together with sudden and necessary deleveraging and cutbacks by consumers, businesses and banks, led to the recession.

The U.S. Trade Deficit

The trade deficit alters the US economy's structure in a negative way. The losing manufacturing area is the sector with the highest rate of capital formation, and therefore also the highest rate of productivity growth also paying the highest wages. US manufacturing sector lost 3 million jobs in the past few years. To be sure, the trade deficit is not its only reason, but a major one. Principally, every increase in spending brings about an equivalent increase in incomes. But this is not true in three cases of spending: first, spending on existing assets; second, spending on imports; and third, Ponzi finance. Ponzi finance means that lenders simply capitalize unpaid interest rates. Ponzi finance creates credit, but it is bare of any demand and spending effects in the economy.

Debt Trap

With stagnant real disposable income and double-digit debt growth, the American consumer is caught in a vicious debt trap. The general idea, certainly, has been to settle debt and debt service problems simply by selling later to the highly appreciated greater fool. During 2000, total financial and nonfinancial credit and debt growth in the US amounted to $1,605.6 billion. In 2005, it had accelerated to $3,335.9 billion; and in the first quarter of 2006, it has run at an annual rate of $4,392.8 billion, and this now with zero income growth. Note that this debt explosion has happened with little change in GDP growth.

In the past, many consumers in America lived on credit, often amazing huge credit card bills spread across multiple cards. At the same time, money was freely loaned to almost anyone, including high-risk people, those with poor credit scores. This became a problem when banks gave high-risk mortgages for home purchases. People had debt that was far beyond their means. When the housing bubble burst, loans were called and / or people tried to sell their home, but the debt totaled more that the house would sell for, meaning the loan could not be re-paid, lending to foreclosure. The same thing happened in auto loan industry.

Impact on Asia

The unfolding global financial crisis is exerting negative impact on Asian economies. But Asian financial institutions' exposure to sub prime-related products has been limited due to three factors:

(i) They have lagged behind global financial institutions in incorporating highly complex financial innovations into their business models;

(ii) Many of them have been cautious in investing in high-risk, high-return instruments—such as mortgage-backed securities and collateralized debt obligations—after experiencing their own financial crisis eleven years ago; and

(iii) Their authorities have strengthened prudential supervision and regulation and risk management practices in their respective financial sectors. For example, Japanese banks fully implemented Basel II in March 2007, ahead of the European Union and the US. In addition, Asian banks and non-bank financial institutions are fundamentally sound, with well-capitalized balance sheets, low non-performing loan ratios (less than 5%), small exposure to real estate, and limited off-balance activities.

The acute global financial crisis and threatening slowdown in the industrialized economies has affected Asia's financial markets through capital flow channels and the real economy through trade channels. Private capital inflows are declining and in some countries these inflows have stopped or even reversed. The global financial crisis has already induced capital outflows from many emerging Asian economies, thereby causing currency depreciation and sharp falls in stock market prices.

The slowdown of the industrialized countries is beginning to have negative effects on Asia's real economic activity through trade channels. Expansion of exports to the US and European markets has been essential for Asia's sustained growth. The prospect of weak demand for emerging Asia's products due to the downturn of US, European, and Japanese economic growth could slow its exports and foreign direct investment inflows, further reducing Asia's economic growth.

In addition, countries with traditionally large remittance inflows from overseas workers such as India, Philippines, Viet Nam, and Indonesia may face declining remittances from abroad. Economic slowdown in industrialized economies could reduce demand for foreign workers in these economies, causing a large drop in remittances. And workers may return home to find that home markets may have difficulty-reabsorbing them.

It is true that exports and profits would be hurt and it is also true that Asia is also exposed to the sub-prime mess. Singapore, Hong Kong and Malaysia have exports to the US, accounting for 20 per cent or more of their GDPs. Singapore's exports to the US fell by 11 per cent and Malaysia's by 16 per cent. Despite all this, one can still be optimistic because China and India's exports to the USA are equivalent to 8.0 per cent and 2.0 per cent of their GDPs respectively. And other important factors are that in East Asia, the macroeconomic fundamentals are strong i.e. they have huge foreign exchange reserves, current account surpluses, strong economic growth rates etc. In addition, their domestic demand is also very strong and governments have more flexibility. And some economies have already decoupled. For instance Malaysia's exports to the USA fell but still their GDP increased from 5.7 per cent to 6.7 per cent in the third quarter of last year.

So, it would be unwise to say that Asian economies will be badly affected. They will be affected but by much less than in the past.

Impact of the Crisis on India

India has by-and-large been spared of global financial contagion for a variety of reasons. Our growth has been largely domestic demand driven with a comfortable level of foreign exchange reserves. The credit derivatives market in our country is at a nascent stage not comparable to the ones prevailing in advanced markets. There are significant restrictions on investments by residents in such products issued abroad and regulatory guidelines on securitisation do not permit immediate profit recognition.

With the increasing integration of the Indian economy and its financial markets with rest of the world, there is recognition that the country does face some downside risks from these international developments. In India, the adverse effects have so far been mainly in the equity markets because of reversal of portfolio equity flows, and the concomitant effects on the domestic forex market and liquidity conditions. The macro effects have so far been muted due to the overall strength of domestic demand, the healthy balance sheets of the Indian corporate sector, and the predominant domestic financing of investment.

As might be expected, the main impact of the global financial turmoil in India has emanated from the significant change experienced in the capital account in 2008-09 so far, relative to the previous year (Table 1). Total net capital flows fell from US$17.3 billion in April-June 2007 to US$13.2 billion in April-June 2008. Nonetheless, capital flows are expected to

Table 2
Trends in Capital Flows (US $ million)

Component	*Period*	*2007-08*	*2008-09*
Foreign Direct Investment to India	April-August	8,536	16,733
FIIs (net)@	April – Sept 26	15,508	-6,421
External Commercial Borrowings (net)	April- June	6,990	1,559
Short-term Trade Credits (net)	April- June	1,804	2,173
Memo:			
ECB Approvals	April-August	13,375	8,127
Foreign Exchange Reserves (variation)	April-September 26	48,583	-17,904
Foreign Exchange Reserves (end-period)	September 26, 2008	247,762	291,819

Note: Data on FIIs presented in this table represent inflows into the country and, thus, may differ from data relating to net investment in stock exchanges by FIIs.

be more than sufficient to cover the current account deficit this year as well. While Foreign Direct Investment (FDI) inflows have continued to exhibit accelerated growth (US$ 16.7 billion during April-August 2008 as compared with US$ 8.5 billion in the corresponding period of 2007), portfolio investments by foreign institutional investors (FIIs) witnessed a net outflow of about US$ 6.4 billion in April- September 2008 as compared with a net inflow of US$ 15.5 billion in the corresponding period last year.

Similarly, external commercial borrowings of the corporate sector declined from US$ 7.0 billion in April-June 2007 to US$ 1.6 billion in April-June 2008, partially in response to policy measures in the face of excess flows in 2007-08, but also due to the current turmoil in advanced economies. With the existence of a merchandise trade deficit of 7.7 per cent of GDP in 2007-08, and a current account deficit of 1.5 per cent, and change in perceptions with respect to capital flows, there has been significant pressure on the Indian exchange rate in recent months.

A detailed study undertaken by the RBI in September 2007 on the impact of the subprime episode on the Indian banks had revealed that none of the Indian banks or the foreign banks had any direct exposure to the sub-prime markets in the USA or other markets. However, a few Indian banks had invested in the collateralised debt obligations (CDOs) / bonds which had a few underlying entities with sub-prime exposures. Thus, no direct impact on account of direct exposure to the sub-prime market was in evidence. Consequent upon filling of bankruptcy by Lehman Brothers, all banks were advised to report the details of their exposures to Lehman Brothers and related entities both in India and abroad. Out of 77 reporting banks, 14 reported exposures to Lehman Brothers and its related entities either in India or abroad. An analysis of the information reported by these banks revealed that majority of the exposures reported by the banks pertained to subsidiaries of Lehman Bros Holdings Inc. which are not covered by the bankruptcy proceedings. Overall, these banks' exposure especially to Lehman Brothers Holding Inc., which has filed for bankruptcy, is not significant and banks are reported to have made adequate provisions.

Indian Financial Markets

Indian growth story has been investment-driven and a decline in foreign investment impacts the growth prospects in the equity market. In the Corporate Bond Markets, the risks of Indian corporates measured by the spread on bonds, have increased significantly in recent months. Though the spreads have lowered in recent days because of numerous policy measures, they are still high compared to 2007 levels. The foreign investors have also withdrawn their monies to support their parent companies. As a result, in the forex market, Indian Rupee has depreciated and has touched ·all time lows. The capital flows in India were so buoyant that they posed a different set of problems for Indian policymakers - appreciating rupee, sterilizing the inflows via government bonds, rising asset prices etc. The situation has reversed now and foreign capital is expected to flow out from the Indian shores.

The Indian Banking System

The Indian banking system is not directly exposed to the sub-prime mortgage assets. It has very limited indirect exposure to the US mortgage market, or to the failed institutions or stressed assets. Indian banks, both in the public sector and in the private sector, are financially sound, well capitalised and well regulated. The average capital to risk-weighted assets ratio (CRAR) for the Indian banking system, as at end-March 2008, was 12.6 per cent, as against the regulatory minimum of nine per cent and the Basel norm of eight per cent.

IT and Real Estate Sector

The key challenges faced by the industry now are investors & the psychological impact of the US crises, leading the companies to hit the pain button. Bonuses, perks, lavish parties & many other benefits are missing as companies look to cut cost. Indian IT export growth is also slowing down. About 15 per cent to 18 per cent of the business coming to Indian outsourcers includes projects from banking, insurance, and the financial services sector that is now uncertain.

Real estate, where building project are half done all over the country, in this tight liquidity situation developers are finding it difficult to raise finances.

Lay Offs & Unemployment

Hundreds of workers have lost jobs in diamond jewellery, textiles and leather industry. Companies in IT industry have stopped hiring & projected lower manpower need. Firms attached to the capital market are laying off people & large companies are putting their future expansion plan on hold.

Industrial Sector

Govt. & other private companies are reluctant in starting new ventures & starting new projects. Projects that are halfway to completion, or companies that are stuck with cash flow issues on businesses that are yet to reach break even, will run out of cash. Car, bike & truck sales are reducing. Steel plants are cutting production Hospitality & airlines are hit by poor demand.

Investments are likely to slowdown because of the industrial downturn and also because of the international trends.

Even so, India is experiencing the knock-on effects of the global crisis, through the monetary, financial and real channels – all of which are coming on top of the already expected cyclical moderation in growth. Our financial markets – equity market, money market, forex market and credit market – have all come under pressure mainly because of what we have begun to call 'the substitution effect' of: (i) drying up of overseas financing for Indian banks and Indian corporates; (ii) constraints in raising funds in a bearish domestic capital market; and (iii) decline in the internal accruals of the corporates. All these factors added to the pressure on the domestic credit market.

Conclusion

The worst global financial crisis since the Great Depression has witnessed failures and collapses of major financial institutions in the United States (US) and several European countries. With the spread of the US sub prime mortgage crisis to the rest of the US financial system and other industrialized countries' financial markets, a significant slowdown in economic growth has taken place in the US, Europe, and Japan. A squeeze on credit falls in house prices and tumbling stock markets are all reinforcing a slump in consumer confidence, consumption and investment.

India has by-and-large been spared of global financial contagion due to the sub prime turmoil for a variety of reasons. India's growth process has been largely domestic demand driven and its reliance on foreign savings has remained around 1.5 per cent in recent period. It also has a very comfortable level of forex reserves. The credit derivatives market is in an embryonic stage; the originate-to-distribute model in India is not comparable to the ones prevailing in advanced markets; there are restrictions on investments by residents in such products issued abroad; and regulatory guidelines on securitisation do not permit immediate profit recognition. Financial stability in India has been achieved through perseverance of prudential policies, which prevent institutions from excessive risk taking, and financial markets from becoming extremely volatile and turbulent.

References

Sivadasan P. (2008), Global Financial Crisis and its impact on Indian Economy, Amity Business Review, Dec.

Global Financial Crisis and Key Risks: Impact on India and Asia by Rakesh Mohan, Deputy Governor at IMF-FSF High-Level Meeting on the recent Financial Turmoil and Policy Responses at Washington D.C. on October 9, 2008.

The Global Financial Turmoil and Challenges for the Indian Economy, Speech by Dr. D. Subbarao, Governor, Reserve Bank of India at the Bankers' Club, Kolkata on December 10, 2008.

The Present Economic Crisis and its Impact on India', Speech by Shri Yogesh Agarwal, CMD, IDBI Bank Ltd., at the Haryana Institute of Public Administration, Dec. 20, 2008.

Asia-Europe Economic Relationships: Prospects and Challenges, Speech by Masahiro Kawai, Dean and CEO Asian Development Bank Institute, Tokyo, Japan at the Asia-Europe Business Forum, 22 October 2008 Beijing, People's Republic of China

Friedman Milton, Schwartz Anna, A Monetary History of the United States, Princeton University Press, ISBN 0691003548.

http://www.Nytimes.com

14

THE IMPACT OF THE CRISIS ON INDIAN BANKING SECTOR: LESSONS FOR FUTURE

Baij Nath Singh

The world is facing challenging times. What started of as a crisis at few financial institutions due to excessive risk-taking on both the asset and liability sides of their balance sheets, quickly spread to the entire financial system? The crisis began in USA and Europe and it has since affected the rest of the world, including Asia, in a bigger way than was thought at, the beginning. According to the IMF report, growth in the European union is expected to shrink this year by 3.2 percent, the U.S economy to 2.6 percent, in Japan by 5.8 percent and in Russia by 6.5 percent. With a contraction in global demand, the financial crisis soon turned into an economic crisis, with consumption and investment demand seeing a slowdown. While developed markets were at the centre of the financial crisis the emerging markets began to feel the impact through reversal of capital flows and particularly in the case of export development economies, through a sharp reduction in export demands. The transmission of financial crisis to the real sector, through the trade and capital channels, has meant that companies across the globe are reworking their expansion plans, and resorting to aggressive cost rationalizations to weathers the economic contraction. This in turn impacts the smaller economic units the small and medium enterprises, down to the last economic unit, the individuals, who faced with uncertain jobs and modest to no increase in pay, cut down on consumption, to save for existing liabilities and for future.

The global banking system is currently dealing with the downside of excessive leverage and aggressive risks taken in their pursuit of returns. They are going through the painful process of adjustment as they manage the depleting effect of de-leveraging and asset write downs through capital infusions governments aware of the systematic implications of failures, are lending their balance sheets, to help repair the impaired banks. Additionally, they are taking measures to rebuild confidence in the economy and kick-start consumption and investment, which would check the economy and the financial system from going into a downward spiral. Given the de-leveraging required in the system, governments and central banks are expanding their own balance sheets to pump money into their economies. India's banking system has been considerably less affected by the ongoing crisis than banking systems in U.S. and Europe. This is because the cause of the crisis in India are quite different from those elsewhere. In the advanced economies, the banking system suffered with huge losses, this led to a collapse in the flow of credit and in confidence and dragged down the real economy. In India, it is the real economy that has been affected through various channels and banks are feeling the effects of a slowing down of the economy.

Why Indian Banks Remain Bright Spot

Indian Banks are well placed to weather this impact. This is not a contrarian view. The RBI itself exudes optimism about the outlook for Indian Banking its report on trend and progress in Banking (2009). "At a time when the financial system across the globe is engulfed in a deep crisis, the Indian Banking system continues to show resilience. The underlying fundamentals of the Indian economy would continue to under pin the robust performance of the banking, which remains profitable and well capitalized". Performance of the Indian Banking system is not more affected by this crisis. These following reasons for such optimism are as follows:-

Volume of Credit

In the west countries where credit supply has collapsed. Unlike in India credit grew at 25 percent in 2007–08. Banks may be expected to slowdown credit growth in 2009-10, given the uncertainties in the environment. But growth of credit of around 20 percent is still and impressive figure. Retail credit is expected to grow up to 575000 crore by 2010. Now 60 percent people of our country has access to banks and only 15 percent out of this has loan accounts and 70 percent farmers have no access to formal source of credit contribution of retail loans to GDP stands merely at 6 percent in India, 15 percent in china and 24 percent in Thailand. It means credit provided by Indian banking system is very low with respect to our just neighbouring countries. There is large scope to enhance credit ratio by Indian banks.

Expansion and Diversified Working

Spreads in the Indian banking system remains high in comparison with other banking system of the world transition from class banking to mass banking and from sellers' market to buyers' market is drastically changing in Indian banking sector. There is an expansion of middle class from 250 to 300 million and they need various banking services. According to Reserve Bank of India, commercial banks' deposits were at Rs. 30,75,224 crore on March14 2008. Presently, total number of banking branches and ATM in India is about 75000 and 35,000 respectively. On the other hand total saving account holders are 37 crore. It means the number of banking branches are meagre for our total population as more than 16,000 people are dependent on a single bank branch.

A recent study at the Indian Institute of Management Lucknow about the scope for expansion of banking in India identifies many new opportunities and avenues from both strategic and operational perspectives. It finds the customer expectations regarding accuracy, security, transaction time, user friendliness, user involvement and convenience as the most important quality attributes in the perceived use fullness of banking services. The study suggests avenues for expansion in the context of opening new branches, financial inclusion, technological up gradation and retail banking by tapping collaborative synergies among various stake holders. It finds that banking has scope for diversification beyond cities to semi urban and rural areas in services like retail banking and micro credit banks need to open Industrial Finance branches selectively. Where they do not find it variable to open branches in rural areas, they may open satellite offices. They need to collaborate with local stake-holders for extending micro credit.

Structure of Banking Sector

India's banking sector is in far better shape than its counterparts in advanced economies. There is heightened appreciation today, even among long standing detractors of Reserve Bank of India that the bias towards caution in matures regulatory has stood India in good stead. Important features of regulation in recent years have been a gradualist approach towards to capital account convertibility, prudence in opening up the sector to private and foreign banks, stringent norms on exposure to sensitive sectors, pre-emptive action in respect of housing, real estate and consumer credit, stricter norms for securitization, prudential limits on inter-bank borrowing and tighter regulation of NBFCS. Many people think earlier the Indian banking system is largely inefficient and that the quickest way to usher in efficiency is to let in foreign banks in a bigger. They are wrong on both counts. Efficiency in Indian banking has improved on a number of parameters in post-reform period return on assets, non performing loans as a proportion of total loans or assets or income. This is too well documented to need elaboration here. As for greater entry of foreign banks, this is largely an academic matter for the next couple of years, given the current state of the leading international banks. Most of these banks are so busy sorting out their problems that they are unlikely to have the appetite for entering into or expanding in India in near future. But even over a longer period, the present crisis has only strengthened regulatory concerns about a great presence for foreign banks. One issue that has long worried regulators is what happens when the parent bank gets into trouble? The leading foreign banks used to laugh away this question saying, it was entirely hypothetical. We are wiser today. We know better about the vaunted efficiency of foreign banks and we also know the costs they can impose on host economies. Emerging Europe faces a serious credit crunch in the present crisis because it has huge foreign banks presence and much of the expansion in local credit in recent years was supported by parent bank funding. There are other regulatory issues as well. The supervision of foreign banks poses huge challenges.

It is easier to get domestic banks to fall in line with local policy imperatives. In the present crisis, for instance, public sector banks have cut their lending rate and maintained high level of credit growth. Foreign banks have not done so. It is hard to think of relaxing entry for foreign banks have not done so. It is hard to think of relaxing entry for foreign banks until many of the regulatory issues thrown up by the present crisis have been addressed. We need to look at other way of increasing competition and fostering greater efficiency in Indian banking in medium term. one way would be to increase domestic competition even more before opening up to greater foreign competition.

Cost of Credit

There is also a clamour for a steep reduction in policy rates to facilitate a sharper decline in lending rates. Policy rates have been falling steeply since October 2008 as out lined above. But lending rates have not followed suit. While the repo rate has declined by 350 basis points, the prime lending rate at Public Sector Banks (PSBS) has declined only by a maximum of 150 basis points and that at private banks by 50 basis points. Private banks are said to be market oriented while public sector banks lending decisions are said to be subject to political direction. It means the action of private banks are more in consonance with market reality. There are sound reasons for lending rates not declining as much as expected and the Reserve Bank of India has spelt out these in its macro economic review of January 2009. These are the following reasons for stable lending rates in credit market.

- Banks face competition for savings from small savings schemes whose rates are administrated and relatively inflexible
- Banks would have mobilized term deposits at higher rates and would face higher cost of funds until such time as the deposits come up for renewal,
- Market borrowings of government are high and will be even higher in light of the fiscal stimuli announced; and
- There is heighten risk aversion and banks will expect higher spreads over the risk-free rate in today's conditions.

These are more fundamental reason why lending rates will not decline when policy rates are cut. These rate reductions are quickly transmitted to the government securities market and result in capital gains on banks' investment portfolios. The fact that Indian banks invest a significant part of their deposits in risk-free government securities provides a buffer for liquidity even in the face of crisis. Moreover, structures with multiple leveraging, which have been at the root of the current crisis, are not prevalent in India. Return on assets in Indian banking system was 1 percent in 2007–08. This figure is widely accepted bench mark for performance in banking. Non - performing Assets (NPAS) are at an all time low. The ratio of NPAS to net advances in down to 1 percent from 9 percent a decade ago.

However the Indian banking system is well placed to withstand these adverse conditions because of a whole set of favourable factors created over decade and half of reforms and five years of buoyant economic conditions Because

- Capital adequacy average is 13 percent

- The level of Non-performing assets (NPAS) to net advances has been bright down to 1 percent and
- Return on assets is 1 percent, which constitute a bench marks for performance for banks world wide.

American and European banks have been undone by problems originating in the housing sector and compounded by investments backed by housing loans. There is as yet no sign of serious collapsed because housing loans are only around 10 percent of over all banking assets. Even if 20 percent of housing loans go bad. A level seen in rule prime-crisis, the maximum impact would be rise in NPA of 3 percent, with an average capital adequacy ratio of 13 percent, banks are well placed to withstand an increase in NPA of this order.

Lessons for Future

In the aftermath of the deep recession in the advanced economies as a part of global financial and economic crisis, the Indian banking policy makers are beginning to recognize some lessons. There is an emerging trend towards protectionism as reflected in the "by American clause" inserted in the fiscal stimulus packages that US in adopting. In any case, the US will have to adjust its consumption pattern to more sustainable levels rather than living on borrowing as in the past. It means that the developing world has to lock for alternative source of demand to sustain the growth rate in coming years. Among the alternative source of demand the most important would be the creation of additional domestic demand. In most of the developing countries, there is substantial incidence of poverty. In India itself a staggering number of people are below poverty line or, are just above it as demonstrated by the recent report of National Commission on Enterprises in Unorganized Sector. The crisis by reducing the demand in west of labour– intensive products such as textiles and garments, gems, jewellary and handicrafts is leading to massive job losses and the number of those below poverty line would go up even further.

Huge investments are required in the infrastructure space especially in transportation and power to support the growth objectives. In this context Nobel prize winner Dr. Amartyasen advised the Indian government to spend more money in social-infra-structure like health, education, food security and nutritional diet. While there is increased spending by the government and investment flowing in through the public-private partnership route, the pace needs significant build up, before it begins to make a meaningful impact. Enabling access to long term finance from the banking or Capital market route, will be essential to spur investment in long gestation infra-structuring projects.

Financial restructuring will be needed to alien the debt of companies to the economic realities. Banks will need to take pragmatic approach and balance asset quality concerns with the need to step in with incremental credit to ease the transition for its borrowers. With proper risk management and prudent leading banks should be able to play the requisite role in the revival of growth in the economy. Infact, once the transition phase is behind us, and with sufficient systematic liquidity, the investment activity of corporate will be restored providing ample growth opportunities for banks.

A new engine of economic growth could be achieved by deepening the regional economic cooperation could help in sharing the dynamism of Asia's economies for mutual benefit several emerging economies of the region including China, India, Indonesia and Bangladesh have been able to grow robustly despite a highly adverse external environment. Regional cooperation involves more than broadening, deepening and consolidating existing regional trade agreements. There is large potential for monetary and financial cooperation that remained to be exploited in Asia.

References

Keynes, John Meynard (1936), The General Theory of Employment Interest and Money, Macmillan and Co. Ltd., London.

Schumpeter Joseph Alois (1942), Capitalism, Socialism and Democracy, George Allen and Unwin Ltd., London.

Glyn A and R, Sutcliff (1972), Capitalism in Crisis, Pantheon Books, New York.

Harvey D. (2005a), A Brief History of Neoliberalism, Oxford University Press, New York.

Subba Rao D. (2009), Impact of the Global Financial Crisis on India: Collateral Damage and Response, Speech delivered in Tokyo, 18 February.

IMF (2006), Global Financial Stability Report, Washington.

IMF (2008), World Economic Outlook, Update 6, November.

Kochhar Chanda (2009), Indian Banking Resilience in Challenging Times, The Hindu Survey of Indian Industry, Chennai.

Ram Mohan T.T. (2009), The Impact of Crisis on the Indian Economy, Economic and Political Weekly, March 28-3 April, Mumbai.

15

The Global Economic Crisis-Its Effect on Indian Economy and Human Resources

B.N. Singh, Anuradha Verma

Introduction

Globalization mean integrating the economy of a country with the world economy. According to the chambers 20th century Dictionary, globalization means "To make global , that is world wide , or effecting or taking into consideration the whole world or all people". Globalization implies having the entire world as one market. It is a process of increasing economic integration and glowing economic interdependence between countries in the world economy, It involves not simply cross-borders movement of goods, services, capital , technology information and people but also an organization of economic activities which crosses national boundaries.

Challenges of Globalisation

The globalization is going on at a fast pace. This rapid move towards greater integration is fuelled by various factors like the spreading political decisions to move towards liberalization and adoption of market economies, the free flow of capital etc. These forces are creating new challenges.

(i) The expansion of global markets and the opportunities of dismantling of protective barriers to trade has enhanced. Due to this the global players are competing with the domestic players. Global players are very big and have the capacity to use their big size to establish monopoly and convert free competition into unfair competition. MNCs are more likely to compete out domestic players as MNCs have several advantages over the local players. There is a biggest challenge to keep the competition fair between local producers and global producers.

(ii) Globalization of the economy and the resultant liberalization within the economic system of the country cannot be reversed. These forces have emerged due to the complex nature of the interaction between the growth of economies of most countries , the resultant trade and market pattern which are unfolding. Business organizations have to reap the benefits of their investments as otherwise the competitors would displace them out of the market.

(iii) In this era of cutthroat competition, it is a great challenge for every management to think innovative and creative in order to ensure its existence. The survival of the fittest is the mantra of globalization. It is possible only when an organization is able to provide its services better than the competitors. This is because now the business is becoming global as compared to the national as earlier. Developed countries have the capabilities to capture the market share in the global business as they have competitive advantages over the developing countries.

(iv) Foreign enterprises are giving stiff competition to the enterprises of the developing countries. MNCs are able to deliver the products and services at lower prices and of better quality. Moreover, the competition, which is an essential element of free economy, is unfair due to the anticompetitive practices of the MNCs.

There is no level playing field for the developing countries.

(v) Global markets are exerting the pressure for economic efficiency on businesses and operations. Developing nations can face these pressures only with enhanced investments in R&D, superior management and easy access to finance. MNCs are accentuating merger and acquisition activity to consolidate and entrench themselves.

These challenges demand a well planned and implemented strategy to cope with the changing business environment. In a globalizing economy, there is a calamitous need for every management to develop the strategies to enhance the competitiveness to become successful in the global competitive market.

Effect of Global Crisis on Corporate Human Resources

One cannot outrun the turbulent economic times in which we find ourselves these days. Whether residing in a nation of struggle or a nation of wealth, people at all levels of society are dealing with the significant changes that seemed to have crept upon us- a time of economic crisis. Whether by accident or malfeasance , the global economic downturn seemed to appear out of the fog with little advances warning. Because historically well-managed organization are also substantially affected by the economic downturn, individual consumers have lost confidence and spending has lurched to a halt. The first faint outlines of necessary major global economic changes are just now appearing. Some economists suggest we have yet to plumb the depths of this downturn and should buckle-up for a long and turbulent ride. The nature of global economic conversation has changed these days, with talks of nationalizing industries (including banking and healthcare), conferences and submits on global economic systems and speeches regarding the needed rescue of entire national markets, one does not have to look far to see a certain level of fear and trepidation in all segments of industry , in all levels of work, and in virtually all nations.

Corporations have been likewise entangled in this worldwide meltdown and have not previously faced such heightened exposure. Organizations are desperately trying to survive and the sad reality is that their survival has required major changes in policy and strategy, most notably dramatic and painful reductions in opportunities for employees. These cuts have ranged from reductions in salary, benefits , perquisites, bonuses, and even the elimination of positions altogether.

Reaction of the Corporate

The primary response to the economic downturn by most organizations has been to enact immediately initiatives to conserve cash, reduce costs and improve efficiency. The fundamental goal is not profits but rather to remain viable or at best, to maintain current market share. Visible action is the preferred mode, often by a new leadership team recently installed in the corporate executive suite. Efforts are made to focus on core activities , develop contingency plans, refine just in- time delivery of raw materials , resulting to shortening of the supply chains, wringing costs out of every element of production , and discarding or extending the use of virtually every corporate asset. The planning horizon is abbreviated, and every corporate function that does not obviously contribute to positive cash flow is halted. In an effort to lower corporate risk, all innovation ideas face heightened hurdle rate and requirements to prove viability and expansive near-term success prior to approval . Previous corporate decisions, plans and methods may be repudiated.

One positive aspect of a severe economic downturn is that it can provide substantial clarity about the historical internal machinations of the corporation that which was hidden or thought inconsequential is suddenly thrust onto center stage. Corporate executives must define reality, and then intentionally clarify the future focus, priorities and plans of the company. The foundation of useful corporate plans is honesty, realism and transparency. Coincident to the development of new corporate focus and plans must be a thought evaluation and refining of corporate metrics or measurements Metrics must be clearly stated, valid, reliable and expansive. The rule of thumb is "what gets measured gets done," so it is essential that leadership winnows the volume of metrics to the half-dozen or so measurements accurately encapsulating the key activities of the company and, specifically, how the company makes money. The new metrics must not be clouded by legacy strategies , should focus more on outputs than inputs, should be appropriately translated into individual day-to-day performance requirements that are clear, aggressive and unconstrained and should motivate ongoing productivity, review and internal conversation.

For the company to remain viable, new plans must have room for innovation, which consistently provides opportunities to grow more rapidly than competitors and to influence ultimately the direction of the industry. Innovation is based on a continuous stream of new, fresh, non-linear ideas that come from an intentionally diverse cadre of employees. Firms must create an environment where appropriate risk is welcome and failure, containing valuable information is encouraged and appropriately utilized. Most organizations, and leadership , and even employees, steer clear of failure basically due to fear of reprisal or retribution; however, the necessity of these times calls for a more risky approach and this approach to innovation and risk might result in some temporary failure, or better put-a path to discovery. Leadership that encourages this freedom to fail, or freedom to risk and innovate, might just find themselves ahead of the curve when better times are in the making , almost as if the organization has taken the downtime and used the time productively.

Employee's Reaction

Corporate deduction in difficult economic times generally causes fear and unease among employees. Their primary goal is to stay "off radar" so not to be identified as a target for additional personnel retrenchments employees do so by avoiding any work that is innovative, requires anything but incremental change, or lies outside the historical corporate trajectory , in other words a safe approach seeking self-sustainability. Emotions such as anguish at the loss of fellow employees, a diminution of confidence in leadership , and an erosion of commitment are common. Formal and informal networks within the organization have been disrupted, employees tend to concentrate on short-term, low-impact projects with a high likelihood of success. In general, employees are busy, but the rate of worth while achievement remains low, not exactly what is needed during these times.

Employees must avoid the pitfall of continual introspection and instead turn their focus outward. The single most important step for a corporation struggling through difficult economic times is to know understand and communicate with Customers at a much deeper and broader level . every business enterprise must be viscerally obsessed with the needs of customers and all possible mechanisms should be employed to recognize both the public and unrecognized needs and desires of current and prospective customers although traditional market research will continue to listening to customers including electronic social networking and empathic research method must also be fully employed. Through intensive study of the broader context of customers lives and activities and a view that extends beyond stele industry orthodoxies and organizational precedent corporation may imagine new and more cost effective solutions to meet customer needs.

Human Resources Reaction

Economics turbulence often means a corporate shift from excess to the essential from routine and comfort and to one of survival. This focus often requires new and unfamiliar priorities, relationships and methods. Corporate leaders are often tasked with creating the strategies to undergird these shifts, meaning making difficult decision, initiating new and sometimes unpopular strategies, all within sustainable budgets. While the activities of the human resource department ara always important to supporting corporate leadership and the organization, ther effort are essential during difficult economic times .the importance of human resource department are always important to supporting corporate leadership and the organization, their efforts are essential during difficult economic times. The importance of human resources transcends the traditional provision of employee cost data to executives during corporate downsizing. To ensure the company thrives in the future, human resources must play a new and expanded role in employee hiring, corporate organization, training , and institutional learning as detailed below:

Employee Recruitment and Hiring

In times of fiscal stress, every new hire bears substantial consequences, both positive and negative, for the organization. In the past,· corporations believed a uniform workforce promoted harmony, unity, and efficiency, and they relied on observable outward characteristics to determine who was the "right sort of person" to fit into the organization. In most industries, current hiring procedures both existing character and orientation of a company, but they do not necessarily strengthen it. The purpose of hiring is quantitative expansion, but qualitative expansion, including enlarging the range of a company's capabilities and the breadth of its vision , is far more important. Employees are the locus of innovative ideas in a corporation and those ideas are limited by employees' rational boundaries. To hire the appropriate mix of employees to support successful innovation and change, there must be internationality in the identification of needed capabilities and recruitment of employees with those characteristics. The concept of diversity itself must be reframed. Innovation driving diversity must include age, race, country of origin, sex, education and other salient personal characteristics. Extreme diversity in a workforce may help the company imagine entirely novel and cost effective solutions to customer needs as it abandons the historical trajectory and the shackles of precedent tradition and orthodoxy.

Corporate Organization

Because most large companies are modeled after the historical organizational hierarchy of the military, rail-roads, and mills, employee roles are rigidly and permanently defined with clear responsibilities, economic incentives tightly linked to those responsibilities and ongoing tasks. Status is primarily based on size of staff and budget. By reorganizing around projects, work has defined limitations, requires extensive interaction with peers and clients, employee capabilities may more easily flow to where they are most useful, and status is based on size of staff and budget. By reorganizing around projects, work has defined limitations, requires extensive interaction with peers and clients, employee capabilities may more easily flow to where they are most useful , and status is based on solving difficult customer problems. Human resources is tasked with developing, initiating, and assessing the appropriateness of the organizational structure, and can make substantive changes to eliminate corporate silos, enhance internal communications, and subsequently speed the development and release of new products and services valuable to customers.

Employee Training

Once corporate executives have defined reality and clarified the focus, priorities and plans of the company, it is a crucial role of human resources to consistently and efficiently educate all employees about the plans and the role of each employee in achieving these important goals. Priorities and plans must be communicated continually through a wide variety of media for them to be appropriately internalized by employees, and substantive training is necessary for employees to develop new and mutually profitable relationships with customers. The ability to communicate, especially in light of the economy where tensions can become strained, becomes of primary important, not only to keep the vision and strategies of the organization front and center, but also to alleviate any questions employees might be having often the leadership of organizations forget this imperative and the vision and strategies can become convoluted, yet if time is taken to be ever present and communicative, employees will feel more engaged in the process as well as the organization.

Institutional Learning

A foundational pillar of companies who succeed during economic downturns is that they internally share information effectively. A diverse employee base and well-de-signed plans are valuable only if the fresh, new ideas acquired by employee can be received , stored and efficiently shared with others in the organization. Institutional learning systems may be either formal or informal , and are crucial to positive organizational change. For learning systems to be rendered effective , internal barriers to communication must be intentionally disassembled and new, non-traditional alliances developed both internally and externally.

Challenges and Opportunities for the Future

Severe economic downturns often provide substantial clarity about the historical internal machinations of the corporation. That which was hidden or thought inconsequential is suddenly thrust onto center stage. The economic turbulence has created many challenges , and yet opportunities also will exist for those who actively seek to be engaged in the process, pro-actively seeking solutions to improve the long-term financial health of the organization. Although human resources has been an important element of the company, it should not "waste a crisis" but should instead seize the opportunity to prove its extraordinary value to the organization. Human resources must serve as the dynamic bridge between the profitable future courageously outlined by corporate executives and the nervous employee base that must somehow translate plans into successful products and services. By aggressively refining policies and procedures related to hiring, organizing the corporation in new and more efficient ways, focusing employees' efforts on new corporate priorities and plans through comprehensive training, and developing an effective institutional learning program, human resources will clearly enunciate its own value to the company.

New Challenges faced by the Indian Mangers in this Era of Global Crisis

While the subsequent global credit crisis (in 2008) has impacted the enthusiasm for such mega-deals for the moment, smaller acquisitions of strategic importance continue to be finalized , with an eye on long-term growth. Let us now examine what this means for the operating mangers in these organizations. The Dominance of the Customer:- A key feature of today's global markets is the emerging dominance of the customer over the companies that compete for her attention and business. Global Crisis has resulted in a vast shift in power-away from the companies , and towards the customer. The Indian manager has to understand and accept this fact, and discard any beliefs to the contrary that he may have. The Importance of the Brand:- As the customer gets used to making choices on a global basis, the brand of the product has become significantly more important than the country of origin or manufacture. Many bands have succeeded in shedding their "nationality" that is the country from which they originally emerged.

The Need for a Global Mindset during Global Crisis

Faced with the global customer , and global competition the Indian manager in the emerging Indian MNC has to work on developing a "global mindset" which is essential for getting a good understanding of today's business dynamics, and developing suitable growth strategies.

Some key elements of his global mindset for the managers during global crisis are as follows:-

- He must being open-minded
- He must be Comfortable with diversity
- He must be Interested in history, geography, and global phenomena
- He should be a person of Integrity- in both intellectual and ethical matters.
- He should have the capability of Abstract thinking.
- He should posses Risk-taking capability.

- He must have managerial skill
- He should have Cultural sensitivity.

Conclusion

Global competition is a complex dynamic process which could not characterize competitive capabilities amongst nations particularly when economic theory and logic rely in restrictive assumptions which have evaporated with open global economy, which today, is the reality of changing times. Globalization has opened up the world as a market place for us, be it for products , people or financial resources. If we have to capitalize on this opportunity, we have to become globally competitive, be it, cost, quality, delivery or any other business parameters.

In the global market place, the competitiveness has been driven by the technology chain over time, which moved from high technology towards commodity classification. Survival in the global competitive market is to be planned through evolutionary process of differentiation and integration, which is further reinforced by the decreasing rigidity of national boundaries. Individuals organizations need this dynamic perspective in the management of the global process. For global competitiveness we need global vision, exceptional human resource capital and consumer insight. Management has to be aware of the measures necessary to be taken for achieving and retaining global competitive edge. Systematic innovation requires a willingness to look on change as an opportunity. Innovations that succeed to so by exploiting change and not attempting to force it.

Will there be problems and pitfalls along the way? Absolutely, and certainly these bumps are eminently manageable. We would do well to remember that there is always hope: some suggest the economic turbulence has an end in sight , perhaps at or near the end of 2009, while others suggest 2010 will be much brighter. Either way, with same creativity, savvy, and good old-fashioned tenacity- it just might prove to be the "finest hour" for human resources. While the world may never be the same and some industries and corporations may face permanent economic white water, the efforts of human resources focused on making the company more nimble and knowledgeable ultimately will help it be more effective and profitable regardless of the new realities ahead.

During the global crisis the managers would need to gear up, in a very short time, the knowledge base needed to face the new challenges they would inevitably face in multiple global markets.

The success of the strategies to be followed in time of meltdown would depend on the ability of their mangers to understand the dominance of the customer and the importance of the brand. Additionally, Indian mangers should develop a "global mindset" that would enable them to understand and manage cultural differences, and lead their organization teams to success.

References

Jorde T. and D. Teece (1992), "Antitrust, Innovation and Competitiveness", New Your: Oxford University Press. Kathuria, V. (1999), "Competition Sans Competitiveness: Need for a Policy," Economic and Political Weekly, Vol. XXXIV, No. 45, Nov.6, pp. 3175-3177.

Rao, V.V. Bhanoji (1993), India's Economic Future-Government , People and Attitudes, New Delhi: Tata Megraw Hill Publishing Co. Ltd.

Sanyal, K.K. (1993), "Paradox of Competitiveness and Globalisation of Underdevelopment," Economic and Political Weekly, Vol. XXVIII, No. 25, June, pp. 1326-1330.

Stiglitz, J. (2002), Globalisation and its Discontents, London Penguin Books.

The ICFAI Journals of 2008&09

Globalization of Business-Durring JH (1993)

Levitt Theodore (1983) 'The globalization of markets", Harvard Business review yipgeorge 5% 1989 Global stategy would of Nations" soon Management Review.

Ohmae, Kenichi (2003), The Borderless World, London, UK: Pro-file Books.

Sirkin , Harold L; Hemerling, James W and Bhattarcharya Arindam K (2008). Globality: Competing with Everyone from Everywhere for Everything, New York: Headline/Business Plus.

16

Global Economic Crisis and Its Impact on the Indian Economy: An Analysis

O.P. Shukla, Vinayak Kant Mishra

The economy which had witnessed high growth till 2007, has slowed down. The GDP growth rate of the last year (2008) has decelerated significantly. Now, it will take longer time for our country to achieve higher growth as witnessed before the crisis. The global economic crisis has been particularly severe in the financial sector however its repercussions are on the real sector of the economy particularly in the export-import sector in the economy. The crisis is global per se. The main cause of the crisis relates to unsettled financial conditions prevailing at the end of 2007, combined with the persistence of global imbalances, have raised the prospect of a slow down in some of the major economies over the period.

IMF projects that the GDP growth of Emerging Market Economies (EMEs) will decelerate to a range of 1.5-2.5% in 2009. This downturn is clear indication that the forces of Globalisation are too strong for the decoupling hypothesis to work. Even across EMEs, there are wide variations - several countries are likely to post negative growth, while significant positive contributions are expected from China and India. The crisis spread from advanced countries to EMEs, through both trade and finance channels. The G-20 commitment to desist from all forms of protectionism and to maintain open trade and investment regimes is a source comfort to EMEs in an otherwise discouraging external environment.

As per RBI estimation, India's GDP growth for 2009-10 would be in the range of 6.5-6.76%, which, however, gets us way ahead of many countries. The RBI said any upturn in the growth momentum is unlikely in view of the projected contraction in Global demand during 2009.

During 2008-09, Indian economy is characterized by lower growth in agriculture sector 1.6% (4.90% last year); manufacturing sector by 2.4% (8.2% last year) and tertiary sector by around 9% (around 11% last year); losing Foreign Instuitional Investors (FIls) and widening trade deficit ($93 bn). Besides, remittances have also fallen. There, however, have been some positive signs, as machinery equipment (other than transport equipment) exhibited double digit growth. In terms of use-based classification, capital goods production registered double digit growth. The community services including social and personal services has increased by 13.1%, as compared to 6.8% last year, reflecting the payout of the sixth pay commission award and other fiscal stimulus measures.

The present paper therefore, seeks to assess the impact of global economic crisis on the employment scenario and exports in India particularly.This paper is being divided into four sections. The introductory section attempts to peep into the nature of the present economic crisis. The second section would look into the brief review of the literature . The third section would try to assess the impact of global economic crisis on the employment scenario and exports of India . The concluding section would thereby highlight some policy responses and conclusions and some suggestions for policy implications.

Global Economic Crisis

After a long spell of growth, the Indian economy is experiencing a downturn. Industrial growth is faltering, the current account deficit is widening, foreign exchange reserves are depleting and the rupee is depreciating. These features can also be directly related to the current international crisis. The most immediate effect of that crisis on India has been an outflow of foreign institutional investment from the equity market. Foreign institutional investors, who need to retrench assets in order to cover losses in their home countries and are seeking heavens of safety in an uncertain environment, have become major sellers in Indian markets.

In 2007-08, net FII inflows into India amounted to $20.3 billion. As compared with this, they pulled out $11.1 billion during the first nine-and-a-half months of calendar year 2008, of which $8.3 billion occurred over the first six-and-a-half months of financial year 2008-09 (April 1 to October 16). This has had two effects: in the stock market and in the currency market. Given the importance of FII investment in driving Indian stock markets and the fact that cumulative investments by FIIs stood at $66.5 billion at the beginning of this calendar year, the pullout triggered a collapse in stock prices. As a result, the Sensex fell from its closing peak of 20,873 on January 8, 2008, to less than 10,000 by October 17, 2008 .

In addition, the withdrawal by the FIIs led to a sharp depreciation of the rupee. Between January 1 and October 16, 2008, the RBI reference rate for the rupee fell by nearly 25 per cent, even relative to a weak currency like the dollar, from Rs 39.20 to the dollar to Rs 48.86. This was despite the sale of dollars by the RBI, which was reflected in a decline of $25.8 billion in its foreign currency assets between the end of March 2008 and October 3, 2008. It could be argued that the $275 billion the RBI still has in its kitty is adequate to stall and reverse any further depreciation if needed. But given the sudden exit by the FIIs, the RBI is clearly not keen to deplete its reserves too fast and risk a foreign exchange crisis.

The result has been the observed sharp depreciation of the rupee. While this depreciation may be good for India's exports that are adversely affected by the slowdown in global markets, it is not so good for those who have accumulated foreign exchange payment commitments. Nor does it assist the Government's effort to rein in inflation. A second route through which the global financial crisis could affect India is through the exposure of Indian banks or banks operating in India to the impaired assets resulting from the sub-prime crisis. Unfortunately, there are no clear estimates of the extent of that exposure, giving room for rumour in determining market trends. Thus, ICICI Bank was the victim of a run for a short period because of rumours that sub-prime exposure had badly damaged its balance sheet, although these rumours have been strongly denied by the bank.

So far the RBI has claimed that the exposure of Indian banks to assets impaired by the financial crisis is small. According to reports, the RBI had estimated that as a result of exposure to collateralised debt obligations and credit default swaps, the combined mark-to-market losses of Indian banks at the end of July was around $450 million. Given the aggressive strategies adopted by the private sector banks, the MTM losses incurred by public sector banks were estimated at $90 million, while that for private banks was around $360 million. As yet these losses are on paper, but the RBI believes that even if they are to be provided for, these banks are well capitalised and can easily take the hit.

In this uncertain environment, banks and financial institutions concerned about their balance sheets, have been cutting back on credit, especially the huge volume of housing, automobile and retail credit provided to individuals. According to RBI figures, the rate of growth of auto loans fell from close to 30 per cent over the year ending June 30, 2008, to as low as 1.2 per cent.

Loans to finance consumer durables purchases fell from around Rs 6,000 crore in the year to June 2007, to a little over Rs 4,000 crore up to June 2009. Direct housing loans, which had increased by 25 per cent during 2006-07, decelerated to 11 per cent growth in 2007-08 and 12 per cent over the year ending June 2008. It is only in an area like credit-card receivables, where banks are unable to control the growth of credit, that expansion was, at 43 per cent, quite high over the year ending June 2008, even though it was lower than the 50 per cent recorded over the previous year.

It is known that credit-financed housing investment and credit-financed consumption have been important drivers of growth in recent years, and underpin the 9 per cent growth trajectory India has been experiencing. The reticence of lenders to increase their exposure in markets to which they are already overexposed and the fears of increasing payment commitments in an uncertain economic environment on the part of potential borrowers are bound to curtail debt-financed consumption and investment. This could slow growth significantly.

Thus, the recession generated by the financial crisis in the advanced economies as a group and the US in particular, has adversely affected India's exports (Table-1), especially its exports of software and IT-enabled services, more than 60 per cent of which are directed to the US. International banks and financial institutions in the US and EU are important sources of demand for such services, and the difficulties they face will result in some curtailment of their demand. Further, the nationalization of many of these banks is likely to increase the pressure to reduce outsourcing in order to keep jobs in the developed countries.

And the slowing of growth outside of the financial sector too will have implications for both merchandise and services exports. The net result would be a smaller export stimulus and a widening trade deficit. While these trends are still in process, their effects are already being felt. They are not the only causes for the downturn the economy is experiencing, but they are important contributory factors (Table-1). Yet, this does not justify the argument that India's difficulties are all imported. They are induced by domestic policy as well. The extent of imported difficulties would have been far less if the Government had not increased the vulnerability of the country to external shocks by drastically opening up the real and financial sectors. It is disconcerting; therefore, that when faced with this crisis the Government is not rethinking its own liberalization strategy, despite the backlash against neo-liberalism worldwide.

Export of India has declined by around 20%. However, most affected sectors are:

Table 1
Exports Decline

Tea	-20%
Handicrafts	-70%
Carpets	-32%
Oil Mills	-50%
Man-made Yarn	-17%
Cotton Yarn	-19%
Marine Products	-19%

Source: Economic Survey (2008-09)

Table 2
Sector-wise Break Up of Decline in Employment

Industry	*Apr.,08–Mar., 09*	*Apr.–Sept., 08*	*Oct.–Dec., 08*	*Jan.–Mar., 09*
Textile	0.307	0.206	-0.107	0.208
Leather	-0.019	0.008	0.006	-0.033
Metals	-0.130	-0.001	-0.100	-0.029
Automobile	-0.175	-0.008	-0.169	0.002
Gems and Jewellery	-0.104	0.022	-0.159	0.033
Transport	0.007	0.007	0.004	-0.004
IT-BPO	0.416	0.258	0.066	0.092
Handloom-Power Loom	-0.023	-0.014	-0.016	0.007
Overall	0.279	0.479	-0.477	0.277

The average decline in employment was 1.01%.

Source: Report on Effect of Economic Slowdown on Employment in India, Ministry of Labour and Employment Labour Bureau, GOI, May, 2009

Brief Review of Literature

C.P. Chandrasekhar and Jayati Ghosh (2009) consider the possible negative effects of the crisis on India and whether the Government's response so far has been appropriate. When the financial crisis erupted in a comprehensive manner on Wall Street, there was some premature triumphalism among Indian policymakers and media persons. It was argued that India would be relatively immune to this crisis, because of the *"strong fundamentals"* of the economy and the supposedly well-regulated banking system. This argument was emphasized by the Finance Minister and others even when other developing countries in Asia clearly experienced significant negative impact, through transmission of stock market turbulence and domestic credit stringency. These effects have been most marked among those developing countries where the foreign ownership of banks is already well advanced, and when US-style financial sectors with the merging of banking and investment functions have been created.

While India is not likely to face a financial meltdown of the kind that was nearly experienced in the US, the global financial crisis will certainly have an impact.

In the *Global Employment Trends Update,* May 2009 the International Labour Office (ILO) issued new labour market projections for 2009, showing a further increase in unemployment, working poor and those in vulnerable employment. In the ILO's Annual International Labour Conference, held in Geneva on 3-19 June, Juan Somavia, the ILO Director-General emphasized the need to consider an emergency "global jobs pact" designed to promote a coordinated policy response to the global jobs crisis.

"We are seeing an unprecedented increase in unemployment and the number of workers at risk of falling into poverty around the world this year. This is cause for grave concern. To avoid a global social recession we need a global jobs pact to address this crisis, and mitigate its effects on people. The choice is ours and the time to act is now".

Juan Somavia, Director-General, ILO.

ILO revised its unemployment projections to levels ranging from 210 million to 239 million unemployed worldwide in 2009, corresponding to global unemployment rates of 6.5 and 7.4 per cent respectively. The Trends report projects an increase of between 39 and 59 million unemployed people since 2007, as the most likely range. Actual outcomes will depend on the effectiveness of fiscal expenditures decided by governments and on a functioning financial sector. Updated projections of working poverty across the world indicate that 200 million workers are at risk of joining the ranks of people living on less than USD 2 per day between 2007 and 2009. The crisis is hitting youth hard. The number of unemployed youth is expected to increase by between 11 and 17 million from 2008 to 2009. The youth unemployment rate is projected to increase from around

12 per cent in 2008 to a range of 14 to 15 per cent in 2009. The ILO cautioned that past experience suggested a considerable lag of 4 to 5 years on average in the recovery in labour markets after economic recovery. There was a risk of the global jobs crisis "persisting" for the next several years. This is why the International Labour Conference is considering a global jobs pact aimed at placing employment creation and social protection at the centre of recovery policies. The aim of the pact is to make sure that both the extraordinary stimulus measures together with other government policies better address the needs of people who need protection and work in order to accelerate combined economic and employment recovery.

The ILO report said 2009 will represent the worst global performance on record in terms of employment creation. The report underlined that the global labour force is expanding at an average rate of 1.6 per cent, equivalent to around 45 million new entrants annually, while global employment growth decreased to 1.4 per cent in 2008 and is expected to drop further to between 0 and 1 per cent in 2009. The ILO also said that in the 2009-2015 periods, around 300 million new jobs will have to be created just to absorb the growth in the labour force.

The ILO Report also provides for the region wise findings regarding the impact of global economic crisis on various regions. Some of the key findings are as follows:

- In the Developed Economies & European Union, total employment is projected to shrink this year by between 1.3 per cent and 2.7 per cent. The region is likely to account for 35 to 40 per cent of the total global increase in unemployment, despite accounting for less than 16 per cent of the global labour force.
- In Central and South Eastern Europe (non-EU) & CIS the number of unemployed could increase by as much as 35 per cent in 2009. Total employment is projected to shrink by between 1 and 2.8 per cent.
- In East Asia, it is estimated that 267 million people, representing more than one third of the total employed, were living on less than 2 dollars per day

at the onset of the crisis. There were around 12 times as many people in vulnerable employment as in unemployment.

- In South East Asia and the Pacific a fairly moderate increase in unemployment is projected for this region, though workers and firms in export-oriented industries are being hit hard.
- In South Asia, approximately 5 per cent of the labour force is unemployed but nearly 15 times as many workers are employed, but in vulnerable employment. The number of workers living on less than USD 2 per day is projected to grow by up to 58 million between 2007 and 2009.
- In Latin America, the unemployment rate is projected to rise from 7.1 per cent in 2007 to between 8.4 and 9.2 per cent in 2009.
- The ILO projects an increase in unemployment of up to 25 per cent in the Middle East and up to 13 per cent in North Africa in 2009 compared to 2007. Vulnerable employment is also expected to increase in both regions. Around one in three workers in each region are in vulnerable employment and this ratio could rise to as much as 4 in 10.
- In sub-Saharan Africa, an estimated 73 per cent of the region's workers are in vulnerable employment, and this could rise to more than 77 per cent this year. The crisis poses a serious threat to investment in infrastructure and capital goods that are crucial for the region's continued development. The potential harm of global trade protectionism in response to the crisis should not be understated.

According to *Rajiv Kumar (2009)* the impact of the global crisis has been transmitted to the Indian economy through three distinct channels viz. the financial sector, exports and exchange rates. The Indian banking sector was not overly exposed to the sub-prime crisis. While exports of both goods and services, still account for only about 22 percent of the Indian GDP, their multiplier effect for economic activity is quite large as the import content is not as high as for example in the case of Chinese exports. Therefore, an export slump will bring down GDP growth rate in this year. The third transmission channel is the exchange rate as the Indian Rupee has come under pressure. In terms of policy response, there is not much room for further fiscal policy action as the consolidated fiscal deficit of the central and state governments in 2008-09 is already about 11 percent of the GDP. Any further increase in fiscal deficit to GDP ratio could invite a sharp downgrading of India's credit rating and a loss of business confidence. It is more important to focus policy attention on removing some of the many remaining structural bottlenecks on raising the potential GDP growth rate. Essentially this will imply efforts at improving the investment climate both for domestic and foreign investors; removing the entry barriers for the entry of corporate investment in education and vocational training; improving the delivery of public goods and services and expanding physical infrastructure capacities including a major effort at improving connectivity in the rural regions.

Bibek Debroy (2009) emphasized that it is widely accepted now that the slowdown in the global economy has impacted the Indian economy though not as badly as those in countries which are more globally integrated. Impacts in India are spatially as well as sectorally differentiated. Despite a variety of media reports about job losses, there is little empirical evidence of this having occurred outside of the export sector, meaning the export of goods sector. It should also be noted that export growth is not evenly spread throughout the country, but is rather concentrated in clusters where the impact of job loss is felt more acutely. At this stage, it is still unclear as to how temporary are these job losses. The media reports about job losses in IT, ITES and financial services are, quantitatively, not that significant. On the positive side, the rural sector, particularly in rice and wheat-growing irrigated areas, seems to have offered some kind of a cushion to India in the growth slowdown. Hopefully, the present episode will lead to policy changes that provide necessary insurance cushions, collectively or individually.

According to *Vijay Mahajan (2009)* the impact of the global economic downturn is beginning to be pervasive. However, its impact for the lower income segments of the population in India seems to be the largest for those employed in export-oriented sectors like diamond polishing, garments, carpets and hosiery. In sectors which cater to the lower end of domestic demand of roti (food), kapda (clothing) aur (and) makaan (shelter) there has been little or no impact. The good news is that the demand for cereals remained robust, despite the slowdown. There does not seem to be any danger of job losses in the food and agriculture sector. In the clothing and textile sector, while demand in the lower end of the market continues to be buoyant, it is not so up-market. The same contrast—stable demand and employment at the lower-end and a downturn at the higher end—can be seen in the makaan or the building materials and construction sector. Going beyond roti, kapda aur makaan, the non-farm sectors most affected are the export-oriented handmade carpet industry, tourism and retail.

K. Seeta Prabhu (2009) in his article emphasized that as the full implications of the global financial crisis unfold, questions are being raised on its impact on India's human development and achievement of the Millennium Development Goals (MDGs). If the national poverty line is used as the definition, the country is generally considered to be well on track to reduce the headcount ratio of poverty, but not if the World Bank's estimates of proportion of population below the newly defined extreme poverty line of USD1.25 per day is considered.

Efforts to Control Crisis

Monetary Policy Response

The Reserve Bank's policy response was aimed at containing the contagion from the outside-to keep the domestic money and credit markets functioning normally and see that the liquidity stress did not trigger solvency cascades. In particular, it targeted three objectives; first, to maintain a comfortable rupee liquidity position; second, to augment foreign exchange liquidity; and third, to maintain a policy framework that would keep credit delivery on track so as to arrest the moderation in growth. This marked a reversal of Reserve Bank's policy stance from monetary tightening in response to heightened inflationary pressures of the previous period to monetary easing in response to easing inflationary pressures and moderation in growth in the current cycle.

Policy packages of RBI included, both conventional and unconventional measures. On the conventional side, we reduced the policy interest rates aggressively and rapidly, reduced the quantum of bank reserves impounded by the central bank and expanded and liberalized the refinance facilities for export credit. Measures aimed at managing forex liquidity included an upward adjustment of the interest rate ceiling on the foreign currency deposits by non-resident Indians, substantially relaxing the external commercial borrowings (ECB) regime for corporates, and allowing non-banking financial companies and housing finance companies access to foreign borrowing.

The important among the many unconventional measures taken by the Reserve Bank of India are a rupee-dollar swap facility for Indian banks to give them comfort in managing their short-term foreign funding requirements, an exclusive refinance window as also a special purpose vehicle for supporting non-banking financial companies, and expanding the lendable resources available to apex finance institutions for refinancing credit extended to small industries, housing and exports. Reflecting the rapid turn of events that could impair assets down the line, we reversed the counter–cyclical regulatory measures introduced in 2006.

Government's Fiscal Stimulus

Over the last five years, both the central and sate governments in India have made a serious efforts to reverse the fiscal excesses of the past. At the heart of these efforts was the Fiscal Responsibility and Budget Management (FRBM) Act which mandated a calibrated road map towards fiscal sustainability.

The depth and extraordinary impact of this crisis, however, clearly indicated the need for counter cyclical public spending. Accordingly, the central government invoked the emergency provisions of the FRBM Act to seek relaxation from the fiscal targets and launched two fiscal stimulus packages in December 2008 and January 2009. These fiscal stimulus packages, together mounting to about 3 per cent of GDP, included additional public spending, government guaranteed funds for infrastructure spending, cuts in indirect taxes, expanded guarantee cover for credit to micro and small enterprises, and additional support to exporters. There stimulus packages came on top of an already announced expanded safety-net for rural poor. A farm loan waiver package and salary increases for government staff, all of which too should stimulate demand.

Conclusion and Suggestions

Thus , to conclude, due to crisis, Indian growth rate declined to 6.5% in 2008 compared to 9.3% in 2007. Demand for labour has fallen causing growth in unemployment. Job losses in export and services sectors particularly IT sector has affected employment tremendously. Reverse migration from urban to rural areas has observed. State intervention is becoming necessary to augment consumption and production patterns. Reform measures have to be adopted to restore stability. More fiscal stimulation packages are required to manage real economy effects. For ensuring stability, banks are required to function within the prudential limits of their inter-bank liabilities in relation to their net worth. It is also necessary to fix ceiling on debt flows to curb undesirable arbitrage. Direct public expenditure should be created towards employment schemes, rural and urban infrastructure and other social upliftment measures.

References

Bala, Shashi (2004), "Skill Development Systems in India", The Indian Journal of Labour Economics, Vol 47, No 4, Oct-Dec.

Bibek Debroy (2009), "*Growth Downturn and Its Effects* ", Business Line, Internet Edition.

Brewer, Laura (2005),"Youth at Risk: The Role of Skill Development in facilitating the Transition to Work", In Focus Programme on Skills, Knowledge and Employability, Skills Working Paper No 19, I L O, Geneva.

Chadha, Meenu (2007), "Developing Employability Skills", Employment News, October 6-12.

Chandrasekhar C. P. and Jayati Ghosh (2009), "India and the Global Financial Crisis", Business Line, Internet Edition.

European Commission (2000), Lisbon European Council, 23 and 24 March: Presidency Conclusions, Brussels.

Fernandes, Oscar (2007), Minister of State for Labour and Employment, in a Conference organized by FICCI, Oct 5, New Delhi.

Gazier, Bernard (1999), "Employability: An Evolutionary Notion, an Interactive Concept", in Bernard

GOI (2001), "Report of Task Force on Employment Opportunities", Planning Commission, New Delhi.

GOI (2001), "Department-Related Parliamentary Standing Committee On Human Resource Development Hundred -Thirteenth Report On Technical Education" (Presented in The Rajya Sabha On 13th December, 2001),Rajya Sabha Secretariat, New Delhi.

GOI (2002), "Targeting Ten Million Employment Opportunities per Year", Planning Commission, New Delhi.

GOI (2007), "Eleventh Five Year Plan", Planning Commission, New Delhi.

GOI (2007), "Towards Faster and More Inclusive Growth: An Approach Paper to 11th Five Year Plan", Planning Commission, Government of India.

ILO (2009), Economically Active Population Estimates and Projections 1980-2020 (EAPEP), Geneva. http://laborsta.ilo.org/.

India Labor Report (2007), "The Youth Unemployability Crisis", A Report by Team Lease Services.

Jayati Ghosh (2009): *"Global Crisis and the Indian Economy "*, Business Line, Internet Edition.

K. Seeta Prabhu (2009), *"Impact of Financial Crisis on India's March Towards MDGs "*, Business Line, Internet Edition.

Karnik Kiran (2005), "Skill Shortage the Looming Challenge for India" NASSCO2M - McKinsey Report.

Khorakiwala, Habil (2007), "Employability, Not Jobs Will be Our Issue", Business Line, January 12.

National Commission on Labour (2002), "Report of the Study Group on Skill Development, Training and Workers Education", Ministry of Labour, Government of India.

Rajiv Kumar (2009), *"Global Financial and Economic Crisis: Impact on India and Policy Response"*, Business Line, Internet Edition.

17

Economic Crisis and Indian Economy Policy Measure Taken By Indian Government-An Assessment

Shobha Jain

When the financial crisis erupted in a comprehensive manner on Wall Street, there was some premature triumphalism among Indian policymakers and media persons. It was argued that India would be relatively immune to this crisis, because of the "strong fundamentals" of the economy and the supposedly well-regulated banking system.

This argument was emphasized by the Finance Minister and others even when other developing countries in Asia clearly experienced significant negative impact, through transmission of stock market turbulence and domestic credit stringency.

These effects have been most marked among those developing countries where the foreign ownership of banks is already well advanced, and when US-style financial sectors with the merging of banking and investment functions have been created.

If India is not in the same position, it is not to the credit of our policymakers, who had in fact wanted to go along the same route. Indeed, for some time now there have been complaints that these "necessary" reforms which would "modernize" the financial sector have been held up because of opposition from the Left parties.

But even though we are slightly better protected from financial meltdown, largely because of the still large role of the nationalized banks and other controls on domestic finance, there is certainly little room for complacency.

The recent crash in the Sensex is not simply an indicator of the impact of international contagion. There have been warning signals and signs of fragility in Indian finance for some time now, and these are likely to be compounded by trends in the real economy.

What is Economic Crisis

After a long spell of growth, the Indian economy is experiencing a downturn. Industrial growth is faltering, inflation remains at double-digit levels, the current account deficit is widening, foreign exchange reserves are depleting and the rupee is depreciating.

The last two features can also be directly related to the current international crisis. The most immediate effect of that crisis on India has been an outflow of foreign institutional investment from the equity market. Foreign institutional investors, who need to retrench assets in order to cover losses in their home countries and are seeking havens of safety in an uncertain environment, have become major sellers in Indian markets.

In 2007-08, net FII inflows into India amounted to $20.3 billion. As compared with this, they pulled out $11.1 billion during the first nine-and-a-half months of calendar year 2008, of which $8.3 billion occurred over the first six-and-a-half months of financial year 2008-09. This has had two effects: in the stock market and in the currency market.

Impact of Global Financial Crisis on Indian Economy

The *Present financial crisis* has been called the most serious financial crisis since the Great Depression by leading economists, with its global effects characterized by the failure of key businesses, declines in consumer wealth estimated in the trillions of U.S. dollars, substantial financial commitments incurred by governments, and a significant decline in economic activity. Many causes have been proposed, with varying weight assigned by experts. Both market-based and regulatory solutions have been implemented or are under consideration, while significant risks remain for the world economy.

The impact of the global crisis has been transmitted to the Indian economy through three distinct channels, viz., the financial sector, exports and exchange rates. The financial sector including the banking sector, equity markets, external commercial borrowings and remittances has not remained unscathed though fortunately, the Indian banking sector was not overly exposed to the sub-prime crisis. Only one of the larger banks, ICICI, was partly affected but managed to thwart a crisis because of its strong balance sheet and timely action by the government, which virtually guaranteed its deposits. The equity markets have seen a near 60 percent decline in the index and a wiping off of about USD1.3 trillion in market capitalization since January 2008 when the Sensex had peaked at about 21,000. This is primarily due to the withdrawal of about USD12 billion from the market by foreign portfolio investors between September and December 2008. The foreign investors withdrew these funds in order to strengthen the balance sheet of their parent companies. Commercial credit, both for trade finance and medium-term advances from foreign banks has virtually dried-up. This has had to be replaced with credit lines from domestic banks but at higher interest costs and has caused the Rupee to depreciate raising the cost of existing foreign loans. Finally, while the latest numbers are not yet available, remittances from overseas Indians have reportedly fallen as oil producing economies in the Gulf and West Asia begin to suffer from decline in oil prices. The second transmission of the global downturn to the Indian economy has been through the steep decline in demand for India's exports in its major markets. The first sector to be hit was the gems and jewellery which felt the impact in November itself and where more than 300,000 workers have lost their jobs. The negative impact has since covered other export-oriented sectors garments and textiles, leather, handicrafts, and auto components. The 21 percent decline in exports in February 2009 is the steepest fall in exports for the last two decades. It is unlikely that exports will recover within this year. While exports of both goods and services, still account for only about 22 percent of the Indian GDP, their multiplier effect for economic activity is quite large as the import content is not as high as for example in the case of Chinese exports. Therefore, an export slump will bring down GDP growth rate in this year. The third transmission channel is the exchange rate as the Rupee has come under pressure with the outflow of portfolio investments, higher foreign exchange demand by Indian entrepreneurs seeking to replace external Commercial borrowing by domestic financing, and the consequent decline in foreign exchange reserves. This is likely to continue because current account will remain in Deficit and the capital account, which has been in deficit in the second and third quarters of 2008-09, will not generate the needed surplus to cover the current account deficit. This will imply further drawing down of foreign exchange reserves and continued downward pressure on the exchange rate. However, with foreign exchange reserves Remaining at 110 percent of total external debt at the end of December 2008, investment sentiments should not be unduly affected in the near-term. The nearly 25 percent Depreciation in the Rupee's exchange rate has partially nullified the benefits from the decline in global oil and gas prices and increased the cost of commercial borrowings.

The weaker Rupee should encourage our exporters and it is possible that with imports declining as sharply as exports, the country's trade deficit may actually improve in the short-run and the external sector balance may remain stable and not pose any major policy issue. Overall, it would be fair to say that the timing of the external shock from the global economic downturn has been rather unfortunate. Coming right on the heels of a policy induced contraction in economic activity, its initial impact, as reflected in the third quarter GDP growth falling to 5.3 percent and the steep decline in exports, has been perhaps exaggerated. This negative impact has been, to an extent, ameliorated by the quick policy response both by the RBI and the Central government. The RBI has infused about USD80 billion, as additional liquidity by cutting the CRR, lowering the SLR and unwinding the MSS. The RBI has also signaled its expansionary preference by cutting its repo rate, at which it lends funds to commercial banks from nine to five percent in less than six months. The reverse-repo rate has also been brought down to 3.5 percent to discourage banks from parking overnight funds with the RBI. Three fiscal stimuli have been announced between November 2008 to February 2009. These amount to about 1.3 percent of the GDP. However, to these stimulus packages we should also add the fiscal outlay of measures announced in the 2008-09 Budget in February 2008. These included some measures that implied a hefty transfer of purchasing power to the farmers and to the rural sector in general. These included, farm loan waivers, funds allocated to the National Rural Employment Guarantee Scheme, Bharat Nirman , Prime Minister's Rural Road Programme, and a large increase In subsidies on account of fertilizers and electricity supplied to the farmers. All this measures, taken more out of political considerations and not in response to the global crisis, have, nevertheless, helped to shore up rural demand for both consumer durables and non-durables. Some of us at the ICRIER have used a model of leading economic indicators to forecast GDP growth for India1. We have modified the model to not only incorporate the impact of the external shock provided by the global economic downturn but also to take in to account the mitigating impact of the monetary and fiscal measures taken by the government. According to this model, Indian economy will grow by about 6.3 percent in 2008-09. The Economic Advisory Council to the Prime Minister has now also brought down its estimate of 2008-09 GDP growth to 6.5 to seven percent and not 7.1 percent as given by CSO in its advanced estimates and used for budget formation by the finance ministry. The GDP growth is likely to further decline to between 4.8 to 5.5 percent in 2009-10. Other agencies like the IMF, the World Bank and the ADB have also estimated Indian GDP growth in 2009-10 at similar levels in their latest forecasts released in March 2009. Thus, Indian economy will come down from the nine percent trend that it had achieved in the last four years. The growth targets for the 11th Five-Year Plan will also have to be surely lowered.

There is not much room for further fiscal policy action as the consolidated fiscal deficit of the central and state governments in 2008-09 is already about 11 percent of the GDP. This is likely to rise further as further necessary public expenditures are announced in the next budget and economic activity slows down. Any further increase in fiscal deficit to GDP ratio could invite a sharp downgrading of India's credit rating and a loss of business confidence. With inflation down at less than one percent and likely to remain below five percent in the coming months, there is room for bringing down the repo rate further. However, the more important issue is to try and induce commercial banks to bring down their lending rates as these currently remain at around 10 percent even for their prime borrowers. This is largely a result of the 'crowding out effect' of the large government borrowing programme. To address it, the government may have to consider monetizing its borrowing requirement so that liquidity is not squeezed out of the system. This poses the danger of stoking inflation in the medium-term but perhaps more importantly the breakdown of macro-prudential discipline that has been achieved after considerable effort. It would seem, therefore, that government's options for taking counter cyclical and reflationary measures in the short term are rather limited. In our view, it is more important to focus policy attention on removing some of the many remaining structural bottlenecks on raising the potential GDP growth rate. Essentially, this will imply efforts at improving the investment climate both for domestic and foreign investors; removing the entry barriers for the entry of corporate investment in education and vocational training; improving the delivery of public goods and services and expanding physical infrastructure capacities including a major effort at improving connectivity in the rural regions. These measures will constitute the package of second generation of structural reforms and will enable the Indian economy to climb out of the downward cyclical phase and then to extend the upward phase for a longer period than was achieved in the last cycle.

Measures Taken By Indian Government and Companies

The Government is committed to taking steps for minimizing the impact of the global financial crisis on the Indian economy. To this end, Government has taken a number of steps since October 7, the most recent being the measures announced on 7.12.2008. These included:

(i) Additional plan expenditure up to Rs.20,000 crore in the current year mainly for critical rural, infrastructure and social security schemes such as Pradhan Mantri Gram Sadak Yojana (PMGSY), Jawaharlal Nehru National Urban Renewal Mission (JNNURM), National Rural Employment Guarantee Scheme (NREGS), Indira Awas Yojana, Accelerated Irrigation Benefit Programme and National Social Assistance Programme .

(ii) Several other measures to support exports, housing, Micro, Small & Medium Enterprises and textile sectors.

(iii) Authorizing India Infrastructure Finance Company Limited to raise Rs.10,000 crore to refinance bank lending for infrastructure projects.

Subsequently, other measures have also been taken such as removal of ban on export of cement.

Additional steps are being taken on the monetary, credit and fiscal front to further strengthen the contra-cyclical stance of policy. The Reserve Bank has today announced a set of measures. In addition, with a view to further liberalizing the policy on External Commercial Borrowing, the Government and the RBI have decided:

(a) The 'all-in-cost' ceilings on such borrowing would be removed, under the approval route of RBI;

(b) To facilitate access to funds for the housing sector, the 'development of integrated townships' would be permitted as an eligible end-use of the ECB, under the approval route of RBI;

(c) NBFCs, dealing exclusively with infrastructure financing, would be permitted to access ECB from multilateral or bilateral financial institutions, under the approval route of RBI.

(d) In order to give a boost to the corporate bond market, FII investment limit in rupee denominated corporate bonds in India would be increased from US$6 billion to US$15 billion.

The decisions at points (a) to (c) would be reviewed after June 30, 2009.

The flow of credit to the economy will be further enhanced by the following:

(i) An SPV will be designated shortly to provide liquidity support against investment grade paper to Non Banking Finance Companies fulfilling certain conditions. Details will be announced separately. The scale of liquidity potentially available through this window is Rs.25,000 crore.

(ii) An arrangement will be worked out with leading Public Sector Banks to provide a line of credit to NBFCs specifically for purchase of commercial vehicles.

(iii) Credit targets of Public Sector Banks are being revised upward to reflect the needs of the economy in the present difficult situation. Government will closely monitor, on a fortnightly basis, the provision of sectoral credit by public sector banks.

(iv) Special monthly meetings of State Level Bankers' Committees would be held to oversee the resolution of credit issues of micro, small and medium enterprises by banks. Department of MSME and Department of Financial Services will jointly set up a

Cell to monitor progress on this front. Matters of MSMEs remaining unresolved with the Banks- SME Helpline for more than a fortnight may be brought to the notice of this Cell.

(v) Recently the guarantee cover under Credit Guarantee Scheme for micro and small enterprises on loans was extended from Rs.50 lakh to Rs.1 crore with a guarantee cover of 50 percent. In order to enhance flow of credit to micro enterprises, it has been further decided to increase the guarantee cover extended by Credit Guarantee Fund Trust to 85 percent for credit facility up to Rs.5 lakh. This will benefit about 84 percent of the total number of accounts accorded guarantee cover.

State Governments are facing constraints in financing expenditure because of slower revenue growth. To help maintain the momentum of expenditure at the state government level, states will be allowed to raise in the current financial year additional market borrowings of 0.5 percent of their Gross State Domestic Product (GSDP), amounting to about Rs.30,000 crore, for capital expenditures.

India Infrastructure Finance Company (IIFCL), which has already been authorized to raise Rs.10,000 crore through tax free bonds by 31.03.2009 for refinancing bank lending of longer maturity to eligible infrastructure bid based PPP projects, will be accessing the market next week for raising the first tranche of the amount. This will enable the funding of mainly highways and port projects on hand of about Rs.25,000 crore. To fund additional projects of about Rs.75,000 crore at competitive rates over the next 18 months, IIFCL is being enabled to access in tranches an additional Rs.30,000 crore by way of tax free bonds once funds raised in the current year are effectively utilized.

Exporters are especially hit by recessionary conditions globally. To support exports a number of steps have been taken. As a further measure:

(i) Taking into account the fact that the rupee has appreciated nearly four per cent against the dollar since November 2008, it has been decided to restore DEPB rates to those prevailing prior to November 2008. In order to provide predictability and stability of regime in the short term for future contracts, the DEPB Scheme would be extended till 31.12.2009.

(ii) Duty drawback benefits on certain items including knitted fabrics, bicycles, agricultural hand tools and specified categories of yarn are being enhanced. These changes will take effect retrospectively from September 1, 2008.

(iii) Exporters have raised a number of procedural issues where modification of procedures could reduce delays faced by exporters. To consider these and similar problems, Government has decided to constitute a Committee under the chairmanship of the Finance Secretary including Secretaries of the Departments of Revenue and Commerce to look into and resolve these issues on a fast-track basis.

(iv) EXIM Bank has obtained from RBI a line of credit of Rs.5000 crore and will provide pre-shipment and post-shipment credit, in rupees or dollars, to Indian exporters at competitive rates.

Other measures designed to counter recessionary trends are the following:

(i) GOI will work with State Governments. to encourage them to release land for low income and middle income housing schemes.

(ii) States, as a one time measure up to 30.06.2009, will be provided assistance under the JNNURM for the purchase of buses for their urban transport systems. A scheme towards this end will be announced shortly.

(iii) Accelerated depreciation of 50 percent will be provided for commercial vehicles to be purchased on or after 1.1.2009 up to 31.03.09.

Government is closely monitoring its spending to expedite the pace of expenditure for all schemes and programmers.

Government will set up a fast track monitoring committee to ensure expeditious approval and implementation of central projects. Chief Ministers are being advised to do the same.

The measures outlined above taken together with steps taken earlier constitute a substantial counter-cyclical stimulus in the current year. Government does not envisage any further measures in the current fiscal year. However, Government is aware that the measures required to provide an economic stimulus to the economy have to extend beyond the current financial year. Towards this end, it is finalizing Plan and Non-Plan expenditure that will be required in the next financial year to maintain the tempo. The Plan for the next year will include proposals for recapitalization of the public sector banks. The recapitalization is expected to be of the order of Rs.20,000 crore over the next two years. This will help to ensure that the banking system will not suffer from capital adequacy constraints in order to provide credit growth needed to sustain the economic momentum in 2009-10.

Evaluation of the Measures taken by Indian Government

In evaluating the measures taken by Indian government for crisis, it is important to remember that although the origins of the crisis are common around the world, the crisis has impacted different economies differently. Importantly, in advanced economies where it originated, the crisis spread from the financial sector to the real sector. In emerging economies, the transmission of external shocks to domestic vulnerabilities has typically been from the real sector to the financial sector.

Countries have accordingly responded to the crisis depending on their specific country circumstances. Thus, even as policy responses across countries are broadly similar, their precise design, quantum, sequencing and timing have varied. In particular, while policy responses in advanced economies have had to contend with both the unfolding financial crisis and deepening recession, in India, our response has been predominantly driven by the need to arrest moderation in economic growth.

The Global Financial Crisis and Short-run Prospects for India

The on-going global financial crisis has cast a shadow over the global economy with world output and trade forecasted by the IMF to shrink in 2009.

Exhibiting a strong dynamism, economic growth in India in 2007–08 was a high 9 per cent despite the fact that the sub-prime crisis had already started to impact the US and other major economies. However, growth rates dropped steadily during the first three quarters of 2008–09. Government forecasts economic growth to be 7.1 per cent during 2008–09 but the fourth quarter growth figures may be overestimates so that growth in 2008–09 may be lower.

Several other indicators, e.g. industrial production and trade, have also pointed toward a slowdown in the economy. Traditional wisdom has it that the GFC should have had minimal impact on India because i) Indian banking had no direct exposure to the sub-prime mortgage crisis, and ii) India's growth is largely based on domestic consumption and domestic investment. External demand as measured by merchandise exports account for less than 15 per cent of India's GDP.

However, the Indian economy has globalizes rapidly during the past few years. The ratio of exports plus imports to GDP increased by more than 50 per cent between 1997–98 and 2007–08 . The growth of financial integration has been even more rapid. During the same 10 year period the ratio of total external transactions more than doubled from 46.8 percent to 117.4 percent. Corporate borrowing from external sources has also increased significantly. In 2007–08 India received capital inflows to the extent of 9 per cent of GDP as against a current account deficit of 1.5 per cent of GDP.

Three different channels of the GFC's impact on India can be identified: i) The financial channel, i.e., the growing integration of India's financial markets with global financial markets; ii) The growing trade links between India and the rest of the world indicate that exports would decline quite sharply, and; iii) A final avenue is the confidence channel. The tightened global liquidity situation following from the failure of Lehman brothers in September 2008 increased the risk-aversion of several banks and other lending institutions.

The short-run outlook for the Indian economy is unclear. Real GDP growth and major sectors have shown strong signs of slipping. But, the stimulus packages announced by the government and the RBI have had their desired effect. Thus, the Indian auto industry, which was heading towards decline recorded positive growth of 0.71 per cent in total vehicle sales in fiscal 2008-09, services and manufacturing sectors are expected to record reasonable growth and investment rates are still high. The sharp fall in inflation has provided room for more aggressive interest rate cuts by the RBI, although the burden of servicing the larger debt because of the stimulus packages will not be insignificant. Although equity markets have registered steep declines the wealth impact on domestic residents is limited since only a small number of Indians participate in equity markets.

Assuming that the global economy starts picking up in 2009-10, of which there are some signs, and provided developed countries do not resort to widespread protectionism, an assumption that may be proved wrong, the Indian economy should be in a good position to register a strong comeback. However, since the stimulus packages have already imposed a significant fiscal burden, the new central government would need to eschew undue populism, failing which high fiscal deficits could again restrict India's growth between potential as was the case in the mid to late 1990s. The chances of this happening are lower now. The Indian economy has certainly grown in terms of sophistication and depth since the 1990s. On balance, there is reason to be guardedly optimistic about the Indian economy in the short run.

To *sum up* the outlook for India going forward is mixed. There is clear evidence of economic activity slowing down. Real GDP growth has moderated modestly in the first and second quarters of 2008/09, and sharply in the third quarter. The services sector, which has been our prime growth engine for the last five years, is slowing, mainly in construction, transport and communication, trade, hotels and restaurants sub-sectors. For the first time in seven years, exports have declined in absolute terms for four months in a row during October 2008 - January 2009. Recent data indicate that the demand for bank credit is slackening despite comfortable liquidity in the system. Dampened demand has dented corporate margins while the uncertainty surrounding the crisis has affected business confidence. The index of industrial production has shown negative growth for two recent months and investment demand is decelerating. All these factors suggest that growth will moderate more than we had earlier thought.

References

The Global Financial Crisis and Short Run Prospects for India Raghbendra Jha 8th May 2008.

Meltdown: A Story of Financial Alchemy? Jaimini Bhagwati March 20,2009.

August 29, 2009 Impact of US Financial Crisis on Indian Outsourcing Industry, September 24, 2008.

http//.www.economictime.com 9.Jan.2009.

http//.www.yahooans.com.29march2009.

http//.www.nscindia.com.

Summary

The *Present financial crisis* has been called the most serious financial crisis since the *Great Depression* by leading economists, with its global effects characterized by the failure of key businesses, declines in consumer wealth estimated in the trillions of U.S. dollars, substantial financial commitments incurred by governments, and a significant decline in economic activity. Many causes have been proposed, with varying weight assigned by experts. Both market-based and regulatory solutions have been implemented or are under consideration, while significant risks remain for the world economy.

The impact of the global crisis has been transmitted to the Indian economy through three distinct channels, viz., the financial sector, exports and exchange rates. The financial sector including the banking sector, equity markets, external commercial borrowings and remittances has not remained unscathed though fortunately, the Indian banking sector was not overly exposed to the sub-prime crisis. The *Present financial crisis* has been called the most serious financial crisis since the Great Depression by leading economists, with its global effects characterized by the failure of key businesses, declines in consumer wealth estimated in the trillions of U.S. dollars, substantial financial commitments incurred by governments, and a significant decline in economic activity. Many causes have been proposed, with varying weight assigned by experts. Both market-based and regulatory solutions have been implemented or are under consideration, while significant risks remain for the world economy.

The Government is committed to taking steps for minimizing the impact of the global financial crisis on the Indian economy. To this end, Government has taken a number of steps since October 7, the most recent being the measures announced on 7.12.2008.like

(i) Additional plan expenditure up to Rs.20,000 crore in the current year mainly for critical rural, infrastructure and social security schemes such as Pradhan Mantri Gram Sadak Yojana, Jawaharlal Nehru National Urban Renewal Mission, National Rural Employment Guarantee Scheme , Indira Awas Yojana, Accelerated Irrigation Benefit Programme and National Social Assistance Programme.

In evaluating the measures taken by Indian government for crisis, it is important to remember that although the origins of the crisis are common around the world, the crisis has impacted different economies differently. Importantly, in advanced economies where it originated, the crisis spread from the financial sector to the real sector. In emerging economies, the transmission of external shocks to domestic vulnerabilities has typically been from the real sector to the financial sector.

In short the Indian economy is unclear. Real GDP growth and major sectors have shown strong signs of slipping. But, the stimulus packages announced by the government and the RBI have had their desired effect. Thus, the Indian auto industry, which was heading towards decline recorded positive growth of 0.71 per cent in total vehicle sales in fiscal 2008–09, services and manufacturing sectors are expected to record reasonable growth and investment rates are still high. The sharp fall in inflation has provided room for more aggressive interest rate cuts by the RBI, although the burden of servicing the larger debt because of the stimulus packages will not be insignificant. Although equity markets have registered steep declines the wealth impact on domestic residents is limited since only a small number of Indians participate in equity markets.

18

Current Financial Crisis: An Overview

R.C. Mishra, K.C. Mishra

Introduction

Since globalization is round the corner, most of the countries of the world are wedded to the philosophy of market economy. Despite a number of advantages, cyclical fluctuation is one of the shortcomings in such an economy. The free play of market forces results in the movement of the economy in a cyclical path such as, prosperity, peak, recession, depression, trough and recovery. Economic recession that takes the form of severe depression had already started in the whole world. The origin of the current recession can be traced back to the mid 2007 in America, but it became severe in 2008. The crisis which was created in America was transmitted to the rest of the countries of the world. As a result, there was world wide recession. However, the paper makes an humble attempt to focus on the following points.

- To explain the causes of recession
- To study the impact of recession on the Indian economy.
- Summary and conclusion.

Genesis of Crisis

There are several causes of the current recession.

First, undue rise in the prices of petrol and diesel is one of the causes of the current financial crisis. In view of the high rate of growth in most of the countries of the world along with America during the last decade, the demand for petrol and diesel went up significantly. Due to the outbreak of Iraq war, there was a decline in the production of petrol and diesel. It is worthwhile to mention that American economy consumes 24% of the total crude oil of the world. In view of the increasing necessity of petrol and diesel in America and declining production of the same, market prices of crude oil went up sharply in America. As a result, Americans started using small cars instead of big cars requiring more petrol/diesel. Those who used to attend their offices from a distant place by car disposed of their houses and settled nearby their offices so as to attend to their offices either on foot or by public bus. Thus, all big companies in America and Japan producing cars using more petrol/ diesel closed down the production of such motor cars and thereby thousands of workers engaged in such Industries were thrown out of employment. Moreover, the prices of petroleum products like plastic, chemical products & cosmetic products went up unduly and thus the demand for these products and its production were adversely affected. Added to it, cost of transportation increased due to the rise in price of petrol/ diesel which adversely affected most of the necessary goods, normal trade and balance of payments of the American economy. Thus, financial crisis began in the American economy.

Secondly, the crisis was intensified to assume its severe form by the indiscriminate supply of home loan in America. Despite rapid growth in American economy during the nineties and the current decade, two numbers of recession of smaller magnitude occurred in America for a short while. With a view to providing more incentives to capital investment and economic growth, the Federal Reserve Bank of America resorted to cheap money policy and reduced the rate of interest continuously. It is worth-mentioning that huge capital was invested in the construction of houses. It is a fact that Americans during their marriage and nurturing their children prefer to have a house of their own. Ordinarily they do not depend on their past savings for buying a house for them. Instead, they borrow loan from banks to purchase/ construct a house. Normally, they borrow 80% to 90% of the cost of house as loans from banks for 20 to 30 years. The house so purchased or constructed is kept mortgaged with the bank until the loan amount is repaid. The borrowers have to decide whether they will borrow loan either at fixed rate of interest or floating rate of interest.

In view of the high rate of economic growth, the interest for constructing a house among the Americans increased and the banks supplied loans to them. The local commercial banks rather than the national level banks supplied this type of loan. But it is a matter of regret that the local commercial banks supplied loans not only to the people with permanent job and regular income but also to the people who do not have regular income and permanent job during this period. Indeed, these banks supplied 100% cost of house as loans to the people for constructing their houses. This type of loan is termed as sub-prime loan. Thus, sub-prime loan refers to a loan given to a borrower who does not qualify for a regular home loan due to a poor credit record, low income and no job security. Such home loans were almost supplied at floating rate of interest.

Since the Federal Reserve Bank had been reducing the rate of interest continuously, it was expected that the interest rate would be reduced still further in subsequent years. Thus, there was an unexpected rise in the demand for house. Further, there was a growing interest among the Americans for speculative buying and selling of houses. One of the reasons for increasing the speculative buying and selling of houses was that in 1997, capital gains tax was repealed. Many people constructed houses through bank loans and after some years sold the houses at higher prices. So these houses became highly valuable and profitable for the borrowers. The sale proceeds were used to purchase various articles for maintaining their standard of living. Thus, it was not possible for them to repay the loan with interest in right time. Hence it had become an important trend of the financial management of the American family.

Truly speaking, the personal savings of American families were zero or negative, since the expenditure was met by loan to some extent. In this circumstance, the Federal Reserve Bank in order to control the symptoms of inflation started increasing the rate of interest in 2007. As a result, it had become an Herculean task for the lower income group to deposit the premium at a higher rate. Finding no other solution, they surrendered their mortgaged houses to the banks and resided in small rented houses. These houses were placed at the disposal of banks. On the other hand, banks were not able to sell these houses to get back the amount because they could not find buyers of houses in the market economic system when there was a continuous increasing rate of interest. Consequently, when houses were lying at the disposal of banks, their values started declining.

This had resulted in a number of adverse effects. The Americans started managing their families according to the principle of 'cut your coat according to your cloth'. Each one felt the need of saving and consumption expenditure was reduced. Consequently, the demand for goods required for the construction of houses was reduced at first and thus, various shops dealing in those goods were closed leading to problem of unemployment. In view of the growing unemployment, the demand for other consumer goods was reduced and thus a number of shops selling those goods and a number of firms producing those goods were closed, leading to the aggravation of the problem of unemployment in America. On the other hand, banks which resorted to such sub-prime loan fell in a critical situation. They borrowed huge loan from the big banks against the mortgaged papers as securities to deal with their transactions. The big banks considered these mortgaged papers very much risky though those were not unnecessary. The small banks were asked to repay the loans but they were not in a position to repay the same. The non-repayment of loan by the small banks had created dangerous situation for the big banks and other big financial institutions. The economic analysts of big banks had packaged these loans to really complicated financial instruments called CDOs (Collateralised Debt Obligation) which were said to be derivatives. Different financial institutions of Europe, Japan, Korea, China and America had invested huge amount of money in these derivatives. The ICICI bank of India had invested in these derivatives.

The economic analysts thought that the risks of derivatives would be distributed thinly and widely and the rating agencies rated most of these derivatives AAA, i.e. the securities are highly secured. But their expectation and calculation did not come true when small banks were unable to repay the loan. They might be good statisticians rather than good market analysts. As a result, the whole derivative market collapsed and thereafter one after another big bank and financial institution closed, vanished or merged with other banks which are not related to sub-prime loans.

Another cause of the crisis was the prevalence of credit card system in America. We know that an ordinary American is a regular customer of credit card system. They can spend huge money in shops and hotels even if they do not have funds in their accounts. This is an indication of negative saving culture of the American society. There was a fear that the consumers were unable to deposit the fund drawn from the banks. Thus, the quantum of NPA (Non-Performing Assets) was increased tremendously and resulted in the collapse of the banking system. So, merger and bankruptcy among banks were seen and accordingly the Government of America provided huge financial help to the banks. What is true for American financial institutions is also true for those of Europe and Asia. Some of them collapsed and some of them are waiting for consequences.

Impact of the Crisis on the Indian Economy

The current financial crisis which was created in America was getting transmitted to the rest of the countries of the world and thereby crisis became worldwide. The current financial crisis has influenced a number of countries including India.

The problems created in India were neither due to her own nor due to the local conditions. The crisis emerged in American economy has influenced our economy in more than one way.

First, when several financial institutions have started collapsing in America, many Americans and financial institutions who had invested in our bonds and securities started selling and withdrawing the funds to meet the crisis. The value of bonds, shares and stocks in Indian stock exchange market reduced sharply. As a result, the income and property of various people dealing with stock exchange market were reduced drastically. Due to this, the consumption expenditure of this section of people was reduced to some extent.

Secondly, the greatest impact is the reduction of export in India. Due to the reduction of demand for various consumers goods in America and other countries, the export of these goods was reduced in India. Cotton industry in India was worst affected. As a result, various dress units and cotton industries were closed leading to unemployment of thousands of people in India. Due to the reduction of demand for iron and steel in America, China, Japan and Korea, the demand for iron-ore and its value have been reduced in India. Unemployment in mines has been increasing in India. Likewise the export of other minerals has been adversely affected in India.

Thirdly, there has been a decline in software maintenance services industry and Business Processing Office (BPO) in India due to the downward movement of American industries. There are highly lucrative industries. In view of the financial crisis some of the employees in these fields lost their jobs; the salary of the employees was reduced and fresh appointment opportunity was reduced in India.

Fourthly, motor car industries and motor car equipments construction industries which exported substantial products reduced their production in India in view of the crisis. Consequently, employment opportunity in these fields was reduced; shift of work was reduced in India. The demand for two wheelers and four wheelers motor cars has been reduced leading to the aggravation of the problem of unemployment in India.

Fifthly, limited employment opportunity and growing unemployment in India reduced the demand for houses. A number of companies in India and foreign companies which were opening their offices in big cities and other towns have changed their decisions. As a result, the value of landed property and houses in towns was reduced drastically.

Sixthly, the demand for various goods and services has been reduced due to the reduction in income of the employees. The production and employment in the field of iron and steel, cement and transportation have been reduced. A number of small steel industry and sponge iron industry in India have already been closed and large scale industries have already reduced their production in India.

On the contrary, while the financial institution of America, Europe, Korea, Japan and China have been worst affected due to the financial crisis, the financial institutions in India remained unaffected fortunately. It is because our banks and other financial institutions were not closely related to those of America. Especially, our financial institutions had not invested capital in the American derivatives. Further, the Reserve Bank of India as compared to the Federal Reserve Bank of America is more influential and active in regulating the activities of our banks and other financial institutions. Loans sanctioned to small and medium industries have mostly increased NPA. Due to the shortage of cash and fear of non-repayment, banks already reduced the lending of term loan and working capital in India. At the same time, since the export sector and private sector in India have relatively less contribution in the aggregate economic activity, the rate of growth has reduced slightly. Unlike America, the rate of growth will not be negative in India.

Suggestions & Conclusions

Since the current financial crisis has affected the Indian economy, it is imperative to take necessary steps to bring recovery to the economy. However, the RBI has already taken steps in reducing the bank rate and the repo rate to bring recovery to the economy so that the rate of growth will be enhanced. Steps have been taken to reduce Cash Reserve Ratio

(CRR) so as to enable the banks to create more credit and the borrowers will be encouraged to borrow at lower interest. But there is no guarantee that such a step would encourage the borrowers to have more funds. This measure would help create more credit, but it is desirable to have larger demand for loan for the recovery of economic activities in India. This will not be possible automatically.

During the period of depression, producers and investors cannot think of the possibility of the recovery of demand and in such uncertainties, banks do not prefer to invest their funds in risk. It is therefore, necessary that like other countries, the Govt. of India should come up for spending more to create various economic activities which would obviously enhance the demand in the economy. It is suggested that Govt. of India should increase expenditure in the field of infrastructure such as national highway, rural roads, railway line, port, hospitals etc.. Such expenditure will help create demand for iron and steel, cement, electricity, oil, unskilled and semi-skilled labour. Such expenditure can not be financed out of tax revenue, since tax revenue is less due to recession and additional tax will adversely affect the demand. Therefore, it can be met by the market borrowing and borrowing from RBI. This would no doubt bring recovery to the economy.

A pertinent question arises whether this kind of market borrowing at a huge scale will be inflationary. Initially, it does not look like so. Because industries are operating below their optimum capacities and small & medium industries would come up quickly by which supply of product will be maintained accurately. Therefore, the appropriate role of the country should be that the funds sanctioned for the projects should be utilized in those projects without pilferage. Otherwise, it will have adverse effect on the economy.

To sum up, while the recovery of the Indian economy depends to some extent, on the recovery of the world recession, our domestic capital formation will help us to recover from recession to a great extent. In the present context, what is required is that there should be massive investment in infrastructure without pilferage. If we fail in this direction, it will create havoc for the economy. It is seen that the current year's budget 2009-10 of the present government proposes massive investment on infrastructure so as to initiate the recovery of the Indian economy. Therefore, we are hopeful that the Indian economy will be recovered from the recession within a short span of time.

References

Barua Abheek (2008), 'Anatomy of a Crisis'; The Times of India, October, 12.

Chandrasekhar C.P. and Jayanti Ghose (2008), 'India and the Global Financial Crisis', Business Line, October, 15.

Dua Ajay (2008), 'The Impact of Slowdown On India', The Times of India, November, 21.

Economic Survey 2008-09, Govt. of India.

Kumar N. Kiran (2009), 'Economic Recession in US and Its Impact on India', Southern Economist, Vol. 48, No. 4, pp. 31-32.

Madhavi N.R. and S.T. Gadade (2009), 'The Impact of Financial Crisis on India', Southern Economist, Vol. 48, No. 1, pp. 27-29.

Satyanarayana G. and Y. Keshava Readdy (2009), 'Global Financial Crisis and Indian Economy'; Southern Economist, Vol. 48, No. 6, pp. 31-32.

Selvaraj Anitha (2009); 'Global Financial Crisis: Its Impact on Indian Economy'; Southern Economist, Vol. 48, No. 2, pp. 5-8.

19

Global Economic Crisis and Indian Price Bubble Home Price Bubble–A Paradoxical Situation in India

Chandeshwari Tiwary

INFLATION whether imported or non- imported has become mostly a regular feature of Indian economy since independence specially under the plans having different impacts on the economy—good for the rich and bad for the poor increasing the gap between the two, causing social, economic and political problems. In July,09, WPI was still negative where as CPI was above 10.5 a situation in which the investors fear of further investment and production due to recessionary trends and on the other, inflation pinches the consumers due to rising retail prices day-by-day making their lives hell, a burning problem for the government and the RBI.

Inflation means sustained increases in the general price level of goods and services. It causes sustained declines in the value of money/purchasing power of money. It is measured in index numbers whether it is price index or value index or volume index. The price index is of the following two types—(1) whole sale price index (WPI) and (2) Retail/Consumers price index CPI). The difference between WPI and CPI is in the different items taken into account, the weights assigned to them. In India, two types of index (1) WPI and (2) CPI are used to monitor inflation. Of the two, WPI is the most widely used in India to measure the changes in the average price level of goods traded in the wholesale market and is available on a weekly basis with the shortest possible time lag only two weeks. But it is measured as an annual per cent increase.

Retail inflation is measured by the following three different sets of CPI - 1. Rural Labourers, 2. Agricultural Labourers, and 3. Industrial Labourers. These variables must be taken into consideration while formulating inflation control measures in a country like India. It is important to ensure that food prices are reasonable. The prices of goods and services of common uses and of other necessaries are also within reach for the masses.

Prices are rising in India but its WPI shows that inflation is still negative- why! , I feel because of the government's indifference towards Consumers price index (CPI). In many developed countries, price indices are prepared on the basis of consumer prices where as in India they are still prepared on the wholesale prices. The following chart shows the changes in the wholesale price index and consumer price index (periods are different):-

Period (averages)	*WPI Inflation Rate*	*CPI Inflation Rate*
1951-52 to 1959-60	1.2	9.6 (1990-99)
1960-61 to 1969-70	6.4	4.5(2000-2007)
1970-71 to 1979-80	9.0	4.8(2003-2007)
1980-81 to 1990-91	8.2	10.2(May 09)
1991-92 (crisis year	13.7	
1992-93 to 1999-00	7.2	
2000-01 to 2006-07	5.1	
2009(May-June)	less than half a percentage i.e. negative	

Reddy (RBI) 2007and World Economic Outlook Database IMF.

It is clear from the above chart that WPI is negative. Ex-RBI governor D. Subbarao also confirmed that wholesale price inflation dropped into negative territory. Still inflation pinches the consumers because consumer price inflation is positive. It means there is paradox between the two. WPI is still down but CPI is up.

The value of money or its purchasing power of goods and services declines in inflation causing various impacts on the economy domestically as well as globally. People lose confidence in the monetary system in case of galloping or rapid inflation as happened in Zimbabwe. It may also lead to undesirable redistribution of income. It may discourage saving since the real value of the sum saved falls through time.

In the sphere of foreign trade, exports decrease and imports increase, leading to declining national income. The balance of payments difficulties also become severe.

High rate of inflation can also be anti-growth because of low saving, and low investment. It increases the di fficulties of the poor but increases the luxuries of the rich causing social tensions and class conflicts. Labour class suffers the most making life hell. There may be malls filled with goods but few customers. Pressures on government, increase leading to deficit financing and foreign borrowing and so on.

Since the middle years of the 1990's decade, global inflationary climate has moved upward. We find a much stronger inflationary impetus from goods which are traded on global markets, particularly oil and commodity prices. The rise in CPI is particularly noticeable in Asia but in the U.K. and some other European countries, inflation has recently reached levels not seen since early1990's. UK CPI inflation reached 3.3% in May 2008, its highest level since July 92, German CPI inflation hit 3.3% in June and French CPI inflation reached the same level in May 2008. U S CPI inflation peaked in September 2005 at 4.7% the highest level since May 1991 thought it has declined to 4.3% in January 2008 and 4.2% in May 2008 and now a recessionary period.

The sustained and prolonged impact of this shift in the global inflation climate is now showing up in higher rates of CPI inflation in most countries around the globe. The pressures are on oil, food and other commodity prices (including metals and non-metals). A cross-country comparison of major EMEs

(Emerging Market Economies) that have adopted Inflation Targeting (IT) indicates that growth in India has been highest after China during 2000-2007 but inflation remains relatively low. Developed economies have performed better than the most EMEs.

From the above facts it is clear that current inflation in India is both due to imported factors as well as domestic factors. Although reasons are various but there are two main theories of causes of inflation:- (1) demand pull theories and (2) cost push theories. In India, both these theories are found in practice. Factors responsible for demand pull inflation are (a) increase in population, (b) increase in money supply, (c) excess government expenditure, (d) increase in monetary income,(e) increase in deficit financing, (f) increase in black money, (g) Sixth Pay Commission's increased salaries and allowances, (h) demonstration effects, (I) increase in foreign investments etc. On the supply side, factors are (a) lower supply of goods and services due to slow growth in agriculture and industries (b) high increase in cost of production, (c) increase in taxes and transport and communication expenditures, (d) global inflation (e) controlled prices and black marketing, (f) speculative activities, (g) lack of basic facilities, (h) moral degradation, (I) nature's calamities like flood, drought and others, (j) increased trade union's power, (k) withdrawal/ reduction of subsidies (l) mismanaged administration and corruptions (m) high profits etc.

Besides, inflation as a feature of capitalist economies was subdued and reined in especially from the early 1980s. This was when monetarist policies were used to great effect to counter the inflationary trends of the 1970s. These policies worked not so much by restricting money supply, as was the explicit claim, but rather by destroying the ability of the working class in the developed countries and commodity producers in the developing world to maintain their income shares even as profit shares soared. The recent expansion of global capitalism in the past decade, with real world output increasing at an annual rate of around 5 per cent and world trade increasing by 8 per cent annually, has been marked by low inflation rates of only around 2 per cent a year.

But all this seems to have changed dramatically, especially in the past two years. While primary commodity prices in world trade have been increasing gradually since2002, there have been significant increases in these since around the middle of 2006. As per IMF data, except for agricultural raw materials whose prices have increased very little, all the other commodity groups have shown sharp rises in prices. Over the past year, the increases have been so marked that they are evident not only in dollars but even in other currencies. While all commodity prices in dollar terms increased by 45 per cent in 2007, they increased by 37 per cent in SDR (Special Drawing Rights) terms. The rise in price levels for metals was the earliest in the recent surge, with the weighted average of metals prices increasing sharply from the last quarter of 2005 and almost doubling in the two-year period. Even after Iraq war, the oil prices have been more volatile, even falling in 2006, and only the past year has witnessed the most rapid price increases for oil since the 1970s. In 2007, other energy prices have also soared. Coal prices more than doubled last year, thereby showing a faster rise than even the oil price.

Food prices, like agricultural raw materials, showed only a modest increase until early 2007. But since then, they have zoomed such that the IMF data showed a more than 40 per cent increase in world food prices over 2007.The food price index of the United Nations' Food and Agricultural Organisation ,which includes national prices and as well as those in cross-border trade, suggests that the average index for 2007 was nearly 25 per cent above the average for 2006. Including sugar, nearly every other food crop has shown very significant increases in price in world trade over 2007, and the latest evidence suggests that this trend has continued and accelerated in the few months of 2008. This is essentially demand-led, the result of several years of rapid economic growth and the voracious demand from some fast growing countries, India and China in particular. It implies that the world economy is heading back to the old Phillips-curve- based scenario, whereby rapid and prolonged growth in a capitalist economy comes up against an inflationary barrier.

The performance of the global economy over the period since 2003 bears out this picture of strong demand particularly driven by growth in developing economies of Asia, Russian and African countries. As per IMF World Economic Outlook, April 2008, the following three reasons for this strong and broadly-based demand are - 1. Investment has been a strong driver of demand growth in these economies—with Asia and other developing regions accounting for over half of the increase in global capital spending since 2000. The production of capital goods and new building work requires large amounts of materials and energy–with steel and cement production being particularly energy-intensive industries. 2. Consumers in richer countries tend to spend a greater proportion of their income on services where as rising consumption in developing and emerging economies is more likely to be spent on physical products - including food. 3. During the period between the mid-1980s and early- 2000s, energy and other commodity prices were generally low and falling in real terms. This was not a climate in which producers were inclined to invest strongly in new capacity or to develop alternatives to traditional sources of energy and raw materials. As a result, supply has not been able to respond quickly to rising demand– particularly in the oil industry.

In the oil market, we can observe directly the contribution of strong demand outside the OECD economies to recent price pressures. In recent years, incremental oil demand in OECD economies has been declining, as economic growth has slowed in a number of economies and higher prices have affected consumption. But incremental demand outside the OECD has continued to grow strongly relative to available supply. The positive impact on oil demand from strong economic growth has offset any dampening effect of higher prices and subsidies have also been used to reduce the extent of price increases in many countries.

For the past two decades and more, international capitalism was able to deal with this and avoid Phillips-curve-type outcomes through political economy processes that restrained the wage and income demands of working classes and primary producers. But there are limits to such a process, and these are now being reached in the form of stagflation - a situation of rising prices combined with output recession or stagnation - cannot be ruled out as is the prevailing conditions in India.

Similarly, there are more than just demand forces at work for rises in food. Four major aspects affecting supply conditions have been crucial in changing global as well as domestic market conditions for food crops: - First, there is the impact of high oil prices, which affect agricultural costs directly because of the significance of energy as an input in the cultivation process itself (through fertilizer and irrigation costs) and in transporting food. Across the world, governments have reduced protection and subsidies on agriculture, which means that high costs of energy directly translate into higher costs of cultivation and therefore, higher prices of output.

Second, there is the impact of both oil prices and government policies in the U.S., Europe, Brazil, and elsewhere that have promoted biofuels as an alternative to petroleum. This has led to significant shifts in acreage as well as use of certain grains. For instance, in 2006, the U.S. diverted more than 20 per cent of its maize production to the production of ethanol, Brazil used half of its sugarcane production to make biofuel, and the European Union (E.U.) used the greater part of its vegetable oil production as well as imported vegetable oils to make biofuel. This has naturally reduced the available land for producing food.

Third, the impact of policy neglect of agriculture over the past two decades is also being felt. The prolonged agrarian crisis in many parts of the developing world; the shifts in acreage from food crops to cash crops relying on purchased inputs; the excessive use of groundwater and the inadequate attention paid to preserving or regenerating land and soil quality; the lack of attention to relevant agricultural research and extension; the overuse of chemical inputs that have long-run implications for both pollution and climate change, including desertification and loss of cultivable land; all these are issues that have been highlighted by analysts but largely ignored by policymakers in most countries. Reversing these processes is possible but will take time and substantial public investment, so until then global supply conditions will remain problematic.

Fourth, there is the impact of changes in market structure, which allow greater international speculation in commodities. It is often assumed that rising food prices automatically benefit farmers but this is far from the case, especially as the global food trade has become more concentrated and vertically integrated. A small number of agribusiness companies worldwide increasingly control all aspects of cultivation and distribution, from supplying inputs to farmers to buying crops and, even in some cases, to retailing food distribution. This means that marketing margins are large and increasing so that direct producers do not get the benefits of increases except with a time lag and even then not to the full extent. This concentration also enables greater speculation in food, with more centralized storage.

Fifth, primary commodity markets are also attracting financial speculators. As the global financial system remains fragile with the continuing implosion of the US housing finance market, commodity speculation is increasingly emerging as an important alternative investment market. It has also affected the minerals and metals sectors without actual benefits to the producers. Such speculations by large banks and financial companies are found in agricultural and non - agricultural commodities causing sharp hikes in prices.

Until the 1990s, both producers and consumers in India were relatively sheltered from the impact of such global tendencies because of a complex system of trade restrictions, public procurement and distribution and policy emphasis on at least food self- sufficiency.

The liberalizing policies that began in the early 1990s have rendered all of that history, since one explicit aim of the reform strategy was to bring Indian prices closer in line to world prices without adverse effect on growth. Our national goal is "to moderate inflation without affecting growth ".

Countries like India seeking to manage this effect of global inflation on domestic prices have to decide how important it is to insulate the domestic economy and the domestic consumers from its effects but both producers and consumers are now more or less directly affected adversely by global and domestic inflationary trends.

The government's response to the domestic price rise, which is already creating panic in official corridors in coming state election years, has been to reduce or eliminate import duties on several food items so as to allow imports to bring the price down. But that is a short sighted and probably ineffective strategy. Because it provides direct competition to Indian farmers and producers and hardship to consumers for leaving the domestic markets open for domestic speculators.

The medium-term outlook for India was also uncertain because the global commodity prices are likely to remain high even if the world economy slows down as there is mismatch between demand and supply. The government is unwilling to reduce duties further because of revenue losses as well as is under increasing pressure to hike oil prices further. As a result, it aggravates an inflationary tendency that is already proving to be economically and politically damaging.

The long term solution lies in the fast growth of the Indian economy with government intervention in several areas for inflation control and recession remedial measures with private co-operation based on indicative planning. The demand is rising in India. People are consuming more. We must increase production and productivity of essential food articles. That is the most durable solution for keeping the primary items under a moderate level of inflation. But the regulation of markets is also essential in the present age of liberalization, privatization and globalization for the poor population. RBI and other authorities must be cautious and watchful with their instruments for the needful steps.

References

Sentence, A. (2007), "The Global Economy and UK Inflation", Speech to Leeds Financial Services Initiative, Bank of England Quarterly Bulletin, Q4.

IMF (2006), World Economic Outlook, Box 5.1," Has speculation contributed to higher commodity prices", September.

HM Treasury (2008), "Global Commodities: A Long Term Vision for Stable, Secure and Sustainable Markets".

Friedman, M. (1970), The Counter-Revolution in Monetary Theory", Institute of Economic Affairs Research Monograph 24, London.

Ball, L and L. Sheridan (2003), "Does Inflation Targeting Matter? , NBER Working Paper No 9577.

Fraga, A.; Minella, A. and Goldfajn, I. (2003), "Inflation Targeting in Emerging Market Economies", NBER Working Paper 10019, October.

Jalan, B. (2002), "Monetary Policy: Is a Single Target Relevant?, In India's Economy in the New millennium: Selected Essays (ed.) B. Jalan, Mumbai: UBS Publishers Distributors.

Mohan, Rakesh (2004), "Challenges to Monetary Policy in a Globalizing Context", RBI Bulletin, January.

——(2007a), "Current Challenges to Monetary Policy Making in India", RBI Bulletin, March.

The Hindu, Wednesday, April 25, 2007.

The Economic Times, 23 June 2009.

Reddy, Y.V.(2007a), Globalization and Monetary Policy: Some Emerging Issues", RBI Bulletin April.

Business Standard, Sunday, Feb. 08, 2009.

Macroscan, C.P. Chandrasekhar and Jayati Ghosh: "Imported Inflation.

C.J. Vinod "A Perspective on Recent Inflationary Pressure". 16 August 2008, Views: 1016, Comments.

Y.V. Reddy (2006), Annual Policy Statement for 2006-07, April. and others— — — —

20

Global Financial Crisis and Indian Economy's Challenges Ahead

Hemlata

The crisis is not merely financial, it is a crisis of the real economy. It is not merely banking, insurance and stock markets which are in crisis. There is a crisis in the real economy in the sense that the industrial output in the advanced capitalist countries is falling. Unemployment is rising. U.S. unemployment rate is currently the highest it has been since 1982, 26 years ago. It is higher than it has ever been after the Second World War. And the only comparison could be with the Great Depression of the 1930s, when unemployment rates reached 25% of the labour force.

A financial crisis in any one country 30-40 years ago would not have impacted so quickly on other countries. Today, because of the processes of global integration, from about the late 1970s, especially from the 1980s onwards, in particular the integration of financial markets on global scale, because of that integration, if U.S.A. sneezes, we do not just catch a cold, we get a fever. That is the degree of integration today in the world financial sector. And this is in fact a key factor underlying the present crisis.

Crisis today in the world economy is not merely one of liquidity, not just of there being not enough money to go around for banks to lend to other banks, and so on. It is the crisis of solvency. In other words, many financial firms are bankrupt. They cannot honour their obligations. This cannot be handled merely by infusing money to some banks. Businessmen are seeing a huge recession. Markets are dull. And demand is not picking up. So nobody wants to invest, no body wants to lend. We have a crisis, not merely of the financial sector, but of the real economy. The crisis is not merely of liquidity, but of solvency. What are the key factors, underlying the global financial meltdown leading to a real economy crisis?

Governments in the western world initially thought that it was a liquidity crisis which could be managed by providing more liquidity to the banking system. It is now clear that it is a solvency crisis. Because banks were lending massively without due diligence to assess whether the borrower can repay or not - this is what is called sub prime lending- many banks found themselves in serious trouble when the housing market weakened. Prime lending is when you lend to some one who is able to return. 'Sub prime' is when this is not the case. But why did sub prime lending take place on such a large scale? Because banks were competing with other financial entities. Non-bank financial institutions-like investment banks and speculators dealing in a range of financial assets-were making huge profits. Banks felt the pressure to expand lending in order to make adequate returns. As the housing sector initially expanded and asset values rose, banks diluted the documentation requirements that borrowers had to meet. These were called 'lim-doc' loans. A number of such loans turned sour and hence became sub-prime when the housing market began to collapse. This is one of the key mechanisms underlying the crisis.

One could say that the burst of the housing bubble in the US is the proximate cause resulting in the financial crisis. *But the key and basic point is the inability of economy to sustain demand at a high enough level to maintain full employment and to avoid cyclical fluctuations in both output and employment.*

The government of India has accepted that there is a crisis but it too initially treated it as a liquidity crisis. The Reserve bank of India lowered the interest rates at which it lends to banks, it lowered the statutory liquidity ratio (SLR) and the cash reserve ratio (CRR). Technicalities aside,it was basically trying to put more money in the hands of banking system.

The government has some reservations about providing an adequate direct stimulus through expenditure. The Reserve Bank of India is afraid of inflation. If they provide too much liquidity, it is argued, that may lead to stoking the fires of inflation. The government has since come out with a very inadequate fiscal stimulus package. The contrast with China is instructive. The Chinese government has not only decided on a huge fiscal stimulus, but it proposes to spend this money on agriculture and rural development, with a view to lessening rural-urban and inter-regional inequalities.

There is a problem that we face but China does not. This is the problem of capital flight. Foreign institutional investors (FIIs) operating in India are taking money out of India. In 2007, these FIIs brought in 20 billion dollars while in the first ten months of 2008 they have taken out 16 billion dollars. Last year 20 billion dollars plus. Now you have minus 16 billion dollars. This is the order of magnitude of change in the flow of foreign finance.

FIIs taking money out currently in order to meet their payment commitments elsewhere leads to a sharp decline in the stock market indices. Secondly, when foreign capital goes out in large amounts, there is a big demand for dollars. This means that the demand for dollars as against the rupee goes up. As a result, the rupee value goes down against the dollar. In last several weeks, the US dollar which used to exchange for Rs. 40 has tended to exchange for Rs. 50. This is a large decline. What does it mean for us? It means our imports became much more expensive. This in turn leads to a generalized pressure on prices. There is a tendency to inflation. Costs of food and other basic commodities rise whenever the rupee declines in value against the dollar. That is occurring now. So, capital flight means stock market declines and currency value goes down. For common people, this translates into a slowing down of investment and therefore of growth and employment. It also means a rise in prices. This is the crisis we are facing. Despite the crash in crude oil prices internationally, inflation rates even as officially measured remain high at around 8 %. On the ground, we know from daily experience that vegetable and other essential commodity prices are in fact rising much faster.

The Indian economy was much less integrated with the global economy than it is today. The combined value of India's imports and exports as a proportion of GDP was not even 10% in 1991. Today, if we add imports and exports, the figure comes to over 40 % as a proportion of GDP. So, our economy today is much more vulnerable to global commodity prices than it was 20 years ago. *More important, it is much more vulnerable to financial flows.*

Declines in rural development expenditure have hurt agriculture and rural development badly over the years since 1991. They have caused considerable rural distress by lowering the purchasing power of the rural population.

Twenty years of liberalization, privatization, and globalization (LPG) policies have greatly weakened agriculture. As is well known, our foodgrains output had been stagnant from 1999 to 2007. The rate of the growth of food grains out put over last 10 years is less than 1 % per year. Population over this period would have grown by at least 10 %. The annual per capita food grain output is now around 155 to 160 kilograms.

There are five ways in which LPG policies have destroyed agriculture. One, with the government cutting back subsidies, input costs in agriculture, i.e. costs of fertilizers, pesticides, transport, and so on, have gone up. Two, with the opening up of the economy to agricultural imports without quantitative restrictions, imports have increased rapidly and output prices of crops such as rubber, spices, coconut, tea and so on have fallen drastically from time to time. Thirdly, the quantum of bank and cooperative credit to agriculture has declined in relation to needs while interest rates rose rapidly until recently.

Fourthly, government has cut back expenditure in the countryside, weakening agricultural infrastructure as well as rural demand. Fifthly, the public distribution system has been greatly weakened and has altogether collapsed in some parts of the country. All these five developments have devastated the rural economy and agriculture. Only in the last two three years, there has been some relief both on account of favourable weather, and more importantly, through interventions such as the national rural employment guarantee scheme under the National Rural Employment Guarantee Act (NREGA) how India should deal with the crisis?

As the crisis and its impact on the Indian economy unfold, it is clear that our exports are declining despite the fall in the value of the rupee against the US dollar while our import costs are going up. There is pressure on our balance of payments, especially with FIIs exiting the country's financial markets, exports declining and imports going up. Contrary to the government's approach, what is required is a strengthening of sector regulations. What is needed is a focus on the real sector of the economy instead of the obsession with the financial markets.

There is now a general consensus even in official circles that besides monetary intervention to enhance liquidity and lower interest rates, the government must infuse demand into the economy by undertaking expenditure.

What is needed is very focused expenditure that will directly benefit the peasantry, rural and urban labour and small and medium industries and enterprises including those which are export oriented and those in retail trade.

One of the key issues in the context of the present economic crisis is the extremely slow growth of foodgrain output over the last decade. So reasonable input prices, remunerative procurement prices and importantly extension of procurement to all major crops and across the country are seen. The third important policy measure has to be the provision of some degree of protection against imports for domestic agricultural output. Trial to enable rapid recovery of the rural and agrarian economy.

Fourth, we must demand that the government of India abandon the system of targeted public distribution of food grains (TPDS) and revert to the earlier system of universal PDS.

References

Narasimham, CRL Fiscal Deficti The Biggest Challenge, *Southern Economist,* 1sy Aug. 2008, pp. 41.

Global Financial Crisis and Key Risk : Impact on India and Asia.

Global Financial Crisis : Reflection on Its Impact on India, Business Line, Nov. 2008.

Global Financial Crisis and Developing Countries, A Background Note.

Government of India, Economic Survey, 2007-08.

21

Global Crisis and the Indian Economy

Ranjit Kumar Singh, Rameshwar Prajapati

Introduction

It took some more time for policy makers and analysts in India to recognize both the speed and intensity of the effects of the global crisis in India. Indeed, there were arguments that India, along with China, is "decoupled" from the global system and capable of becoming an autonomous growth pole, based on its recent high growth from a low per capita income base, and a young population leading to falling dependency ratios. In addition, the "strong" domestic financial sector was also seen to be immune to shocks from the international financial system.

However, it turns out that this presumption was wrong, and even involved a faulty assessment of the previous boom. Recent high economic growth in India was fundamentally dependent upon the greater global integration and related to deregulation of finance combined with fiscal concessions that spurred a deflationary fiscal policies, poor employment generation and agrarian crisis kept mass consumption demand low. The substantial rise in profit shares in the economy and the proliferation of financial activities combined with rising asset values to enable a credit-financed consumption splurge among the rich and the middle classes, which in turn generated higher rates of investment and output over the upswing. This was therefore, quite similar to speculative bubble-led expansion in several other countries in the same period. This also made the growth process more vulnerable to internally and externally generated crisis.

By the middle of 2008, even before the global crisis really in India, this process too was reaching its limits. the crisis made matters much worse by causing sharp declines in exports of manufactures and reversal of capital flows such that both current and capital accounts of the balance of payments have worsened .the macro issues have been much commented upon, but the pacific impact upon certain groups has been much less wildly noted. the crisis have been accompanied by changes in employment and relative prices that have adversely impacted especially upon three sections of the population that were already very venerable cultivators,Migrant workers and home-based women workers. In addition, it has sharply affected food insecurity which was already a problem in the country.

Cultivators

The impact of the crisis on agriculture is much more severe than has been recognized. Cultivators in India have already been through more than a decade of agrarian crisis, which persisted even through the period of rising international crop prices. The problems of farming in India are both deep and varied. They include weather problems such as less reliable monsoons, more frequent droughts and floods, soil degeneration, lack of institutional credit and insurance leading to excessive reliance on private moneylenders, problems in accessing reliable and reasonably priced input, difficulties in marketing and high volatility of crop prices.

Except for the first set,these are all related to public policies from the early 1990s onwards,that systematically reduced the protection afforded to farmers and exposed them to import competition and market volatility ;allowed private profiteering in agricultural input supply and crop purchess without adequate regulation;reduced critical forms of public expenditure;tried t cu t subsidies by increasing the prices of important inputs like fertilizer and water and electricity rates , ran down or destroyed impportnt public institutions that have direct rebelence for farming , including public extension services and marketing arrangements;and did not adequately generate other non-agricultural economic activities.

At the same time that various foprms of public protection for cultivation were being reduced,trade liberalization meant that Indian farmers had to operate in ahighly uncertain and volatile international environment. They were effectively competing against highly subsidized large producers in the development countries,whose average laevel of subsidy amounted to many times the total domestic cost of production for many crops.in addition to increasinfg the risks of farming, volatile crop prices also generated misleading price signals.Indian farmers tend to respond quickly and extensively to price signals by shifting to more high-priced crops. This caused large and often undesirable shifts in cropping patern which ultimately rebounded on the frmers themselves.

In dry land areas, traditional staple crops such as millets and sorghum were abondaned in favour of oil seeds such as groundnut which require more irrigation and purchased inputs, and which have also faced major volatility in crop prices. As a result of shift away from the traditional staple grains to cash crops, there as much greater use of a range of purchased inputs, including new varieties of seed and related inputs marketed by major multinational companies.small cultivators, who took on debt in order to pay these cash inputs, then found themselves in real difficulty if crops failed or output prices remained low.

So the inevitable uncertainities associated with weather fluctuations weer compounded by further problems of extrmly volatile crop prices, which were no longer inversely related to harvest levels but followed an international pattern. Further, this dramatic volatility of output prices was associated with continuosly rising prices of inputs.this was especially marked because of government attempts to reduce fertilizer subsidies , and progressive deregulation of supply of inputs such as seeds and pesticides.

Such explosure to global price volatility was associated with a growing reliance on private debt, because of the lack of extension of institutional credit, but things got much worse after 1993. financial leberelisation measures caused a significant slow down in the growth of Bank credit, particularly from commercial banks to rular areas, and a relative fall in proportion of bank credit following to the priority sectors, especially agriculture. The im pact of theslow down in the rular banking disproportionally on poor and small borrowers.

Volatility of output price remains a huge problem for farmers and the central questioin of the huge burden of farm debt has really not been solved, despite "the loan waiver" for farmers announced in the 2008-2009 budget. This is because most farmers operate in the informall credit market, and go to private sources who are typically either rular money lenders or input dealers.the real problems of rular debt cannot be addressed without dealing with cases of both public and private debt and recapitalizing the money lenders to alleviate the problems of borrowers and keep private rular credit channels following.

Meanwhile, crop price volatility has been become most worse in past year, dramatically increasing the difficulties of cash crop producers.farmers did not benefit from such as short-lived price boom, especially if they produce cash crops.instead, they now face lower prices of their output even as food prices have continued to increase.this is particularly to for cultivators of cotton and oilseeds, prices of which have crashed compare to a year ago.cultivators who opted to sow these crops when there prices were at their peak now face a completely different environment with very different configurations of cost and prices that could easily make the cultivation process financially completely unviable.

Migrant Workers

Official sources suggest that there has already been a sharp fall in employment in the export-oriented sectors like textiles and garments and gems and jewellery, and even in industries catering more to the domestic market like metal products, automobiles and construction. Many newly unemployed are migrant workers, often short-term migrants with casual contracts whose very existence tends to be ignored by our official statistics. The economic boom of the past decade relied heavily on such workers: Not just in the sectors mentioned above but in labour -intensive services, such as cleaning, maintenance, private security, driving and related services. These were not simply informal activities; many of them catered to the requirements of the expanding corporate sector, and in effect subsidized it by providing a cheap and flexible external labour force.

Such workers are now forced either to stay in precarious condition in urban areas,or go back to their places of origin-villages or smaller towns. They consequently change from becoming providers of remittance incomes to their households, to becoming of these households, even as these households face more fragile material circumstances than before.,many of these migrant orkers, for obvious reasons,come from the most depressed and backword regions of the country. unsurprisingly, they are lso the regions in which extremist maoist activity is widely prevalent,because of the nger bred by persistent backwardness and rising inequalities.

Home-Based Workers

As opportunities for paid employment have dwindled, even during the boom, home-based subcontracting activities, or work in very small units that do not even constitute manufactories ,often on price-rate-basis and usually very poorly paid and without any known none-wage benefits, substituted to some extent .there are estimated to be more than 15 million women workers in the unorganized sectors , and more than a half of them are women involved in home-based work for different types of industry, dominantly on a price-rate basis .this includes ZARI,CHARKHA or other handloom work; BINDI,labels,stiching;food processing, and also potentially hazardous work involving acids and chemicals.

Surveys show that most of them are very poorly paid price-rate workers providing specific products or intermediate goods for manufacturing industries such as textiles and garments engineering and chemical industries, leather and misclanious production such as imitation jewellery and petty cosmetic items. Such work typically does not get incorporated in the employment statistics which are based on employees records. Very recent micro-evidence conforms the poor and sometime even deterioting conditions of such work.even during the boom, their was pressure on price rate wages because of competion from other and newer centres of such production, both inside the Country and Outside.

The marginal utilization of women workers in a manufacturing industry is typically at the lowest and poorest paid parts of the production chain such women workers are effectively deprived of ll the benefits that may accure from outside employment except for the low nominal returns that they receive from piece - rate work.this means that any downswing is directly reflected in both the declining orders or contacts and falling rates of remunation.

Very recent evidence suggests that as export -based inustries such as garments face highlitened competitive pressure, they pass this pressure on to home-based women workers by reducing the effective retes for ppiece -rate work.even nominal piece reate wages have fallen in many such activities,even as price of necessities such as food have continued to increase.

Food Security and the Price of Essential

Much has been made of the slow down in inflation rates to almost zero, and there are those who have pointed out that this reflects the decline rate of economic growth and could even led to a deflation that is damaging for growth.

But what is often not noted that even within this overall stagnation in prices, food prices have continued to entries. food grain prices have gone up the most , by more than 10 percent in the year April 2008 to March 2009.this cannot be blamed on higher procurement, prices alone , since the [prices of pulses, which are not covered public procurement ,have also gone up just as much,

The prices of fruits and vegetables and eggs, fish and meat have also increased, even if not by as much as food grains. The only food category for which prices have fallen is eatable oils, which reflects the decline in oil seed prices as world prices have crashed. Other food articles" have increased by more than one fifth in this one year.

This obviously, effects household budgets, especially among the poor for whom food still accounts for more than half of total house hold expenditure.mean while, non -food primary product prices have already changed.

What is to be Done?

What is immediately require is significantly increased public expenditure, directed towards particular areas –expansion of the employment guartee scheme within rular areas and extension to urban areas, creative use of nregs, especially in urban areas, to enable productive use of tremendous wealth of labour resources available, especially women workers.

If this can be done, the current crises might ever be worth the pain that is now delivering to so many millions.

References

International Economics by "Soderften"

Economic Development in Third World by "M.P. Todaro".

New Reality by "Draker P.F."

World Bank Development Report 1999.

Economic Survey Govt. of India.

International Economics by "Salvatore-D".

22

GLOBAL FINANCIAL CRISIS AND THEIR IMPACT ON INDIAN ECONOMY

Brajesh Srivastava

The intensification of the global financial crisis following the bankruptcy of Lehman Brother in September 2008 has made the current economic and financial environment a very difficult time for the world economy, the global financial system and for central banks. The proximate cause of the current financial turbulence is attributed to the sub prime mortgage sector in the U.S.A. At a fundamental level, however, the crisis could be ascribed to the persistence of large global imbalance, which, in turn were the outcome of long period of excessively loose monetary policy in the major advanced economies during the early part of this decade.

The immediate cause of trigger of the crisis was the bursting of the United States housing bubble which peaked in approximately 2005-06. High default rates on subprime and adjustable rate mortgages (ARM), began to increase quickly thereafter. An increase in long incentives such an easy initial terms and a long term trend of rising housing prices had encouraged borrowers to assume difficult Mortgages in the belief that they would be able to quickly refinance at more favorable terms. However, once interest rates began to rise and housing prices started to drop moderately in 2006-07 in many parts of the U.S., refinancing become more difficult. Defaults and foreclosure activity increased dramatically as easy initial terms expired, home prices failed to go up anticipated, and ARM interest rates reset higher. Foreclosure accelerated in the United States in late 2006 and triggered a global financial crisis through 2007 and 2008.

In the years leading up to the crisis, high consumption and low saving rates in the U.S. contributed to significant amounts of foreign money flowing into the U.S. from fast growing economics in Asia and oil producing countries. This inflow of funds combined with low U.S. interest rates from 2002-04 resulted in easy credit conditions, which fueled both housing and credit bubbles. Loans of various types (e.g. Mortgage, credit and auto) were easy to obtain and consumers assumbed an unprecedented debt load. As part of the housing and credit booms, the amount of financial agreements called mortgage-backed securities (MBS) which derive their value from mortgage payments and housing prices, greatly increased. Such financial innovation enabled institutions and investors around the world to invest in the U.S. housing market. As housing prices declined, major global financial institutions that had borrowed and invested heavily in sub-prime MBS reported significant losses. Defaults and losses on other loan types also increased significantly as the crisis expanded from the housing market to other parts of the economy. Total losses are estimated in the trillion of U.S. dollar globally.

Contrary to the "decoupling theory" emerging economies too have been hit by the crisis. The decoupling theory which was intellectually fashionable even as late as a year ago, held that even if advanced economies went into a downturn, emerging economies will remain unscathed because of their substantial foreign exchange reserves, improved policy frame work, robust corporate balance sheets and relatively healthy banking sector. In a rapid globlizing world the decoupling theory was never totally persuasive given the evidence of the last few months-capital flow reversals, sharp widening of spreads on sovereign and corporate debt and abrupt currency

Table 1

Global Economic Outlook for 2009 (percent)

Indicator	*Month of Forecast*											
	April 2008	*July 2008*		*October 2008*		*November 2008*		*January 2009*		*April 2009*		
1.	*2*	*3*	*4*	*5*	*6*	*7*	*8*	*9*	*10*	*11*	*12*	*13*
1. Global Growth	3.7	3.8	4.1	3.9	3.9	3.0	3.4	0.5	3.4	0.5	3.2	1.3
(a) Advanced Economies	1.3	1.3	1.7	1.4	1.5	0.5	1.0	-2.0	1.0	2.0	0.9	3.8
(b) EME's	6.7	6.6	6.7	6.9	6.9	6.1	6.3	3.3	6.3	3.3	6.1	1.6
2. World Trade Volume	3.7	3.8	4.1	3.9	3.9	3.0	4.1	2.8	4.1	2.8	3.3	11.0
3. Consumer Price Inflation												
(a) Advanced Economies	2.6	2.0	3.4	2.3	3.6	2.0	3.5	0.3	3.5	0.3	3.4	0.2
(b) EME's	7.4	5.7	9.1	7.4	9.4	7.8	9.2	5.8	9.2	5.8	9.3	5.7

Source: World Economic outlook various issue International Monetary Fund.

depreciations---the decoupling theory stands totally invalidated. Reinforcing the nation that in a globalize world no country can be as island, growth prospects of emerging economies have been undermined by the cascading financial crisis with, of course, considerable variation across countries. The global economic outlook deteriorated sharply over the last quarter. Global growth for 2009 which was seen at a healthy 3.8% in April 2008 is now projected to contract by 1.3% (IMF, 2009 C) (Table 1). Recent evidence suggests that concretionary forces are strong; demand has slumped.

Production is plunging, job losses are rising and credit markets remain in seizure. Most worryingly; world trade-the main channel through which the downturn will get transmitted on the way forward is projected to contract by 11% during 2009 as against the robust growth of 8.2% during 2006-07. Private capital inflows (net) to the EMEs fell from the peak of us 617 billion$ in 2007 to US 109 billion$ in 2008 and are projected to record net outflow to US 190 billion$ in 2009. The sharp decline in capital flows in 2009 will be mainly on account of outflows under bank lending and portfolio flows. Thus, both the slowdown in external demand and the lack of external financing have dampened growth prospects for the EMEs much more than that was anticipated a year ago.

Impact of the Crisis on India

The initial impact of the sub- prime crisis on the Indian Economy was rather muted .As the impact on India unfolds, there are two frequently asked questions; first how is that India is affected when it came out of the Asian crisis relatively unscathed? Second, why India is affected even when its exports account for only 15% of its GDP? The answer to both the questions lies in globalization. We are certainly more integrated into the world economy today then ten years ago at the time of the Asian crisis. Integration into the world implies more than just exports going by the common measure of globalization India's two way trade (merchandise exports plus imports) as a proportion of GDP grew from 21.2% in 1997-98, the year of the Asian crisis to 34.7% in 2007-08. If we take an expanded measure of globalization that is the ratio of total external transactions (gross current account flows plus gross capital flows) to GDP, this ratio has increased from 46.8% in 1997-98 to 117.4% in 2007-08. These numbers are clear evidence of India's increasing integration into the world economy over the last 10 years. We must also note another important difference between the crisis in the advanced countries and the developments in India. While in the advanced countries the contagion spread from the financial to the real sector, in India the slowdown in the real sector is affecting the financial sector, which in turn has a second order impact on the real sector.

The effect of the global crisis have directly impacted some important macroeconomic variables Three such indicators stand out in terms of their quite sudden deterioration since the middle of last year. The decline in the foreign exchanger reserves held by the Reserve Bank of India the fall in the externals value of the rupee especially vis-à-vis the U.S. dollar and the decline in stock market indices.

Chart 1 shows how foreign exchange reserves, which had been increasingly steadily over the past years, started declining after June 2008. Not that the earlier build up of reserves reflected any great macroeconomic strength, since unlike china it was not based on current account surpluses. Instead the Indian economy experienced an inflow of hot money especially in the form of portfolio capital of investment.

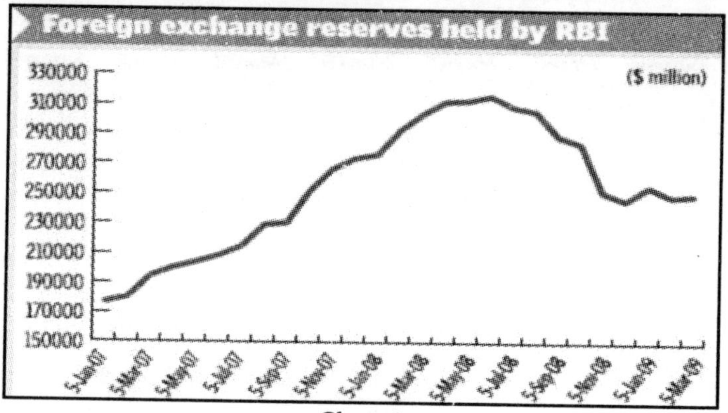

Chart 1

Domestic macro policies combined with the need to prevent exchange rate appreciation to prevent increased domestic absorption of such resources as a result of which these were largely added to reserves since they were based on hot money inflows. It was only to be expected that they would reverse with any bad news and that is essentially what was happened over the past eight months, In the bad news coming from the U.S. and other developed markets rather than from the Indian economy. But that movement of foreign institutional investors was in turn related to the sudden collapse of the rupee, shown in Chart 2. Early in march 2009 the rupee when breached the line of Rs. 51 per dollar and it may continue to fall, there are those who argue that this depreciation is positive since it will be exports but conditions prevailing in the world fared market with falling export volumes and values does not give rise to much optimism in that context. India currently has a current account deficit including a large fared deficit and also quite significant factor payments; a broad the falling rupee will imply rising factor payments (such as debt repayment and profit repatriation) in rupee terms, which is not good news for many companies or for the balance of payments. Associated with all this is the evidence of falling business confidence expressed in the stock market indicators.

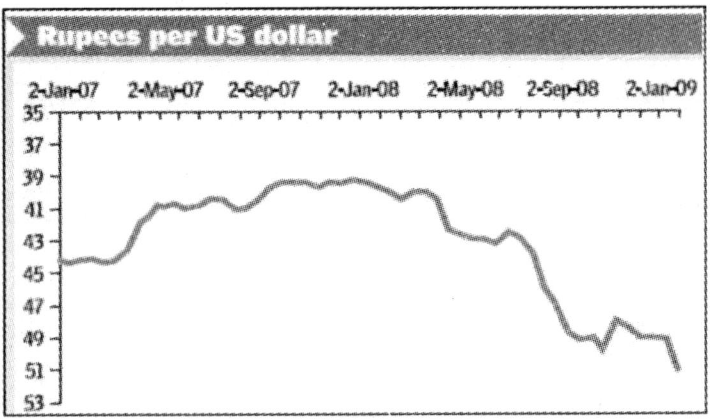

Chart 2

How much of all this is due to the behavior of foreign investors rather than domestic investors? Chart 3 tracks the changes in total foreign investment split up into direct investment and portfolio investment over the period since April 2007. It is evident that both have shown a trend of increase followed by decline FDI has been more stable with relatively moderate fluctuations even through it does include some portfolio type investments that get categorized as foreign direct investment. It peaked in February 2008 and thereafter has been coming down but is still positive portfolio investment which includes both FII investment in the domestic share market and GDRs/ADRs has been extremely volatile and largely negative indicating net outflows since the beginning of 2008 and this has dominated the overall investment trend.

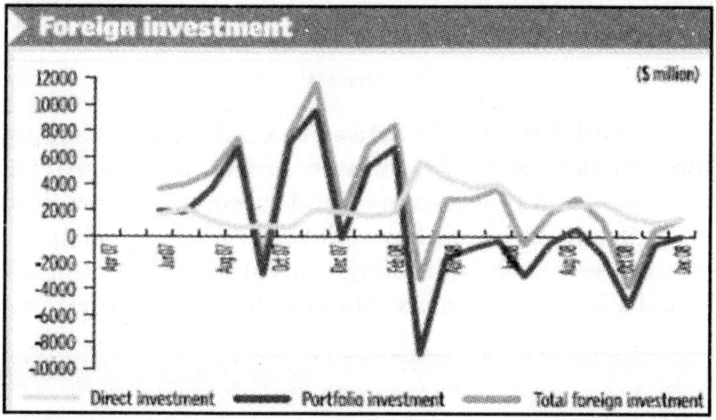

Chart 3

As a result as Chart 4 shows the cumulative value of the stock of Indian equity held by FIIs fell quite sharply by 24% between may 2008 and February 2009. This is not likely to be due to any dramatically changed investor perceptions of the Indian economy. Since if anything GDP growth prospects in India remain somewhat higher that in most other developed or emerging markets. Rather, it is because portfolio investors have been repatriating capital back to the U.S. and other Northern markets. Whatever the causes the impact on the domestic stock market has been sharp and direct, since then

Indian stock market is still relatively shallow and FII activities play a disproportionately strong role in determining the movement of the Indices. It is not surprising that this outward flow has been associated with the overall decline in stock market valuations.

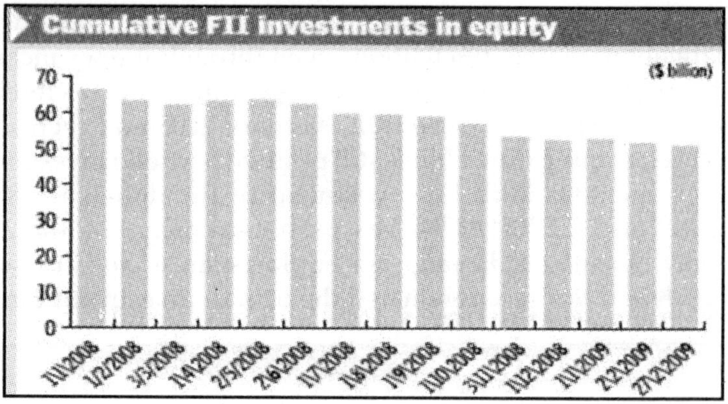

Chart 4

As Chart 5 shows the Sensex has moved generally in the same direction as net FII inflows. In fact, movements in the latter have been much sharper and more volatile, suggesting that domestic investors have played a more stabilizing role over this period. Overall foreign investment flows (Including not just FII but direct investment) have also, predictably,

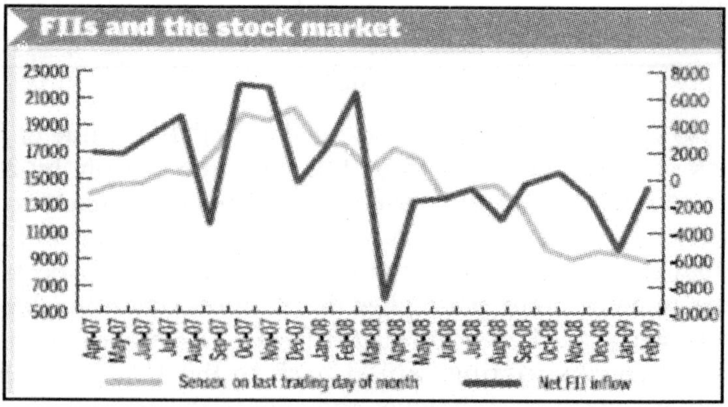

Chart 5

played a role in determining the level of external reserves. Chart 6 shows the pattern of aggregate foreign investment and change in reserves since April 2007.

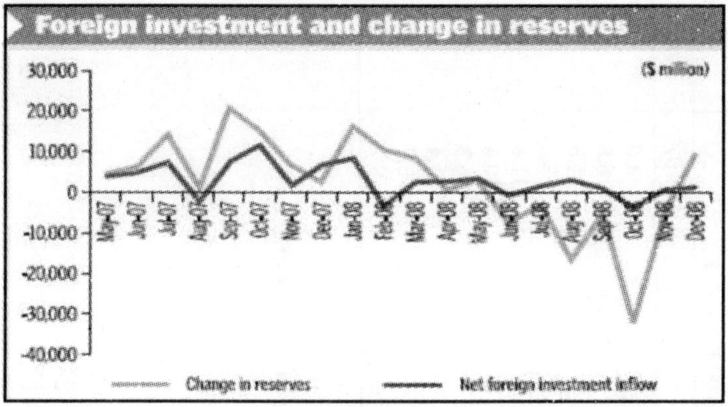

Chart 6

It is apparent that the Indian banks and financial system had only negligible direct exposure to the type of toxic assets that have contaminated the western countries' banking system, bank's credit quality remains of high quality. Although bank credit growth was quite high at around 30% per annum during 2004-07. It would appear that there was no significant relaxation of lending standards. Bank's loans to Individuals for housing have been backed by prudent loan-to- value rations. However, in view of the rapid credit growth to certain sectors, the reserve bank had pre-emotively tightened prudential norms, provisioning requirements and risk weights for these sectors in order to safeguard financial stability: provisioning norms for standard assets were also raised across the board except for agriculture and SMEs. These tightened provisioning norms and risk weights have now been rolled back in the wake of slowdown in order to ensure flow of credit to the productive sectors of the economy. This "dynamic provisioning" approach have facilitated adequate buffers within the banking system. Such "dynamic provisioning" is now being advocated as general practice internationally. Therefore, unlike the banking system in the western world,

Table 2
Rate of Growth at Factor Cast at 1999-2000 Price (%)

Sector	*03-04*	*04-05*	*05-06*	*06-07*	*07-08*	*08-09*
Agriculture and forestry and fishing	10.2	0.0	5.8	4.0	4.9	1.6
Mining and quarrying	3.1	8.2	4.9	8.8	3.3	3.6
Manufacturing	6.6	8.7	9.1	11.8	8.2	2.4
Electricity, gas and water supply	4.8	7.9	5.1	5.3	5.3	3.4
Construction	12.0	16.1	16.2	11.8	10.1	7.2
Trade,hotal & Restaurants	10.1	7.7	10.3	10.4	10.1	**
Transport, storage and Communication	15.3	15.6	14.9	16.3	15.5	**
Financing,insurance,real estate and business services	5.6	8.7	11.4	13.4	11.7	7.8
Community, social and Personal services	5.4	6.8	7.1	5.7	6.8	13.1
Total CDP at factor cast	8.5	7.5	9.5	9.7	9.0	6.7

Note: Plan period is simple average

Source: Central statistical organization.

* Trade, hotel and restaurants, transport and communication (together) grew at 9%, 2008-09.

domestic banks have not recorded losses so far and there has been no need for any government bailout.

Table 3
Key Indicators of Scheduled Commercial Banks in India (%)

Item	*04-05*	*05-06*	*06-07*	*07-08*
Capital to Risk Weighted Assets Ratio (CRAR) (%)	12.8	12.3	12.3	13.0
Of which; Tier 1(CRAR) (%)	8.4	9.3	8.3	9.1
Net- Non Performing Assets (% to net Advances)	1.9	1.2	1.0	1.0
Net- Non Performing Assets (% to Assets)	0.9	0.7	0.6	0.6
Net Profit (% to Assets)	0.9	0.9	0.9	1.0
Net Interest Margin (% to Assets)	2.8	2.8	2.6	2.3

Source: Report on Trend and Progress of Banking in India, 2007-08, Reserve Bank of India.

Policy Response to the Slowdown

To counter the negative fallout of the global slowdown on the Indian economy the government responded by providing a substantial fiscal expansion in the form of tax relief to boost demand and increased expenditure on public projects to create employment and public assets. The net result was an increase in fiscal deficit from 2.7% in 2007-08 to 6.2% of GDP in 2008-09.

The RBI took a number of monetary easing and liquidity enhancing measures including reduction in CRR, SLR and Key policy rates. The objective was to facilitate the flow of funds from the financial system to meet the needs of productive sectors. The breadth and depth of the global crisis and the uncertainty and the fear surrounding it, required use of fiscal policy to supplement monetary policy. It was therefore necessary to ensure adequate coordination between the two, so that they did not work at cross-purposes. The government also announced specific measures to address the impact of global slowdown on India's exports. These includes extension of export credit for labor-intensive exports, improving the pre and post -shipment credit availability, additional allocation for refund of terminal excise duty /CST and export incentive schemes, and removal of export duty and export ban on certain items. Though, it is not possible to substitute for the dramatic fall in foreign demand, these measures would be helpful in facilitating the adjustment of companies and worked to the new reality and to survive the temporary setbacks.

There has been an increase in foreign direct Investment (FDI) during 2008-09 over the previous yeas. More importantly, there are signs that foreign Institutional investors who had recorded net outflows in 2008-09, may have returned to the Indian Market in the last two months. The credit market appears to be working normally and there is no dearth of liquidity in the economy. Inflation is no longer an area of concern. With the Index of Industrial Production showing clear sign of revival in the month of April it is likely that the two worst quarters since the global financial meltdown in September 2008 are behind us. Indeed the stock market in the last few weeks (of May- June 2009) May have already picked up their early signs of the rebound.

Reference

Rakesh Mohan (2008), 'Global Financial Crisis and Key Risks: Impacts on India and Asia" Remarks prepared for IMF-FSF High Level Meeting on the Recent Financial Turmoil and policy Responses at Washington D.C. 9 October.

Rakesh Mohan (2009), 'Global Financial Crisis and Key Risks: Impacts Policy Responses and Lessons', RBI Monthly Bulletin May.

Duvvuri Subbarao (2009), "India-Managing the Impact of the Global Financial Crisis', speech at the confederation of Indian Industry's National Conference and Annual Session 2009. New Delhi: 26 March.

"The Limits of Decoupling"-The Economic Times, 13 July 2009.

"Money Markets Hit Indirectly"- The Economic Times, 3 July.

C.P. Chandrasekhar and Jayati Ghosh- "The Global Crisis and Indian Finance" Business Line Tuesday, Mar. 10, 2009.

Wikipedia " Sub prime Mortgage Crisis"

"Wall Street Crisis: Implications for India" The Economic Times 15 October, 2008.

INDEX